FAITH STORIES

~

*Devotional Thoughts
from the
Lives of Missionaries*

~

C. JOANNE SLOAN
CHERYL SLOAN WRAY

Woman's Missionary Union
Birmingham, Alabama

Woman's Missionary Union
P. O. Box 830010
Birmingham, AL 35283-0010

For more information, visit our Web site at www.wmu.com or call WMU Customer Service at 1-800-968-7301.

©2000 by Woman's Missionary Union
All rights reserved. First printing 2000
Printed in the United States of America
Woman's Missionary Union®, WMU®, Christian Women's Job Corps®, Girls in Action®, and Acteens® are registered trademarks.

Dewey Decimal Classification: 242.2
Subject Headings: DEVOTIONAL CALENDARS
　　　　　　　　　 MISSIONARY STORIES

　　Scripture quotations identified NIV are from the Holy Bible, New International Version. Copyright ©1973, 1978, 1984 International Bible Society. Used by permission of Zondervan Bible Publishers.
　　Verses marked TLB are taken from *The Living Bible,* copyright 1971 by Tyndale House Publishers, Wheaton, IL. Used by permission.
　　Scriptures identified RSV are from the *Revised Standard Version of the Bible.* Old Testament: Copyright 1952 by Division of Christian Education of the National Council of the Churches of Christ in the United States of America; New Testament: Copyright 1946, by Division of Christian Education of the National Council of the Churches of Christ in the United States of America.
　　Scripture quotations marked KJV are from the King James Version of the Bible.
　　Scripture quotations identified CEV are from *Contemporary English Version.* Copyright ©American Bible Society 1991. Used by permission.

Design by Janell E. Young

W004116•0700•5M1
ISBN: 1-56309-338-3

This book is dedicated to history's dauntless missionaries and today's dedicated ones who follow in their footsteps.

May their stories inspire us all to follow the admonitions of our Lord:

"'Go therefore and make disciples of all nations, baptizing them in the name of the Father and of the Son and of the Holy Spirit, teaching them to observe all that I have commanded you; and lo, I am with you always, to the close of the age'" (Matt. 28:19 RSV).

"'For I was hungry and you gave me food, I was thirsty and you gave me drink, I was a stranger and you welcomed me, I was naked and you clothed me, I was sick and you visited me, I was in prison and you came to me'" (Matt. 25:35 RSV).

Acknowledgements

We would like to thank all of the missionaries and missions organizations that supplied with us valuable information. They are too numerous to list separately, but we are indebted to them for their cooperation and willingness to help. You will all continue to be in our prayers.

We also want to thank our many family members and friends who encouraged us in writing this book and prayed for us as we labored. Especially, we are grateful to David, Gary, McKenna, and Delaney, without whose love and support we could not have accomplished our task.

Changing the World

They changed the world. The stories of their lives can change your life.

Much of the population knows nothing of the great accomplishments of missionaries, those unsung heroes of our past. Maybe it is time to change that.

The lectern from which Scripture is read at coronations, royal weddings, and daily evensong in London's Westminster Abbey is dedicated to William Carey. The words on the lectern—"Attempt great things for God, Expect great things from God"—come from his now famous sermon of 1792. That seems a fitting memorial to a humble Baptist minister who started one of the most extensive global movements ever in human history—the modern missionary movement.

Missionaries before and after Carey have been evangelizers, Bible teachers, preachers, pastors, explorers, doctors, nurses, translators, and fund-raisers.

They have led millions to become Christians, fed the hungry, formed missionary societies, translated Scripture into numerous languages, and started rescue missions. They have built hospitals, established orphanages, founded colleges, taught people to read, cared for refugees, introduced new crops, stimulated trade, and written books. In the forefront of social change, they have battled superstition, slavery, suttee, female circumcision, temple prostitution, and the killing of twins.

Missionaries teach us about commitment, persistence, and endurance. Tireless workers, some labored five and even six decades on the missions field. Many literally "burned themselves out for God."

Above all, they teach us about love and sacrifice. They were killed by cannibals, starved to death in concentration camps, executed by those who opposed them, and died from tropical diseases.

Missionaries are visionary. They see a need and work and pray to see it to its fruition. From William Carey, a revolutionary who dared advocate evangelizing in foreign lands, to Bob Pierce, who founded World Vision, they are ahead of their times.

They show us that each of us can be involved in missions. They have come from all walks of life—a cobbler, parlormaid, and a gardener all went on to become famous missionaries.

Women have made a tremendous contribution to the history of missions. This book contains many of their moving stories. The women's missionary movement was the largest women's movement in the early decades of the twentieth century. Beginning with the nineteenth century, women were sent out in large numbers to the missions field. Many single women established women's work; evangelized; and founded colleges, hospitals, and schools.

Missionary women were often "firsts." From the first woman to speak in a public meeting in South Carolina to the first American woman to go to China, they were pioneers.

Black women have played a significant role in missions. Five Presbyterian pioneers from the South were trailblazers in Africa. Others such as Amanda Smith and Eliza Davis George battled racism to make their significant mark.

Missionary stories are some of the greatest of all stories. From Quaker Mary Fisher walking 600 miles to evangelize the sultan of Turkey to David Livingstone opening up Africa fighting slavery along the way to Mildred Cable and the two French sisters crossing the Gobi Desert in China five times to spread the gospel, these stories can inspire us.

From St. Patrick in the fifth century to J. Hudson Taylor and Lottie Moon in the nineteenth century to Eric Liddell and Mother Teresa in the twentieth century, missionaries have left us a heroic legacy. May the historical devotionals in this book inspire you to take the best of their lives and apply it to yours.

And the Work Goes On

As we wrote this book, my mother and I emailed our research

notes and our devotions to each other. I read her devotional stories with interest and often amazement: these great missionaries of the past did such pioneering work and had such awe-inspiring faith. Their unswerving faith in God and in their work sometimes cost them the ultimate sacrifice—their lives.

In learning about missions activities and organizations today, and in interviewing contemporary missionaries about their work, I was impressed by something: these missionaries of today (and all Christians) stand on the shoulders of the giants who came before them.

In Hebrews 11 we learn about the faith of our forefathers and foremothers. Noah, Abraham, Joseph, Moses, Rahab, David—they all make up our faith heritage. They inspire us to live faithfully in God's presence and continue to do His work today.

Consider what verses 39 and 40 of that chapter proclaim: "These were all commended for their faith, yet none of them received what had been promised. God had planned something better for us so that only together with us would they be made perfect" (NIV).

These words impart to us one of the great epiphanies I received in writing this book. It tells us that we continue the works of faith started by those before us.

Today's missionaries—whether they are career missionaries, administrators for missions or relief organizations, volunteers in short-term missions, or missions workers in their local church—are there because of the people before them. The faith of a Pandita Ramabai working with widows and orphans can inspire those who toil in the inner city with AIDS-stricken mothers or lonely children. The faith of a Mary Slessor trekking into Calabar, West Africa, can motivate and encourage those who work in the interior villages of South America.

In turn, they can inspire, motivate, and encourage each one of us.

This book's daily devotional thoughts will introduce you to a variety of missionaries who work in a myriad of ministries today. You will meet those who work within the boundaries of the United States. They work in the inner cities, on Native American Indian reservations, in Appalachia, on beaches, in foster homes, at campgrounds, in health-care clinics, in food banks, on the streets, in literacy classes, and in so many other places.

You will meet those women and men who work across our borders and across the oceans. They minister to Kenya's street children, provide disaster relief in Turkey, reach out to the hungry in Honduras, uplift new Christians in Russia, defeat spiritist forces in Brazil, reach out to the blind in Nigeria, and work through so many other missions outreaches.

You will meet women and men just like you who saw a need for human love and the good news, and did something about it. They organize building projects through their community's churches, reach out during the holidays to those in need, travel on missions trips to deliver physical and spiritual help, volunteer through church and ecumenical outreach organizations, and do so much more in the name of Christ.

You will meet people from all walks of life, from all Christian denominations, with all different types of talents and gifts. The similarity among them all is that they each have felt God's call on their lives to do something with their faith.

Olga Carter, who coordinates trips between American and Ukrainian churches through the Missions Our Mission organization, says of her call: "I have never thought of myself as a missionary. I do my part, God does His."

Dellanna O'Brien, the former executive director of WMU, echoes that sentiment when she says that all Christians need to simply be open to God's call. She says: "Wherever you are, the safest place is where God leads you."

Let those words and this book become a challenge to you. Read the stories of the great missionaries throughout history and meditate on what they did. Read about today's missions workers and ask yourself what you can learn from their experiences.

We are all missionaries, for Christ challenged us all to "love one another" (John 15:17). What better way to love the hurting, hungry, and lost in the world than to reach out with your time, talent, prayers, and hands?

Take your faith to greater heights and become involved in missions in your own corner of the world. Create your own faith stories.

C. JOANNE STUART SLOAN

CHERYL SLOAN WRAY

January 1: Following in His Steps

"Direct my footsteps according to your word" (Psalm 119:133 NIV).

Does God direct your footsteps? Are you willing to step out in faith and follow Him?

Angela Payne stood in the middle of an open square in Russia, holding one remaining Bible. She prayed for the right person to receive it.

"Two precious *babushkas* (grandmothers) saw me and the Bible and were gesturing to me. I was absolutely thrilled to give it to them," Angela recalls.

"As I was reaching toward their open hands, a woman in her late 20s, dressed professionally, ran up to me. There was desperation on her face, and she frantically motioned for me to give her the Russian Bible. It was if she were pleading with me."

Praying all the while, Angela felt she should give it to the young woman. The older women looked on, tears rolling down their cheeks. Moments later, Angela caught up with a teammate and told him her story. He pulled one last Bible out of his backpack, and Angela rushed off to find the women. "I threw myself around their necks, kissed their cheeks, and breathlessly gave the Bible to them."

This experience is just one of many for Angela, who has also traveled on short-term missions trips to China, Hong Kong, and Romania. "I feel a deep stirring in my heart that I will never be satisfied living a status quo life," she says. "I will always have a world vision."

∼

Unveil to me the opportunities I have to serve You, Lord.

January 2: A New Beginning

"Praise be to the God and Father of our Lord Jesus Christ! In his great mercy he has given us new birth into a living hope through the resurrection of Jesus Christ from the dead, and into an inheritance that can never perish, spoil or fade—kept in heaven for you" (1 Peter: 1:3–4 NIV).

It has been said that she was "instrumental in saving more fallen women than any other person."

The remarkable Emma Whittemore founded Door of Hope missions around the world. She established her first mission home for street girls in New York City in 1890. At the time of her death in 1931 there were almost 100 such homes in major cities in the United States, Canada, Western Europe, Africa, China, Japan, and New Zealand.

Growing up in affluence and marrying into even more wealth, Emma involved herself in numerous social activities until a back injury left her an invalid. After she was miraculously healed, she began her active inner-city ministry work.

Her work focused on girls who in many instances had been taken advantage of because of poverty or family problems. The street girls needed a refuge where they could turn their lives around. In the slums of Shanghai as well as the urban ghettos of New York City, Door of Hope missions often provided their only avenues of escape.

Does your life exhibit the new hope that you have found in Christ?

∽

God, guide me today to those in despair who need the Living Hope.

January 3: Liberty

"Because the creation itself will be set free from its bondage to decay and obtain the glorious liberty of the children of God" (Rom. 8:21 RSV).

Have you found liberty in Christ?

Lott Cary (c. 1780–1828), the first American missionary to Africa, did. He also found liberty from slavery and died defending liberty.

Born on a plantation near Richmond, Lott grew up hearing stories about Jesus. Hired out by his master to work in a tobacco warehouse, he was soon living a loose life. One Sunday afternoon in 1807 in response to the minister's text, "You must be born again," he became a Christian.

By 1813 he had saved enough money to buy his freedom. Two years later he helped found the African Baptist Missionary Society. In January 1821 the society sent Lott; his wife, Nancy; and five others to Africa.

After facing numerous hardships including his wife's death, Lott founded a colony named Liberia "because the love of liberty brought us here." The town was named Monrovia after President James Monroe.

In addition to being a doctor, teacher, and preacher, Lott served as acting governor of the colony. In November 1828 a Spanish slave ship attacked. As Lott was loading shells in the fortress, a child accidentally knocked over a candle. When the gunpowder blew up, Lott and seven associates were killed.

Lott's legacy lives on today in the Providence Baptist Church of Monrovia.

Thank You, Lord, for the liberty Christ offers.

January 4: A New Name

"No longer will you be called Abram; your name will be Abraham, for I have made you a father of many nations" (Gen. 17:5 NIV).

Names say a lot about a person. In the Bible, names are especially important, as their meanings reveal truths about a person's relationship with God.

For a young man in Tanzania, his name became an important facet of his new Christian walk. It continues to serve as a witness to his Muslim community.

Southern Baptist missionaries Margaret and Dennis McCall met this man through their work in the Ten Mile community of Tanzania. Now a member of one of the local churches, he once served as the teacher of the Koran for the village school.

One day he suffered a mental breakdown and had nowhere to go, since very few hospitals in Africa provide help for mental illnesses. He was bound and isolated from others.

One night after reading the Bible, he prayed to Jesus: "If You are real and will heal me, I will believe in You and serve You the rest of my life." He woke up the next morning healed and changed his name to Zaburi, which is Swahili for "a praise song to God."

Margaret says that he "continues to be a strong witness for the Lord."

If God gave you a new name, what would it mean?

∼

Abba, Father, Savior, I praise You for Your many names. Help my life today be a witness for You.

January 5: Your Place

"And having chosen us, he called us to come to him; and when we came, he declared us 'not guilty,' filled us with Christ's goodness, gave us right standing with himself, and promised us his glory" (Rom. 8:30 TLB).

Do you ever wonder if you are in the place God wants you to be? Have you ever wondered why God allowed you to be in a certain place, time, or situation?

When situations are especially stressful or trying, it may be even harder to answer such questions.

Dellanna O'Brien, the former executive director of national WMU and a former missionary to Indonesia, looks at it this way: "Wherever you are, the safest place is where God leads you."

In their years of service in Indonesia, Dellanna and her husband, Bill, endured some trying times. During the Communist coup of the country in 1965, for example, Dellanna says her family experienced divine protection. Her son was born around that time. "We knew God had a special purpose in his safe birth and continuing life," she says.

In the ensuing years, the encouragement and prayers of other missionaries and Christians from around the world reaffirmed their belief that they were in the right place. "God gives you fellow missionaries as brothers and sisters who are often closer than blood kin," says Dellanna.

Give me confidence, O Lord, that when I am where You want me to be, You will abide in me.

January 6: Fighting Evil

"Deliver me from evildoers . . . for you are my fortress, my refuge in times of trouble" (Psalm 59:2,16 NIV).

When she arrived in 1888, the village was deserted. Everyone was at the funeral of the chief's mother. When he returned, the chief happily told her he had killed 24 people to be buried with his mother.

Mary Slessor (1848–1915) wrote, "The tribe seemed so completely given over to the devil that we were tempted to despair."

One evening she heard screams in the Okoyong village and forced her way into the center of a crowd. A young woman was tied to stakes on the ground; a man was ready to scald her with boiling oil. Because she had given food to a starving male slave while her husband was away, she was deemed unfaithful. Mary rushed between the woman and the man with the oil and refused to budge. Mary prevailed, and the assailant backed off. Taking the woman with her, Mary praised God for this protection.

These villagers held the belief that twins were children of the devil and consequently abandoned them at birth. Mary adopted dozens of twin babies—some of which she found in the village dump.

When the Presbyterian missionary died in January 1915, after four decades of sharing the gospel in Calabar (Nigeria), she was held in such high esteem that she was known as Eka kpukpro Owo—Mother of All the Peoples.

What is your response to evil?

∽

God, give me courage and wisdom to fight evil.

January 7: Angels Among Us

"Are not all angels ministering spirits sent to serve those who will inherit salvation?" (Heb. 1:14 NIV).

Stephen and Carol Strong arrived at New York City's John F. Kennedy Airport more than two hours before their scheduled flight to Los Angeles. The flight served as the first leg of their trip to Bangkok, Thailand, where the couple would begin their work as Christian and Missionary Alliance missionaries.

Upon arriving at the airport, long lines stretched in front of them. They settled in to wait with their nine-month-old son Joshua. Moments later, a stranger came and took them to the front counter. He showed their tickets to the representative, who announced that their flight had been canceled. Another one left in 15 minutes if they wanted to try and make it.

They changed flights, raced toward the gate, and boarded the plane just moments before takeoff.

Today, Stephen works with Bangkok's Mahapawn Rangsit Church, and Carol manages the city's Alliance Guest House. Their family has grown to include two other sons, Jordan and Justin.

Stephen says he often thinks of the stranger at the airport. "I have often thought that he may very well have been an angel that God sent to enable us in our moment of need," he reflects. "An angel who served us by helping us board the flight to Los Angeles and in turn begin our trip to Thailand as missionaries smoothly."

Can you think of a time when angels might have ministered to you?

Thank You, Eternal God, for Your ministering angels.

January 8: A Full Life

"And to know the love of Christ which surpasses knowledge, that you may be filled with all the fulness of God" (Eph. 3:19 RSV).

The martyred missionary had kept a journal in which he recorded his spiritual growth. Some of his statements have become memorable quotes:

"He is no fool who gives what he cannot keep to gain what he cannot lose."

"Live to the hilt every situation you believe to be the will of God."

"I seek not a long life but a full one, like You, Lord Jesus."

Philip James "Jim" Elliott (1927–1956) was born in Portland, Oregon, and graduated from Wheaton College. Representing Christian Missions in Many Lands, he went to Ecuador in 1952 teaching and ministering to the Quechua Indians.

In 1955 he and four other missionaries—Pete Fleming, Ed McCully, Nate Saint, and Roger Youderian—began efforts to reach the Aucas, a primitive Ecuadorian tribe. After making carefully planned weekly visits by air for three months over the remote village, they landed on a sandbar of the Curaray River. They were encouraged by friendly contact with three Indians, but two days later on January 8, 1956, they were attacked, and all were speared. Many people became followers of Christ after hearing of the obedience of the Auca Five. All five Indians who killed the missionaries are now strong believers.

Are you living your life to the fullest?

∽

I praise You, Lord, for those willing to give their lives to minister to unreached peoples.

January 9: Open Doors

"Here I am! I stand at the door and knock. If anyone hears my voice and opens the door, I will come in and eat with him, and he with me" (Rev. 3:20 NIV).

For people to open the doors of their hearts to God, they must first be able to learn of Him. Society's closed doors sometimes prevent this.

Open Doors International reaches others with the gospel by getting past the barriers governments and societies erect. It started in 1955 with the work of Brother Andrew, who was appropriately called God's Smuggler because of the Bibles he carried into hostile areas. Bible delivery and leadership training programs are still part of its work.

John Mathews, a volunteer with Open Doors, says he has seen an insatiable need for God's Word and the encouragement of other Christians in every country he has visited.

Of his trip to Albania in 1992 he says, "Everyone would listen to us as we shared about Jesus. Everyone would accept a Bible or tract."

His experiences in Cuba left an indelible impression. "It is a country just 90 miles off our coast and yet they don't have total freedom to worship," he says. "On my last trip they took most of my Bibles at the airport. I was able to get in a few and the believers I gave them to were so appreciative."

How can you open doors for Christ?

Our God, thank You for opening doors that have long been closed.

January 10: Mother to Orphans

"In thee, the orphan finds mercy" (Hos. 14:3 RSV).

She found her first orphan in a squalid hut. After the child's mother died, she rented a house and started the orphanage work that would distinguish her ministry for 50 years.

"I wanted to look after every neglected child that I saw," Lillian Trasher (1888-1961) once said.

Because she felt God was calling her to go to Africa, Lillian went to Egypt in 1911 with no financial support of any mission board. After 5 years of enduring hardships, 50 children were under her care. With help from those who believed in her ministry, she was able to purchase property and construct buildings.

Her work was strengthened when the newly formed Assemblies of God accepted her as one of their missionaries. By 1923 her orphanage had 300 children who were cared for by both Egyptian and American women.

Despite many setbacks in her ministry, she also witnessed miracles. During World War II when the orphanage desperately needed help, a Red Cross shipment of clothing, bedding, and food on its way to Greece was unexpectedly diverted to Egypt.

When she died, 1,400 children and widows were living at the orphanage. She had helped over 8,000 orphans during her lifetime. Lillian touched thousands of lives as shown by the outpouring of emotion in Assiout when she died.

Are you familiar with the work of your denomination's children's homes?

∽

God of mercy, help me today to take seriously what the Bible teaches about taking care of orphans.

January 11: Miracles on Mission

"And we know that in all things God works for the good of those who love him" (Rom. 8:28 NIV).

Mary Daniel says she has seen many miracles in her years as a missionary in East Africa.

Mary and her husband, Wayne, are the founders and field missionaries for the interdenominational African Children's Mission, a ministry to poor, orphaned, and abandoned children. ACM is a faith mission supported solely by contributions.

On a 1995 trip home from Nairobi, Kenya, to Meru, Uganda, they drove their car up and down steep, twisting mountain roads. Sheer cliffs dropped off the side of the road. They could see the remains of wrecked vehicles below them. Praying fervently for safe passage, they praised God when they arrived home safely.

A short while later, Wayne went to start the car again. "When he turned the wheel, it was free-spinning, completely disconnected from the steering gear box," Mary remembers. "He opened the box and found that all the ball bearings which connect the steering column to the drive shaft were missing. There was nothing to allow the car to be steered!"

Mary says that experience reminds them of God's ever-present providence. "We are sure of God's sovereign charge over us and confident of His desire to give us faithful care," she says. "No circumstances are too adverse for Him to use for our good."

When have you been part of a miracle?

∽

O God, we praise You for using all circumstances for Your glory.

January 12: Exploring and Evangelizing

"They left and went up into the hill country, and came to the Valley of Eschcol and explored it" (Deut. 1:24 NIV).

What was the driving force behind the work of missionary explorers?

"Our grand aim was but the spreading of the kingdom of God," German Lutheran explorer Johannes Rebman (1819–1876) said of his travels.

Pioneer missionary of the Church Missionary Society to East Africa, Rebman, together with J. L. Krapf (1810–1881), established Rabai Station, 1,000 feet above Mombasa in 1846. They made six exploratory trips with Rebman discovering Mount Kilimanjaro in May 1848. Never returning to Europe, Rebman was blind during his last two years.

One of the greatest explorers, Baptist George Grenfell (1849–1906), worked under the (British) Baptist Missionary Society. He explored the Congo up to the equator establishing stations at numerous sites. With his river steamer *Peace* he undertook six exploratory voyages which resulted in the formation of several more mission stations. He was honored with a founder's medal by the Royal Geographical Society.

Plymouth Brethren missionary Frederick Stanley Arnot (1858–1914) explored much of central Africa making nine journeys. Suffering incredible hardships, he founded many missions.

Daniel Crawford (1870–1926), a Plymouth Brethren missionary, opened a chain of stations from the Atlantic Ocean across Angola and into southern Zaire. Crawford had a unique gift of presenting the gospel convincingly to masses of people and of identifying with the people and their customs.

Thank You, Lord, for giving explorers a missions calling.

January 13: Treasure in Heaven

"'Sell everything you have and give to the poor, and you will have treasure in heaven. Then come, follow me'" (Luke 18:22 NIV).

When he received his father's inheritance of $150,000, he gave it all away after reading what Jesus said to the rich young ruler.

Son of a wealthy plantation owner, C. T. Studd (1862–1931) was educated at Cambridge University where he won fame as a cricket player. After his conversion at one of evangelist D. L. Moody's revivals at Cambridge, he devoted himself to missionary work. He and six friends he recruited became known as the Cambridge Seven. They laid the foundation of the Student Volunteer Movement with its purpose of recruiting college students as foreign missionaries.

In 1885 they arrived in China and worked with Hudson Taylor's China Inland Mission. When his father died, C. T. gave away his fortune. On January 13, 1887, he wrote out nine checks to various Christian organizations such as the Salvation Army, Moody Bible Institute, and George Muller's orphanages.

Returning to England because of poor health, he then traveled to America inspiring many college students. He went to southern India in 1900 where for six years he served as a pastor. Poor health again led him to give up this work; but 1910 found him in central Africa where he established the Heart of Africa Mission. Completely spent for the Lord, he died in Africa.

Are you being obedient to God's calling?

Lord, make me Your willing follower each day.

January 14: Homes of Hope

"'In everything I did, I showed you that by this kind of hard work we must help the weak, remembering the words the Lord Jesus himself said, "It is more blessed to give than to receive"'" (Acts 20:35 NIV).

The Egyptian woman cried when asked how she felt about soon having her own home. She and her family stayed in a cramped, one-bedroom apartment while waiting for their new Habitat for Humanity home to be built. The tiny conditions aggravated the rheumatic fever of one of her sons. Through tears, she said she'd never dreamed it could happen.

Susan and Matthew Maury—program coordinators for Habitat for Humanity in Zambia, Malawi, and Kenya—often meet women like this in their work. Experiences like this, in fact, reinforce their belief that Habitat is a wonderful way to reach out in Christ's name.

"We continue with Habitat because of the way Christ's love works through this ministry and shares good news with people like this Egyptian woman," Matthew says.

Habitat, they say, transforms people's physical and spiritual lives. Not only does the organization use grass-roots efforts and self-help methodology, it also provides spiritual hope.

"People have learned what it means to sleep without the rain falling on them, and some have come to know Christ in a way they never had before," they say.

Have you considered working with Habitat for Humanity?

∽

Give me empathy, God, towards the homeless in my own community and around the world.

January 15: God Working in You

"For it is God who works in you to will and to act according to his good purpose" (Phil. 2:13 NIV).

At her death on January 15, 1947, more than 2,000 people followed her body to the cemetery at Temuco, Chile.

Often referring to Philippians 2:13, Agnes Graham (1888–1947) once wrote that "it was God who was working in me both to will and to do his good pleasure. . . . It was he who first guided me in my desire to teach in my own country and later to bring his message to the young people of Chile."

The 11th of 13 children, Agnes was born on a farm near Kansas, Texas. After earning her teaching certificate, she taught school for 2 years and was a principal for 9 years. Her dream to attend the University of Texas was fulfilled when her widowed mother sold the family farm to finance her education. During her senior year she volunteered for mission service. While attending the WMU Training School, she was asked to found and develop a Baptist school in Chile.

In June 1920 she became the first single missionary appointed by the Foreign Mission Board (now International Mission Board) for Chile. She established the Baptist Academy in Temuco, one of the first coeducational ventures in Chile. She was a highly respected educator in Chile for over 26 years.

Are you allowing God to work in your life?

∽

Lord, guide my thoughts and actions so that Your work will be done through me.

January 16: Closed Doors

"'I was in prison and you came to visit me'" (Matt. 25: 36 NIV).

"Nobody wants to come."

These words greeted Ken and Grace Young, area missionaries with the American Missionary Fellowship, when they stepped through the front doors of a jail in Idaho. They, along with three other Christians (including Mary Jane, a former inmate at the jail), planned to hold a Good Friday service for any interested inmates.

Their hearts fell when the head jail matron told them, "There's not going to be a service because nobody wants to come."

Instead of leaving, though, Mary Jane ventured back into the cell block while the rest of the group stayed behind and prayed. Moments later, two inmates joined them for a service of singing, testimonies, and a short Bible message.

At the end of the service, both inmates said they believed in Christ and wanted to start a Bible study. Today the inmates and missionaries continue to meet together for Bible study. The new Christians are growing closer to Christ.

Ken and Grace say that the experience shows how God can open any closed doors. "Just like God's Word says, prison doors were opened," they say. "Through His power we gained a victory over closed doors and closed hearts."

Are you discouraged from closed doors you see in your life? How can you break through them in order to reach others for Christ?

∽

God, thank You for Your power over closed doors and closed lives.

January 17: Funding Missions Efforts

"Jesus traveled about from one town and village to another, proclaiming the good news of the kingdom of God. The Twelve were with him and also some women. . . . These women were helping to support them out of their own means" (Luke 8:1,3 NIV).

To raise money for Christian women's colleges in Asia, she talked John D. Rockefeller Jr. into pledging $1,000,000 if she could match it two to one. She collected $2,942,555!

Did you know that Lucy Peabody (1861–1949) was one of the largest fund-raisers for missions causes?

Lucy was a missionary before she was a missions organizer. She and her husband, Norman Waterbury, served 5 years in India until his death in 1886. She and her two children then returned to Rochester, New York.

Moving to Boston in 1889, she became head of the Woman's Baptist Foreign Missionary Society. In 1900 she organized and led for 28 years the Central Committee for the United Study of Foreign Missions.

Her marriage to Henry Wayland Peabody, a wealthy Boston businessman, ended 2 years later with his death. She then gave her wealth and energies to missions.

In 1911 she organized rallies across America to celebrate the 50-year celebration of the Women's Union Missionary Society of America for Heathen Lands, helping raise over $1,000,000.

In 1913 she and fellow mission supporter Helen Montgomery traveled around the world visiting mission sites. Her active work in missions continued until 1934 when she turned to writing.

Thank You, Gracious God, for gifted and generous organizers.

January 18: Come As Children

"Jesus said, 'Let the little children come to me, and do not hinder them, for the kingdom of heaven belongs to such as these'" (Matt. 19:14 NIV).

We often encourage people to come to Christ as little children—innocent and filled with childlike faith. But do we really mean it?

Jane Carole Meredith, a Southern Baptist missionary serving in Penza, Russia, works at a children's orphanage. In teaching English to the children, she yearned also to teach them the gospel story.

The Christmas season gave Jane the opportunity she had been praying for, as she planned a Christmas pageant. None of the children knew the Christmas story, so Jane shared it with them and then gave each of them Bibles of their own.

In January, after they had performed the drama, Jane began to talk with the children about loneliness and rejection. She shared with them how Jesus helped her through such problems, telling them that Jesus was her best friend.

Soon after, she and a Russian friend asked five girls to Jane's house to share testimonies. When she asked if any of them would like to know Jesus, all five yelled out in unison, "Me!"

Jane remembers what happened next: "Standing quietly aside, I watched as my Russian friend led each child in a prayer of repentance. God is faithful to bring these precious children into His kingdom."

∽

Dear Jesus, help me accept You without doubt, as a child so readily does.

January 19: A Life Transformed

"Here is a trustworthy saying that deserves full acceptance: Christ Jesus came into the world to save sinners" (1 Tim. 1:15 NIV).

On the bitter cold night of January 19, 1897, homeless Mel Trotter (1870–1940) had sold his shoes for one last drink and was headed for Lake Michigan to commit suicide. Rescue mission worker Tom Mackey found him in the Chicago blizzard and pushed Mel into the warm Pacific Garden Mission where a gospel service was going on.

"Jesus loves you, and so do I," said Harry Monroe, the mission's superintendent. "He wants to save you tonight. Put up your hand for prayer. Let God know you want to make room for Him."

Mel raised his hand. Staggering to the altar, he gave his life to Christ.

Growing up with an alcoholic bartender father, Mel had also become an alcoholic. Prior to his conversion, he had been on a six-year cycle of drunken binges and sober resolves. It took his conversion to Christ to set him free.

In 1900 he became superintendent of the Mel Trotter Rescue Mission in Grand Rapids, Michigan, a position he held until his death. He became an ordained minister in 1905 and helped supervise 68 rescue missions, many founded by former alcoholics. He also led crusades for two decades in America and Great Britain.

Do you know someone today who needs these words: "Jesus loves you, and so do I"?

Savior, thank You that through salvation empty lives can be transformed into meaningful ones.

January 20: Living Waters

"'Whoever believes in me, as the Scripture has said, streams of living water will flow from within them'" (John 7:38 NIV).

A simple well-drilling operation resulted in many Indians coming to Christ. Missions volunteer Lisa Coggin calls it a miracle.

Lisa participates in missions trips through Global Outreach, an ecumenical organization that sends volunteers and missionaries to witness for Christ and provide resources for the poor. The group currently works in Belize, Chile, Haiti, Honduras, India, Uganda, Brazil, Equador, Southeast Asia, Romania, Poland, and Mexico. This miracle took place in India, where Lisa worked with missionaries Sundar and Helen Singh.

One day after hiring well diggers, a local Hindu man came by saying, "Do not drill here. You will not get water." He proceeded to put a curse on the area they prepared to dig.

The Christians laid their hands on the drill and prayed. Sundar, in his native language, prayed, "Jesus, You are Living Water; I ask You to bring that Living Water for our souls and living water for our land, for it is Your land." The people watching them laughed.

Two hours after they started drilling, they hit water at 70 to 75 feet. By 250 feet, they hit a river. Lisa remembers: "People were coming from all around and saying that our God *is* God. A group from one of the villages wanted us to come and pray for them. Helen shared the gospel, and all believed."

∼

I praise You, Lord, for Your Living Water.

January 21: Believing Prayer

"'Whatever you ask for in prayer, believe that you have received it, and it will be yours'" (Mark 11:24 NIV).

Have you experienced the power of prayer?

Missionary J. Hudson Taylor (1832–1905) learned about the power of prayer early in life. His conversion came after the fervent prayer of his mother.

One day at 17 while alone at home he went to his father's library to find a book to read. He selected a religious leaflet. "I sat down to read the little book in an utterly unconcerned state of mind," he later said, "believing indeed at the time that if there were any salvation, it was not for me."

Hudson didn't know that his mother 70 miles away was praying for his conversion. She had resolved not to leave her room until her prayers were answered. Hour after hour she prayed for him until she "was constrained to praise God for that which His Spirit taught her had already been accomplished—the conversion of her son."

While she was praying, Hudson was reading the tract and was impressed with the phrase, "The finished work of Christ." He thought, "If the whole work was finished and the whole debt paid, what is there left for me to do?" He then fell on his knees and accepted Christ.

Days later when his mother returned home he told her he had good news. She said, "I know, my boy, I have been rejoicing in the glad tidings you have to tell me."

Lord, help me to pray believing.

January 22: Untiring in Missions Work

"She must be well attested for her good deeds, as one who has brought up children, shown hospitality, washed the feet of the saints, relieved the afflicted, and devoted herself to doing good in every way" (1 Tim. 5:10 RSV).

She was once referred to as "the guiding light of practically every benevolent project in New York City."

Remembered for her founding of the Woman's Union Missionary Society of America for Heathen Lands in 1861, Sarah Doremus (1802–1877) was involved in a vast array of Christian endeavors. Her compassion extended from her immediate family of nine children to needs around the world. She was the first director of the Women's Prison Association in New York where she served 32 years. She was manager of the City and Tract Society for 36 years and the City Bible Society for 28 years. She founded and directed the New York House and School of Industry, the Nursery and Child's Hospital, the Woman's Hospital of New York State, and the Presbyterian Home for Aged Women. Her international work included the formation of the Society for Promoting Female Education in the East.

Known as the Mother of Missions, Sarah died on January 22, 1877, after a fall in her home. E. P. Rogers, pastor of the South Dutch Reformed Church in New York, aptly eulogized her using 1 Timothy 5:10.

Have you ever thought about which Bible verse others would choose to illustrate your life?

Holy God, show me what good deeds I can do in Your name today.

January 23: A New Life

"Therefore, if anyone is in Christ, he is a new creation; the old has gone, the new has come!" (2 Cor. 5:17 NIV).

Are you depressed, need to change jobs, have low self-esteem, or need spiritual guidance?

Tammy Gaither, filling out an application for government-assisted housing, read these words on a sign on the wall. "Boy, that's me," she thought as she wrote down the phone number from the sign. The number was for the York County, South Carolina, Christian Women's Job Corps® office.

Tammy, a single parent, became homeless after her paycheck couldn't pay the bills. She moved into a friend's house. There, she got her first taste of hope.

Returning a call left on her answering machine one night, Tammy found herself talking to someone who'd actually dialed the wrong number. The man on the other line led Tammy to Christ. Still, Tammy didn't know how to turn her life around.

She moved into a homeless shelter and called the Christian Women's Job Corps (CWJC℠), a ministry of WMU that mentors and teaches life skills to women. Through CWJC, she has met four goals: a closer relationship to God, a better job, health insurance, and her own home.

"God said He would open up the windows of heaven, and there'll be so many blessings you won't be able to receive them," Tammy says. "I believe that. I am a living testimony!"

Have you ever felt hopeless? Has God ever turned your life around?

∼

Lord, thank You for second chances.

January 24: The Power of Prayer

"'When you pray, go into your room, close the door and pray to your Father, who is unseen. Then your Father, who sees what is done in secret, will reward you'" (Matt. 6:6 NIV).

After his death, family and friends discovered two ridges, or grooves, in the wooden floor by his bed. Kneeling to pray, George Muller (1805–1898) had literally worn two depressions into the floor.

Born in Prussia, he became a Christian at a prayer meeting at the age of 20. He moved to London in 1829 and joined the Plymouth Brethren movement. When he began his first pastorate at Ebenezer Chapel, he took no salary and began his life of trust and faith for his needs. While pastoring a church in Bristol in 1834, he founded the Scripture Knowledge Institution for Home and Abroad, which promoted education of biblical principles, circulated Scriptures, and supported missionary work.

He opened his first orphans home in 1835. Beginning with only two shingles (50 cents) and a few orphans, he eventually housed and educated 2,000 children in five houses on Ashley Down near Bristol. He never asked for money. Yet, in response to his faith, God sent over $7 million.

When he was 70, he and his wife set out on a worldwide missionary tour that lasted for 17 years and led to the establishment of orphanages based on his faith principles.

Do you pray believing that God will provide all of your needs? Covenant to do so during this month's National Week of Prayer.

Thank You, O God, for daily answering my prayers.

January 25: A Healing Touch

"People brought all their sick to him and begged him to let the sick just touch the edge of his cloak, and all who touched him were healed" (Matt. 14:35–36 NIV).

His heart broke at the sight of little Baby Selva. Although a year old, she weighed just ten pounds. Assembly of God missionary Mike Files realized that Selva would die if she did not receive immediate treatment.

Selva's mother had taken her to the village witch doctor, and he had instructed her not to feed her for ten days. Miraculously, though, Mike and his medical team saw Selva on their trip to the Health Care Ministries clinic set up in a school in Santa Cruz, Bolivia. They stayed with her through the night, afraid she would die before morning. Then they transferred her to a local hospital.

They spent months on Selva's physical healing and also prayed daily for God to bind the power of the witch doctor and to reach Selva's mother.

More than a year later, Mike returned to Santa Cruz and anxiously asked for any word of Selva and her mother.

"Within 20 minutes, I was thrilled to see a very healthy two-and-a-half-year-old little girl. I could hardly contain my emotions," Mike remembers. "As an added bonus, Selva's mother is now saved, attending our church there, and working at the school."

Where have you witnessed God's healing power?

Dear God, I praise You for Your power over sickness.

January 26: True Time Management

"Be very careful, then, how you live—not as unwise but as wise, making the most of every opportunity, because the days are evil" (Eph. 5:15 NIV).

Alarm clocks. Daily planners and organizers. To-do lists.

We tend to be ruled by the clock. We want to know exactly what's on our schedule and become stressed when we don't do everything on our list for the day.

Susie Edworthy, a Southern Baptist missionary in Poland, feels that flexibility is the greatest lesson she's learned on the missions field. She has realized that people in Poland aren't time-bound as Americans are.

One year Susie had just 1 free day amidst 54 straight days of overnight guests. On that 1 free day—a day she had anticipated with excitement—she came home to find another missionary visiting with her husband. He was seeking spiritual counseling.

"I realized that our schedule, no matter how busy, must allow us the opportunity to meet the needs of others," she says. "What would our witness have been had we turned them out?"

She now sees interruptions and hectic days as opportunities to reach out to others.

"If my plans are too rigid, I may miss having the opportunity to share Christ with someone."

Do you let alarm clocks and calendars rule your life? Do you need to be more flexible with your time?

∽

God, enable me to look at every moment of my day as an opportunity to live for You.

January 27: A "Royal Doctor"

"And who knows but that you have come to royal position for such a time as this?'" (Esther 4:14 NIV).

She was court physician to a Muslim prince's wife and her court where she not only ministered to their medical needs but spread the gospel.

A native of Castile, New York, Clara Swain (1834–1910) taught school near her home before entering the Women's Medical College of Philadelphia.

After graduation she went to Bareilly, India, in 1870 to teach medicine at a Methodist girls orphanage. Representing the Woman's Foreign Missionary Society of the Methodist Episcopal Church, she was the first woman missionary doctor overseas.

In 1873 Clara helped establish the first women's hospital in India. The 40-acre site was the gift of the Nawab of Rampore, a Mohammedan prince, who once bitterly opposed Christianity.

By 1880 she was treating around 7,000 patients a year. She also trained nurses and native midwives. Although a doctor, she considered herself primarily an evangelist to women.

In 1885 she accepted a position as court physician to Rani, wife of the Rajah of Khetri, Rajputana. After Rani's health improved so much, she opened a dispensary for other women of the area. Always a witness for Christ, she distributed copies of the Bible and taught hymns to women for ten years before going home to New York.

Are you allowing God to use you—whatever your role is—to spread the gospel?

God of healing, empower me today to be a witness for You.

January 28: Write It All Down

"This word came to Jeremiah from the Lord: 'Take a scroll and write on it all the words I have spoken to you'" (Jer. 36:1–2 NIV).

Journaling—the practice of writing down your thoughts, meditations, and prayers—can be a powerful spiritual discipline. Writing can be God-inspired, as it was for Jeremiah.

Many missionaries journal on a regular basis and say that it's extremely important to their spiritual growth and their daily life.

Christian and Missionary Alliance missionary to France Bev Hawkins says: "One of my favorite things to do is journal and write poetry. It helps me process what the Lord is doing inside of me. It is often encouraging to be able to look back on for a tangible record to remember where the Lord has brought me from."

Former Nazarene missionary to Denmark John Nielson says: "I reflect on life and the situations I met, the things I experience—drawing spiritual lessons from them and writing them as prose, poems, or devotions. It's my way of both meditating and journaling, as well as praying and studying the Bible."

Volunteer Quaker missionary Sandy Farley says: "I journaled every day in Kosovo. I used the practice of sitting in silence as a means of reaching clarity regarding some course of action."

Have you given thought to keeping a journal? Perhaps you should consider doing so.

Thank You, God, for the power of words.

January 29: Expand Your World

"'Enlarge the place of your tent, stretch your tent curtains wide, do not hold back; lengthen your cords, strengthen your stakes'" (Isa. 54:2 NIV).

Do you go outside your comfort zone to reach others for Christ? Do you have the courage to enlarge your world?

God often calls Christians to do just that, and many missionaries find this to be their reality.

The above words from Isaiah serve as Southern Baptist missionary Joy Oglesby's clarion call. "My worldview has been changed, and God has enlarged the place of my tent and stretched me to my limits," she says.

Joy and her husband, Butch, work in English-language ministries for Belgium, the Netherlands, Germany, Finland, Sweden, and Denmark. They live in Germany. When they first arrived on the missions field, they served with the International Baptist Church in Cologne. There Joy learned that being a Christian involves experiencing new things.

"I have learned there are many ways to worship, and in our church I truly got a glimpse of heaven," she remembers. "On any given Sunday we would have 20 to 50 different nationalities present all worshiping together. What an experience it has been, to hear so many different languages singing the same songs."

Joy's journey began years ago as a young girl in the Girls in Action® missions organization. She and Butch began their overseas service after their children went to college.

~

Give me courage, Lord, to enlarge the place of my tent. Help me enlarge my dreams for You.

January 30: Found Faithful

"Be faithful, even to the point of death, and I will give you the crown of life" (Rev. 2:10 NIV).

A missionary martyr, she was a faithful follower of Christ.

Betty Olsen grew up in Africa with missionary parents. After her mother died when she was 16, she rebelled and suffered depression. A youth counselor, Bill Gothard (who developed the Basic Institute of Youth Conflicts), helped her overcome her problems. She became a warm and caring person. Accepted by the Christian and Missionary Alliance, she was sent to Banmethuot, Vietnam—a place where the most terrible missionary massacre of the Vietnam War would occur.

On January 30, 1968, the Tet offensive began. Vietcong attacked Banmethuot killing five missionaries and a child. Betty and missionary Hank Blood were taken captive with Mike Benge, an AID (Agency for International Development) worker. They endured agonizing tortures on insect-infested jungle trails. After five months of suffering, Hank died. At the end of eight months, Betty and Mike were walking corpses. Two days after her 33rd birthday she died of dysentery and starvation.

Mike was imprisoned as a POW in North Vietnam. When released in 1973, he spoke of Betty's courage. Calling her the most unselfish person he had ever known, he said, "She never showed any bitterness or resentment. To the end she loved the ones who mistreated her."

Are you living your life unselfishly?

God, help me daily to be found faithful.

January 31: Pioneer in China

"The grass withers and the flowers fall, but the word of our God stands forever" (Isa. 40:8 NIV).

Do you understand how precious the Word of God is?

English missionary Robert Morrison (1782–1834) did. He spent many years translating the entire Bible into Chinese.

Known as the founder of Protestant missions in China, Robert became a Christian at the age of 15 while apprenticed to a shoemaker. After years of theological preparation and studying the Chinese language, he was appointed the first missionary of the London Missionary Society to China. He left London on January 31, 1807, and arrived in Canton to discover that the Chinese government forbade the preaching of Christianity and the printing of Christian books. He was allowed to stay, though, because of his proficiency in Chinese. Appointed interpreter for the East India Company, he held that position until his death.

Under the most unsuitable missionary conditions, he began the translation of the Bible into Chinese. In 1814 he had completed the New Testament, and with the aide of his colleague William Milne, he finished the Old Testament comprised of 21 volumes in 1821. He completed a Chinese dictionary in 1823.

Taking his first vacation in 17 years, he returned to England a famous man. He presented King George IV with a Chinese Bible. Returning to China, he died after 27 years of devoted service.

Dear Lord, I pray that Your Word will change people's lives in China today.

February 1: Unconditional Love

"Love is patient and kind; love is not jealous or boastful; it is not arrogant or rude. Love does not insist on its own way; it is not irritable or resentful" (1 Cor. 13: 4–5 RSV).

"To love a human being means to accept him, to love him as he is.... I must accept the pain of seeing him with hopefulness and expectancy," she once said.

Florence Allshorn (1888–1950) was an English missionary leader whose life exemplified unconditional love. William Paton, secretary of the International Missionary Council, said of her: "I think she has the greatest spiritual insight of anyone I have ever known."

Perhaps Florence's secret was her understanding of Christian love.

In 1920 she served with the Church Missionary Society in Uganda as the director of a girls boarding school. Seven young missionaries had preceded her, but none had stayed because of the unhealthy climate and because of the difficult senior missionary. Almost in despair one day because her relationship with her female colleague also seemed to be a failure, Florence began to pray fervently about the situation. She also read 1 Corinthians 13 every day and would continue to do so for a whole year. Slowly things improved as she began to respond to her colleague with Christlike love.

Is God leading you to demonstrate unconditional love toward a friend or a colleague?

~

God, help me today to grasp the profound words of 1 Corinthians 13 and apply them to my life.

February 2: Kenya's Street Children

"If I speak in the tongues of men and of angels, but have not love, I am only a resounding gong or a clanging cymbal" (1 Cor. 13:1 NIV).

The boy, just eight years old, roams the streets of Kisumu, Kenya, in search of food and shelter. He scavenges for food in garbage cans and often resorts to begging and stealing to make it through the day. Abandoned by his family years ago, he can rely only on himself—for he is truly an outcast of society.

Darla Calhoun, a missionary nurse with Medical Ambassadors, regularly saw such children in her work and felt deeply moved by their plight. She began organizing weekly outdoor meetings and Sunday afternoon soccer games for the street children.

In 1993, Darla founded the Agape Children's Ministry (ACM) to reach out formally to Kenya's street children. The organization provides a home for 24 young boys. A literacy school teaches them basic math, reading, and English skills. People from around the world also sponsor individual children.

Darla says that street children are a worldwide phenomenon. "Throughout the world there are millions of abandoned and homeless children living in the streets," she says.

The answer to helping them, she says, is love. ACM strives "to provide a Christian family atmosphere of love and acceptance."

Hence the organization's name—*agape* is the Greek word for love.

Won't you pray today for the world's street children?

I pray, God, that You will bless the children of the world who feel abandoned and alone.

February 3: A Door Closes—But Another One Opens

"Knock, and the door will be opened" (Matt. 7:7 NIV).

"There are no openings in Africa for black missionaries."

Her letter of rejection shattered her dream to become a missionary.

Educator and advocate for black women, Mary McLeod Bethune (1875–1955) never went to Africa, but other doors opened for her in America.

She was the only 1 of 17 children in her family to attend Mayesville (S.C.) Presbyterian Mission for Negroes. Her education continued at Scotia Seminary (N.C.) followed by graduation at Moody Bible Institute in 1895. At Moody she was part of the inner-city missions teams. She said of her time there: "At Moody we learned to look upon a man as a man, not as a Caucasian or Negro. A love for the whole human family entered my soul."

After being rejected for foreign missionary service, she and her husband, Albertus Bethune, started a mission school in Palatka, Florida. She opened a mission school in Daytona in 1904. After buying an abandoned garbage dump called Hell Hole, she established the Daytona Beach Literary and Industrial School for Negro Girls. In two years it had 250 students. In 1923 the school became Bethune-Cookman College. She served as college president until 1942.

Mary founded the National Council of Negro Women in 1935. In 1936 she organized the Federal council on Negro Affairs, also know as the Black Cabinet.

Have you allowed rejection to defeat your purposes?

Thank You, Loving God, that when doors close, others open to endless possibilities.

February 4: A Simple Hug

"Now about brotherly love we do not need to write to you, for you yourselves have been taught by God to love each other. . . . Yet we urge you . . . to do so more and more" (1 Thess. 4:9,10 NIV).

"As I drive down the street, I see kids and teens standing on street corners ready to die for a lack of love."

Kids are dying for love—this is the message that Ken Brown and his wife, Kathy, have for Christians. In their work as Assemblies of God missionaries in inner-city Washington, D.C., they see children begging for a loving touch. "I'm amazed at the love starvation factor here," Ken says.

Missionaries Bill and Cheryl Gray agree. They work in 13 inner-city housing projects in Mobile, Alabama. Cheryl says that she daily sees children as young as five out on the streets, watching adults act in very unloving ways. And at home, things aren't much better, as many see drug addiction or domestic violence firsthand.

The result is that many children don't know how to receive love. "We give them a hug, and they don't know how to respond," Cheryl says.

The Grays and Browns say that we must remember the children of America's inner cities.

What can you do for the many children in your own community who don't know the meaning of love?

~

Dear God, bless the children in my world who don't receive love. Make me a vessel of that love.

February 5: Maintaining Fortitude

"But we have this treasure in jars of clay to show that this all-surpassing power is from God and not from us. We are hard pressed on every side, but not crushed; perplexed, but not in despair; persecuted, but not abandoned; struck down, but not destroyed" (2 Cor. 4:7–8 NIV).

When her husband, Adoniram, was arrested and imprisoned for 21 months in a filthy, vermin-infested Burmese prison, she moved nearby and regularly ministered to him bringing him food and nursing him through fevers.

Ann Judson's amazing capacity to suffer through the most perilous adversities bears witness that her power came from God.

The first woman missionary to the Far East, Ann (1789–1826) opened a school for Burmese girls and helped her husband translate the New Testament into Burmese. (She sewed his manuscript into a pillow and smuggled it to him while he was in prison.) Her first child died of jungle fever, and she constantly had tropical diseases that left her in a weakened state.

Ann's health deteriorated while caring for Adoniram in prison. She died shortly after he was released. Her daughter's death followed hers in six months. Her missionary career of 14 years may not have been long, but her legacy of spiritual fortitude lives on.

Are you allowing the adversities of life to destroy your spirit and witness?

Sustaining God, give me strength today when situations are difficult and seem overwhelming. Empower me with Your love and constant care.

February 6: Generosity Out of Poverty

"Out of the most severe trial, their overflowing joy and their extreme poverty welled up in rich generosity. For I testify that they gave as much as they were able, and even beyond their ability" (2 Cor. 8:2–3 NIV).

She had a "missionary" hen that contributed $8.00 for missions and a row of sugar cane that brought forth $6.00.

Former slave Hester Williams presented the $14.00 to the Louisiana Annual Conference of the Woman's Home Missionary Society in 1882 as a challenge to the Methodist Episcopal Church to match her funds in order to start more schools. Aunt Hester had little formal education; yet, she was a pioneer in starting schools for freed girls and women in Baton Rouge, Louisiana.

In 1886 she traveled to Detroit to plead for funds to open the Hester Williams Industrial Home. At this annual meeting of the Woman's Home Missionary Society she received $200.00, which she used to start five schools in addition to the home founded in her name. Traveling by foot, horseback, wagon and mule, boat, and train, she established schools teaching the Bible, catechism, and sewing to her girls.

Have you ever felt that your resources were inadequate to meet needs around you? May the legacy of Aunt Hester show us that a little can have a great impact.

Today, Lord, reveal to me where needs exist. Enable me to give beyond my means to meet them in Your name.

February 7: Favorite Verses

"I have hidden your word in my heart that I might not sin against you" (Psalm 119:11 NIV).

What is your favorite Bible verse?

Missionaries have their own favorite pieces of Scripture. They give assurance to their call and help them in the struggles they often face.

These verses can speak afresh to us by reminding us of the call we each have to missions and by providing us with confidence amidst any struggles we may face.

Mitch Land, former Southern Baptist missionary to the Ivory Coast, says that John 14:6 is his favorite verse. It reminds us of the message we are delivering to the world: "Jesus answered, 'I am the way and the truth and the life. No one comes to the Father except through me.'"

Bonnie Harvey, a volunteer who has gone on a number of missions trips through her Georgia Presbyterian church, says that Romans 8:28 gives her strength and confidence. It says: "And we know that in all things God works for the good of those who love him, who have been called according to his purpose."

Mark and Carolyn Lozuk, Southern Baptist missionaries to Bolivia, remind us that Proverbs 3:5–6 gives us instruction for living a Christ-filled life: "Trust in the Lord with all your heart and lean not on your own understanding; in all your ways acknowledge him, and he will make your paths straight."

Thank You, God, for the powerful and encouraging words You give us through the Bible.

February 8: Honoring God

"Those who honor me I will honor"' (1 Sam. 2:30 NIV).

A note slipped into his hand before he ran the 400-meter race at the 1924 Paris Olympics reminded him of the passage in 1 Samuel.

Before this race, Eric Liddell (1902–1945) had truly honored God. He had refused to compete in the 100-meter race that he had trained for because the event was held on a Sunday. Criticized by many for being legalistic, Eric stuck to his convictions. He entered the 200-meter race winning a bronze medal and the 400-meter for which he won a gold, broke the world record, and received worldwide honors.

The 1981 Oscar-winning movie, *Chariots of Fire*, which chronicled Liddell's victory, brought renewed fame to "Scotland's greatest athlete." The movie, though, told only part of his story.

Graduating from Edinburgh University in 1925, Eric followed in his missionary father's steps and joined the London Missionary Society as a teacher at the Tientsin Anglo-Chinese Christian College. He served there and as a rural evangelist near Siachang until the Japanese held him in a camp in 1942. In prison he served others energetically. Totally expending himself and not realizing he had a brain tumor, he died in February 1945.

Eric Liddell took every opportunity to honor Christ as an athlete, missionary, and prisoner. Do you honor God in everything that you do?

∽

Worthy Lord, today and every day, help me to honor You with my life.

February 9: The Blind Can See

"'The blind receive sight, the lame walk'" (Luke 7:22 NIV).

The city of Kano, Nigeria, is often called a "blind town" because it is home to thousands of blind and handicapped people. Peter and Miriam Fretheim, Society of International Missions missionaries to Nigeria, helped start an outreach in the area that treats the sick with medicine and also shares God's love.

Peter says that one day the blind chief of Kano, one of the most prominent chiefs of thousands in West Africa, shared some incredible news with the missions team. More than 40 of his people had told him they had been healed of their sicknesses. He also felt healed and knew that Jesus was the reason for his newfound health.

Peter adds: "He did not use the Islamic title for Jesus, which is Isa, but instead used the name Jesus which is amazing by itself!"

Soon after, Peter learned of another prominent leader who had become a Christian. When missionaries met with the man, he requested someone who could secretly disciple him and teach him more about Jesus and the Bible. "He also told us that he is not the only one," Peter says. "There are seven others who have placed their trust in the Savior."

Isn't it amazing how God can change the lives of those who trust in Him?

∼

Thank You, God, that You have made me to see. I rejoice in the new spiritual sight I have because of You.

February 10: A New Language

"Paul stood on the steps and motioned to the crowd. When they were all silent, he said to them in Aramaic" (Acts 21:40 NIV).

If you were traveling to an unfamiliar country, what would be your main concern? I would be concerned that I wouldn't be able to communicate with anyone. I would have trepidation about learning the language of the land.

Many missionaries have the same concerns, realizing that the practicality of learning a new language sometimes has to take precedence over the spiritual work they are ready to do.

Southern Baptist missionaries David and Tami Wood have had to learn not just one, but several new languages. When first appointed to the Niger Republic in West Africa, they spent nine months in French language study and then another three months in studying Zarma, a language of Niger. Several years later they relocated to the neighboring country of Burkina Faso and had to learn still another language.

"A new country meant learning a new language, a new culture, a new job, and a new ministry," Tami says. "We spent the first few months in Mooré language study."

Leona Choy, former missionary to China, says the Chinese language is especially challenging. Although the written form of Chinese is uniform, the way it is pronounced varies from people group to people group. "Their pronunciation may be almost unintelligible to someone from another part of China," Leona says.

~

Lord, I recognize the dedication of missionaries serving You in foreign nations. Give them skill in learning new languages.

February 11: Living for Christ

"For to me, to live is Christ and to die is gain" (Phil. 1:21 NIV).

Soon after his death, his Chinese friends risked danger to erect a marker for him. The Scripture verse they chose for his grave was Philippians 1:21. They knew that the doctor had lived only to serve them.

Are you familiar with the indomitable Southern Baptist missionary who died in February 1951 in a Communist prison?

Bill Wallace (1908–1951) was a resident in surgery at Knoxville General Hospital in Tennessee when he applied to the Foreign Mission Board (now International Mission Board). "I do feel God can use my training as a physician," he wrote in 1934. "As humbly as I know how, I want to volunteer to serve as a medical missionary."

Bill's application was welcomed because a surgeon was direly needed at Stout Memorial Hospital in Wuchow. Arriving in China in 1935, he soon endeared himself to his patients bringing physical as well as spiritual healing to them. In 1938 when war between Japan and China started, he worked at the hospital around the clock. In World War II he served until Japanese forces neared the city. He then evacuated the hospital, taking all the equipment, until it was safe to return.

When the Communists invaded Wuchow in 1949, he remained at his post, even caring for the sick. An intense anti-America campaign in 1950 led to his arrest. Falsely accused of spying, he was imprisoned and died 53 days later.

~

Lord, today I want to serve You.

February 12: Truly Praising God

"How good it is to sing praises to our God, how pleasant and fitting to praise him!" (Psalm 147:1 NIV).

Although pastors shouldn't do it, Sam Wolff couldn't help but dread the upcoming church service a little bit. He was running behind schedule as it was, and the service he would oversee that morning would be an extended one. There was confirmation, baptism, communion for at least 1,000, and performances by many guest choirs. It was a big day for the Nairobi church, but it would also be a long one.

Sam, who works as a pastor under the Division for Global Mission of the Evangelical Lutheran Church in America, started for the church well ahead of time, and then, unexpectedly, his Land Rover broke down. He called the church, telling other leaders that he might be an hour late and to start the service without him.

Three hours later, he breathlessly entered the church. He was amazed to find that the service had still not begun. Fighting exasperation, he wondered what had kept them from starting without him.

Then, he realized the truth and was suddenly humbled. For three hours the Kenyans had truly praised God. They prayed, talked, read from the Bible, and mostly sang. "They sang as only Africans can," Sam remembers.

The experience, Sam says, was "humbling and life-changing."

Do you ever miss opportunities to praise God because you are too busy or too stressed?

∼

Reveal to me more ways to praise You every day, Lord.

February 13: An Almost-Perfect Soul

"Share with God's people who are in need. Practice hospitality" (Rom. 12:13 NIV).

The grandeur and history of St. Petersburg awaited Sharon and George Bretherick. The day of sight-seeing, though, became more of a lesson about the heart of the Estonian people than a tourist experience.

Sharon and George, who traveled to Tallinn, Estonia, on an 11-month missions trip to equip Estonian and Russian educators to teach Christian ethics and missions, took a two-day break to visit the former capital city.

Maxx, the son of their Estonian next-door neighbor, took it upon himself to be their guide. Maxx and two other neighbors took turns showing Sharon and George the sights of the city. Sharon says that their generosity amazed her, making her wonder if she would treat total strangers in such a kind way. She also says that it gives a glimpse into the Estonian and Russian soul.

When she asked Maxx why they were doing so much for them, he seemed taken aback. "Oh, it is nothing," he said. "Any Russian would do this for you. That's the way we Russians are."

Looking back, Sharon reflects: "The Russian spirit is one of indescribable buoyancy, indomitable spirit, impassioned love, and loyalty. All the Russian soul is lacking to be a perfectly packaged partner for us who love the Lord is our everything, Jesus Christ our Lord."

When have you experienced such hospitality and kindness?

Thank You, God, for the hospitality of strangers. Remind me to practice hospitality today.

February 14: Ministering in Love

"Do everything in love" (1 Cor. 16:14 NIV).

She left the world some memorable quotes about love:
"We can do no great things; only small things with great love."
"There is no greater sickness in the world today than the lack of love."
"People who love each other fully and truly are the happiest people in the world."
Mother Teresa (1910–1997) epitomized love. Her selfless acts of charity endeared her to millions throughout the world.

Born Agnes Gonxha Bojaxhiu to Albanian parents in Yugoslavia, she joined the Sisters of Loretto, an Irish order of missionary nuns. After studying in Ireland, she moved to Calcutta and taught history and geography at her order's high school for 17 years.

Sensing God's call to work among the poor, she founded the Missionaries of Charity in 1950. The nuns took four vows: poverty, chastity, obedience, and free service to the poor. Her Calcutta work included a home for the dying, an orphanage, a leper colony, medical centers, and shelters. Her ministries to the "poorest of the poor" eventually spread around the world. She received the first Pope John XXIII Peace Prize in 1971, the first Templeton Prize in 1973, and the Nobel Peace Prize in 1979. She accepted all prizes in the name of "the hungry, the naked, the homeless."

How can you reach out in compassion to those around you?

God, thank You that because of Your great love toward me, I want to minister to others in Your name.

February 15: Everyone's Mission

"For Christ's love compels us, because we are convinced that one died for all, and therefore all died" (2 Cor. 5:14 NIV).

So you think you can't be a missionary? Perhaps you're one already and don't even realize it.

Deborah Brunt says that her own experiences prove that God sometimes leads people to missions, and they don't even realize it's happening. A Christian's call to missions can be, as hers was, a "surprise call."

Deborah is the women's missions and ministries specialist for the Baptist General Convention of Oklahoma. She administers and guides the missions activities and education for the Baptist group, but she says that her purpose is really deeper than that.

"I have a missionary purpose, and it is to challenge women to know Christ, grow in Christ, and to echo God's heart for the world," she says. It is a purpose we should all strive to fulfill.

As a child, Deborah told God she would be a missionary if He wanted her to be one. Life went on, and she began to serve God through writing, speaking, and performing drama. Was she a missionary, though? She wasn't quite sure.

Deborah soon realized, though, that those activities were both her talents and her mission. In writing, speaking, and performing, she was encouraging other women to be on mission.

"Isn't God amazing?" she asks. "He led me to become a missionary without my even realizing it."

Your love compels me to be on mission for You, Lord. Remind me today to show that love to others.

February 16: Return to the Lord

"'Come let us return to the Lord. . . . Let us acknowledge the Lord; let us press on and acknowledge him. As surely as the sun rises, he will appear'" (Hos. 6:1,3 NIV).

Bev Hawkins likes to remind people that missionaries are very human—just like all Christians. "Missionaries are not exempt from temptation, sin, discouragement, and rebellion, and we need much grace," she says. "How wonderful that God's grace is as amazing as it is, that is extends to every one of us ragamuffins equally."

Bev and her husband, Tom, serve as Christian and Missionary Alliance missionaries in Vélizy, France. They both work in administrative capacities, supporting the work of other missionaries in the area. They also reach out in their community, sharing the gospel message with neighbors.

"I try to do outreach in the community," Bev says. "This happens mainly through monthly craft meetings with neighbor friends and an annual Thanksgiving dinner, as well as day-to-day contacts."

The above verses in Hosea give Bev strength for whatever job she is doing. It reminds her that all Christians sometimes wander from their call.

"I find myself often in a position of having to return to the Lord. I am so prone to wandering," she says. "I find assurance in knowing that His coming to me is certain."

When are you prone to wander from God? Do you realize you can always return to Him?

Eternal God, thank You for Your unfailing love toward me even when I wander.

February 17: A Person of Prayer

"Epaphras, who is one of you and a servant of Christ Jesus, sends greetings. He is always wrestling in prayer for you" (Col. 4:12 NIV).

One observer described his praying as "dry, choking sobs that showed how the depths of his soul were being stirred."

John Hyde (1865–1912), known as Praying Hyde, would sometimes pray for over 40 hours on his knees.

One of the most fervent persons of prayer in Christian history, Hyde was the son of a Presbyterian minister. After graduating from Carthage College in Carthage, Illinois, and the Presbyterian Church's McCormick Seminary in Chicago, he went to the Punjab region of India as a Presbyterian missionary in 1892. As soon as he arrived in India, he started praying for revival. He learned several of the local languages and taught Bible in a boys high school. He often traveled to remote villages leading people to Christ and praying with stumbling converts.

In July 1904 he began a 30-day prayer vigil for a spiritual life convention to be held in August in Sialkot, India. Vigilant, intensive praying by the participants led to many conversions as revival broke out. For years Hyde led prayer sessions for the annual conventions.

Completely worn out by his labor, he returned to New York in 1911 and died of a brain tumor on February 17, 1912. His last words were, "Bol Yisu Masih, Ki Jai!" (Shout the victory of Jesus Christ!)

Do you "wrestle" in prayer for the lost?

Holy God, make me diligent in my prayers.

February 18: Showers of Blessings

"I will bless them and the places surrounding my hill. . . . There will be showers of blessings" (Ezek. 34:26 NIV).

Stark constrasts surround her. Beautiful white clouds serve as a canopy for the green Andes mountains. Below the mountain peaks stand shabby huts and dirty faces.

Southern Baptist missionary Dana Seale faces poverty every day in her work in lush, naturally beautiful Venezuela. She sees children who are hungry and swollen by parasites and houses that are nothing more than dirt floors and thatched walls.

A worship experience at an open-air church, however, taught Dana that God's blessings abound.

At the service, villagers sang praise songs in their Yukpa language. They laughed, shared, and sang joyfully.

Then the village chief stood up and thanked the missionaries and volunteers for the improvements they had made. He thanked them for the medicine, food, and school supplies they had brought over the mountains.

"We have everything we need," the chief told them.

Dana stood in awe at his words. How could he be thankful when his villagers still faced the reality of infant mortality and ever-present hunger?

She realized that it was the work of the Holy Spirit. He had taught them to count their blessings, instead of cursing their hardships.

Do you sometimes forget to praise God for the blessings He has showered upon you?

∽

Lord God, today thank You for the many blessings You have given me. Help me to be mindful of them every day.

February 19: America's First Missionary Hero

"Now you have observed my teaching, my conduct, my aim in life, my faith, my patience, my love, my steadfastness, my persecutions, my sufferings" (2 Tim. 3:10–11 RSV).

When he returned home in 1845 for his first and only furlough, he was revered as a saint. A Brown University professor described people's feelings toward him: "Hundreds were gazing for the first time upon one, the story of whose labors and sorrows and sufferings had been familiar to them from childhood, and whose name they had been accustomed to utter with reverence and affection."

Did you know that Adoniram Judson (1788–1850) was the first great American missionary hero?

Born in Malden, Massachusetts, Adoniram graduated from Brown University and attended Andover Seminary. He married schoolteacher Ann Hasseltine on February 5, 1812. They sailed on February 19 with the first team of missionaries commissioned from America. Through Ann's letters and journals from Burma, Americans learned about the couple's sacrifices and sufferings and felt as if they knew them.

Supporters rejoiced in May 1819 when the Judsons baptized their first convert and the next year when their small church baptized ten members. They grieved when Adoniram, accused of spying, was confined in a vermin-infested "death" prison for a year and a half and when Ann and children died.

Despite many sufferings, Adoniram experienced success. He translated the Bible into Burmese, produced a dictionary, composed much literature, and trained pastors and evangelists.

Almighty God, help me through times of sufferings to persevere.

February 20: Spread the Word

"In this way the word of the Lord spread widely and grew in power" (Acts 19:20 NIV).

More than 440 million people have yet to hear the Word of the Lord in their own language.

For Kurtis Smith, a missionary with Lutheran Bible Translators, that fact motivates him. "Should we sit on our couches of security and pity the people who haven't heard of salvation by grace? We must not."

When Smith visited the Enga people of Papua New Guinea, he realized the importance of Bible translation. The Enga, who already had the Old Testament, were asking now for a translation of the New Testament.

One day Smith stood outside with a group of missionaries and villagers and noticed one man in particular:

"His leathered face was wrinkled with years of wisdom. His steel machete protected his life as well as his wealth. And wealth this man had as he proudly displayed on a long bamboo necklace. Thirty-nine pigs he owned, each pig represented by a small shoot of bamboo sewn together with bark string and decorated with local seeds. He was a big man from the Enga Province."

The wealthy villager taught Smith something. "We have the Word of God in our own language—in fact, in over 400 English versions," he says. "We have wealth equal to thousands of pigs and yet we often don't realize that we have the good news."

Are you grateful today for the good news?

~

Dear Lord, I thank You for Your Word. May I appreciate it more.

February 21: Home As A Mission

"As Jesus and his disciples were on their way, he came to a village where a woman named Martha opened her home to him" (Luke 10:38 NIV).

"I invited a few to meet with me at my home for a prayer service," the dedicated missionary wrote. "Fifty have been coming, and we have emerged into a missionary society whose aim is to care for the sick... and help others in need."

Lucy Gantt Sheppard (1867–1955) formed the first women's society of the Presbyterian Congo Mission in her home. One of the first black missionary women to the Congo, Lucy had already opened her home at Luebo as a place to train girls of the Pantops Home. She said that "the making of a Christian home was part of my missionary task and I was glad that my house could be used."

Lucy was born on February 21, 1867, in Tuscaloosa, Alabama, to Eliza Gantt, an orphaned ex-slave. After graduating from Talladega College in 1886, she taught school until her marriage to William Sheppard in 1894. That year they sailed for the Congo where Lucy served as a teacher, evangelist, and nurse. Assigned to the new Ibanche station in Bakuba territory in 1899, she founded the first school there with 15 students. In 1901 it had grown to 70 students.

Is God calling you to use your home for missions work?

Lord, thank You for my home. Show me today how I can utilize it for Your service.

February 22: Joy in Ministry

"And he took the children in his arms, put his hands on them and blessed them" (Mark 10:16 NIV).

As Doug and Nancy Soderdahl journeyed through the beautiful east African landscape, they knew little of what to expect. They were traveling to northeast Nairobi, Kenya, to visit Joy Town, a Salvation Army home for crippled children. A urologist and a nurse, they didn't know what medical needs they might encounter.

Arriving at Joy Town, a boarding school for 500 children in grades 1–12, they admired the beautiful campus. They enjoyed tea with the assistant principal and prayed with him for wisdom and power.

Moments later, the scene changed. They encountered 19 children with severe spina bifida. They all had poor or no lower limb function, and little or no bladder and bowel control. Doug shook his head as he saw children in urine-soaked diapers and teenagers with bedsores aggravated by constant soiling. They were racked with shame and low self-esteem.

Miraculously, Doug and Nancy had brought the right types and quantities of medical supplies. They taught the children and many workers how to alleviate the problems.

Doug says he experienced real joy in a depressing situation. "It is thrilling to see God so obviously at work," he says, "in the joy of the disabled children, in the love of the staff, in the unity of fellow Christians ministering with a cup of cold water in Christ's name."

∼

We praise You, God of joy, for Your power over distressing circumstances.

February 23: Complete Love

"Dear friends, since God so loved us, we also ought to love one another.... If we love one another, God lives in us and his love is made complete in us" (1 John 4:11–12 NIV).

Do you love others completely?

British Methodist missionary David Hill (1840–1896) did. He died of typhus after contracting the disease while caring for famine victims in China.

Independently wealthy, David gave his income to Christian work. Representing the Wesleyan Missionary Society, he worked as an evangelist and church planter. He trained missionaries, pastors, and lay workers in central China. He founded secondary schools, schools for the blind, orphanages, and homes for the aged. His varied ministries included founding the Christian Literature Society and fighting the opium trade. His special vocation lay in famine relief.

David's most famous convert was Pastor Hsi (1830–1896) who became one of China's greatest preachers. At the age of 49, Hsi was dramatically converted after reading the Gospel of Matthew in order to enter a literary contest arranged by David. Hsi worked with David and later with the China Inland Mission. A man of strong faith and prayer, Pastor Hsi became a spiritual giant. Because of his own former bondage to opium, he opened rehabilitation centers where opium addicts, through the power of Christ, could be delivered from their addiction.

Thank You, our Liberator, for the example that David Hill and Pastor Hsi have left us in their love for You and for others.

February 24: Surviving Loss

"I consider everything a loss compared to the surpassing greatness of knowing Christ Jesus my Lord, for whose sake I have lost all things. I consider them rubbish, that I may gain Christ and be found in him" (Phil. 3:8 NIV).

During their years as Southern Baptist missionaries in West Africa, Mary Lou and Fred Levrets suffered many losses. They lost their home and all their earthly possessions two separate times as a result of the country's civil wars. They also lost a son at the age of 35.

Still, despite these losses, the Levretses say as they look back at their missionary service that they have only one regret—the fact that they couldn't serve more. "A large part of my heart remains in West Africa," Mary Lou proclaims. "There is still so much more to be done!"

Now retired, the couple recalls with fondness the work they did in God's name and the foundation they helped lay for future generations of missionaries.

"When we went to Africa, we hoped to be able to work ourselves out of a job," she explains. "That is exactly what happened. Today we see capable, qualified Baptist partners able to carry on much of the work."

Today, they continue spreading word of the work God enabled them to do and that He enables others to do in West Africa and around the world.

What losses have you encountered in your lifetime? How has God used them for His good?

∼

Thank You, Lord, for missionaries and their dedication, even in loss.

February 25: Labors of Love

"They will rest from their labor, for their deeds will follow them" (Rev. 14:13 NIV).

Did you know that some missionaries served over 60 years?

Evelyn "Granny" Brand toiled 63 years in southern India reaching the impoverished people on six mountain ranges of the Mountains of Death. Anne Luther Bagby served 61 years in Brazil, the longest tenure of any Southern Baptist missionary. David Zeisberger labored 60 years among the Delaware Indians.

Consider the "roll call" of service over 50 years: Amy Carmichael served 56 years in India, without a furlough. Mabel Francis labored 56 years in Japan, several in internment during World War II. Ludwig Nommensen worked 56 years in Indonesia. Lucy Thurston spent 56 years in Hawaii. R. H. Graves, a Southern Baptist physician from Maryland, served in China for 56 years from 1856 to 1912.

Cornelius Van Alan Van Dyck worked 55 years in Syria. Malla Moe served in Swaziland for 54 years preaching in places no one had ever gone. Henry Jessup was a missionary in Syria for 54 years. Robert Moffat spent 53 years (with one furlough) and Mary Moffat 52 years in South Africa. Robert Laws ministered 52 years in Africa as a doctor and educator. Lillian Trasher, Assemblies of God missionary, toiled 50 years in Egypt in orphanage work.

God, help me labor in the task You have given me—as long as You give me strength.

February 26: Loving God Completely

"'Love the Lord your God with all your heart and with all your soul and with all your mind and with all your strength'" (Mark 12:30 NIV).

"I want people to be passionately in love with Jesus," she said, "so that nothing else counts."

To missionary physician Helen Roseveare medicine was her way of introducing others to Christ.

She was converted while attending college at Cambridge University. In 1953 she arrived in Ibambi, Belgian Congo (Zaire), representing the Worldwide Evangelization Crusade (WEC).

Setting up a dispensary, she built a hospital and trained African nurses. After she moved to Nebobongo, she established a hospital, a training center, and clinics. After five years, she went on furlough in England for more training.

Immediately after returning to the Congo in 1960, civil war broke out, and violence against Whites began. She continued her medical work amid harsh conditions. In the next four years she was attacked, beaten, and brutally raped. Imprisoned for five months by rebel Simba soldiers in 1964, she was able to comfort other rape victims. After she was freed, she returned to England in 1965, vowing never to return. Following a plea from a doctor, she returned to Nebobongo establishing the Evangelical Medical Center. In 1971 she turned the accredited hospital over to the nationals.

Returning to England in 1973, she became an author and an international speaker for WEC.

Do you love God with all of your being?

~

Help me, God of grace, daily to put You first in my life.

February 27: Sowing Where the Spirit Leads

"Other seeds fell on good soil and brought forth grain, some a hundredfold, some sixty, some thirty" (Matt. 13: 8 NRSV).

The Holy Spirit has taught her that she works in partnership with Him, and her part is to simply plant seeds.

Martha Golson, the director of the International Weekday Program at First Baptist Church, Tuscaloosa, Alabama, says that she used to worry about the ministry's results. She has learned, though, that she can only do her part.

"I do my part and answer the call," Martha says. "I've done all I can, and I rest in that."

Waiting for people to believe the Christian message is oftentimes a long process in international work. "Their opinion of Christians is usually not good," she says. "And they wonder why we do this for them. When they ask, then we say we do it because God loves us and we want to serve others." Many people participate only in the English classes and nothing more. Some, though, take the bold steps to make friends and learn about the gospel."

The program—which is part of the larger International Ministry started by Lillian Hinton, Betty Hollingsworth, and Vial Fontenot more than 20 years ago—holds English classes, craft classes, two Bible studies, and a family supper each week. More than 1,200 students from 68 different countries have participated.

Do you ever want to hurry along the work of the Holy Spirit?

∽

Loving God, remind me today that sowing seeds for You is so important.

February 28: Christ in You

"I have been crucified with Christ and I no longer live, but Christ lives in me" (Gal. 2:20 NIV).

She founded Mount Holyoke Female Seminary to "cultivate the missionary spirit among its pupils; the feeling that they should live for God and do something as teachers, or in such other ways as Providence may direct."

Mary Lyon (1797–1849), the founder and first president of what is now Mount Holyoke College, was born on a remote farm in Buckland, Massachusetts, on February 28, 1797. An interest in missions that began in childhood prompted her to organize the first mission society in Buckland.

After years of teaching, she started a campaign in 1834 to raise funds for a women's college that would be similar to those for men. As she traveled through small towns in New England, her health declined; but she refused to quit. Her sacrificial spirit toward Mount Holyoke is evident in a letter to her mother: "Had I a thousand lives, I would sacrifice them all in suffering and hardship for its sake."

Mount Holyoke opened in 1837 with a purpose of equipping Christian teachers with a mission to convert their students. During its first 12 years, 12 of its students became missionary teachers to the American Indians. By the time of her death, 70 students had become foreign missionaries.

Are you allowing God to work through your vocation to accomplish His purposes?

Dear God, may my life daily exemplify Christ living through me.

February 29: International Friendships

"'For there is no difference between Jew and Gentile—the same Lord is Lord of all and richly blesses all who call on him'" (Rom. 10:12 NIV).

My community has a large Hispanic population. My mother's, a university town, has a large Asian population. People from all different cultures and countries make their lives in our midst. Our country truly is a melting pot.

Perhaps you feel a special urge to make friendships with international individuals in your area. Maybe God wants you to break down the barriers and prejudice that often exist between different culture groups.

The Southern Baptist International Mission Board says that there are some easy ways to minister to internationals: (1) Invite an international (a student, immigrant, family) to your home for a meal. (2) Invite an international to your home to celebrate a holiday. (3) Volunteer to teach English-as-a-second-language classes at your church. (4) Purchase a Bible in the language of your international friend. (5) Locate the nearest migrant camp and volunteer your help. (6) Call a local Christian college and ask about the needs of international students. (7) Sponsor a potluck International Night at your church and ask internationals in your community to share their favorite dishes.

Which of these things can you do today or this week?

~

You are the Lord of all people. Open my eyes to any prejudice or ill feelings I may have toward people of other cultures. Open my heart to love them more.

March 1: Role Models

"To this you were called, because Christ suffered for you, leaving you as an example, that you should follow in his steps" (1 Peter 2:21 NIV).

Missionaries not only serve Christ and others, they also become great role models for other missionaries.

David Brainerd and David Livingstone were two who have inspired and motivated countless others.

David Brainerd (1718–1747), missionary to the American Indians, lived only 29 years, but through his diary he influenced many missionaries. Anglican missionary Henry Martyn felt called to missions after reading the life of Brainerd. Martyn, in turn—after his death at 31—influenced many others to missions through his *Journals and Letters*. While English cobbler William Carey began to develop a biblical perspective on missions, he read Brainerd's writings. Methodist Thomas Coke also read the diary on his voyage over to America to evangelize.

Missionary explorer David Livingstone (1813–1873) opened up the continent of Africa and inspired many to follow him. After reading Livingstone's *Travels*, Scottish missionary Robert Laws followed in his footsteps the year after Livingstone's death. That same year—1875—Mary Slessor, another Presbyterian, offered herself to the mission board. Impressed by Livingstone, Scottish Frederick Stanley Arnot felt God calling him to Africa in 1881. He became a great explorer and, like Livingstone, brought others to Africa including Daniel Crawford who had a remarkable ministry.

God, thank You for the ripple effect that committed lives to Christ can have on others. May my life so reflect Christ that others can see Him, not me.

March 2: What Are Your Hobbies?

"And pray for us, too, that God may open a door for our message, so that we may proclaim the mystery of Christ" (Col. 4:3 NIV).

Sometimes Christians don't know where to begin in ministering and witnessing to others.

In looking for ways to share Christ with others in Portugal, Southern Baptist missionary Tina Butts came up with a plan: she would use her hobbies to build relationships. She looked at two of her hobbies—crafts and music—and asked how she could use them in Christian ministry.

Tina's answer was to teach women to make crafts and to give music lessons to children. The music lessons are especially popular because Portuguese public schools don't teach music and private lessons are too expensive for ordinary citizens. Tina is also considering using her talent for sign language to start a deaf ministry.

Tina's days are full—in addition to the crafts and music lessons, she works in church planting with her husband, John, and homeschools her three children—but filled with opportunities and blessings. She says that she and her husband are "in the best place in the world" because they are open to God's will for their lives.

How can you use your talents and hobbies for God's glory?

Dear Lord, reveal to me how I can use my hobbies for You. Then make me willing to use them to tell others of Your love.

March 3: Doing Missions

"Jesus went through all the towns and villages, teaching in their synagogues, preaching the good news of the kingdom and healing every disease and sickness. When he saw the crowds, he had compassion on them" (Matt. 9:35–36 NIV).

What could a poor Honduran woman teach an Alabama Baptist minister?

Gil McKee says his most humbling experience during his two missions trips to Honduras involved a woman who needed a pair of shoes. A 90-year-old woman came through the medical clinic at Atima, a poverty-stricken remote area. Gil discovered that he wore the same size shoes as she. After putting a pair of his new socks and his new canvas shoes on her old crusty feet, he felt truly humbled.

"I will never forget her face," Gil says. "You would have thought I'd given her a million dollars. Her face glowed." Although she couldn't speak English, and he couldn't speak her language, there was no need for words. Her sense of gratitude said it all.

The son of a minister, Gil had been taught missions since childhood. He believes, though, that missions must be "caught" by doing.

"People soak up what you have to say after you have met their physical needs," says Gil, who led many to Christ through his street evangelism work while in Honduras.

∼

Lord, help me to be attuned to the physical and spiritual needs of people I meet. Teach me humility through my service to them.

March 4: Let Your Light Shine

"'Let your light shine before men, that they may see your good deeds and praise your Father in heaven'" (Matt. 5:16 NIV).

In war-torn Kosovo, hatred abounds. There is hate between the Kosovars and the Serbians who displaced them and made them refugees. There is even hate for Christians, who are often perceived as the enemy.

Amidst such hatred, it is challenging to be a witness for Christ. For Sandy Farley, though, the answer is to be a witness through her lifestyle and actions.

Sandy is supported by the Kosovo Project of the Palo Alto Friends Meeting, a Quaker ministry, and works through the Balkan Sunflowers (a European secular group caring for refugee children).

The children in the area are confused about the situation, but they are still children. Sandy and others, then, spend a lot of time playing.

"We play with the kids in what I call therapeutic recreation," she says. "We juggle; practice origami (Japanese paper-folding art); play soccer, volleyball, chess, dominoes, and Parcheesi."

Such actions and others, such as teaching English and helping in cleanup, go a long way in showing that Christians care.

Sandy says her goal always is to live up to the advice of George Fox, the Quaker founder, who said in 1656: "Be patterns, be examples in all countries, islands, nations, wherever you go, so that your carriage and life may preach among all sorts of people, and to them."

Does your life "preach" to others of God's love?

God in heaven, may my life be a witness for You.

March 5: Three Knocks in the Night

"While Peter was still thinking about the vision, the Spirit said to him, 'Simon, three men are looking for you. So get up and go downstairs. Do not hesitate to go with them, for I have sent them.' Peter went down and said to the men, 'I'm the one you're looking for. Why have you come?'" (Acts 10:19–21 NIV).

One evening in 1893 as she sat by a lamp writing letters she was interrupted three times by knocks at her door. Three Indian men—a Brahmin, another high-caste Hindu, and a Muslim—knocked on her door pleading for her to help their wives who were having complications during childbirth.

"But I know nothing about doctoring," she told each one. "It's my father who is the doctor." Her father could not go because it was not the custom in India for a man outside the family to enter a woman's quarters.

She learned the next morning that all three women had died because there was no woman doctor available.

That night Ida Scudder (1870–1960) received the call to become a medical missionary. After earning her degree from Cornell Medical College, she returned to India in 1900. As the founder of a medical college and a women's hospital, she was always there for any knocks in the night.

Have you ever had to say no to someone who asked for help?

∽

Dear God, equip me to be Your instrument in meeting the needs around me.

March 6: A Good Name

"A good name is more desirable than great riches; to be esteemed is better than silver or gold" (Prov. 22:1 NIV).

"Dr. Ida, India."

A letter to missionary doctor Ida Scudder (1870–1960) reached her addressed this way.

The name Scudder had made a mark well before Dr. Ida was born. Her grandfather, John Scudder, was the first American missionary doctor. Representing the Reformed Church in America, he had 7 sons who became missionaries to India. In all, 43 members of the Scudder family gave over 1,100 years in missionary service.

Dr. Ida arrived in Vellore, India, in 1900 to join her father, John Scudder Jr. Opening a women's hospital in 1902, she treated over 12,000 patients the first year. By 1906 the number of patients had risen to 40,000.

Dr. Ida started a small nursing school in 1909. It grew throughout the years until, in 1946, it became the first graduate school of nursing in India. In 1918 she opened a medical college for women.

Her decades of labor resulted in broad international and interdenominational support for her Christian Medical College and Hospital. Today the hospital with its almost 800 doctors and nurses treats nearly 2,500 patients each day.

Is it any wonder a letter addressed only to Dr. Ida found her in a nation of 300 million?

Do you desire a good name above material riches?

Holy God, help me to live my life so others will associate my name with Your work.

March 7: The Power of Faith

"'If you have faith as small as a mustard seed, you can say to this mountain, "Move from here to there" and it will move. Nothing will be impossible for you'" (Matt. 17:20 NIV).

To realize her dream of providing furniture for the homeless, Carol Kane sold her home, gave up her own belongings, and put her total faith in God's care.

Carol volunteered for years with homeless ministries in the Orlando, Florida, area. Much of her joy in this endeavor, however, was seasoned with a sad realization: "I've brought these people to their new homes, and now I realize they have absolutely nothing to put in them. They all huddle up on the floor with just an old jacket spread over them. I can't walk away from that."

This dilemma gave birth to the Mustard Seed Furniture Bank, an organization that provides household goods, furniture, appliances, clothing, toys, and games to the homeless and others in need. The ministry serves more than 1,200 families each year.

Carol has endured many struggles over the years. Once her husband, John, lost his job, and they sold their house to fund the ministry. They used the proceeds from the sale to buy furniture for upcoming months.

People often asked Carol how she could give up her house and her own furniture to help total strangers. She always answered, "How could I not?"

Do you have that kind of loving concern for others and that kind of faith in God?

Give me more faith, Lord.

March 8: Triumphant over Weakness

"But he said to me, 'My grace is sufficient for you, for my power is made perfect in weakness'" (2 Cor. 12:9 NIV).

Do you think of missionaries as being healthy, robust individuals?

Consider these dauntless missionaries.

Mary Webb (1779–1861) had a crippling disease at the age of five that kept her in a wheelchair for the rest of her life. Yet, in 1800 she helped form the Boston Female Society for Missionary Purposes and remained active in missions throughout her life.

Missionary to China, Samuel Schereschewsky (1831–1906) experienced a paralyzing disease in 1881. He still translated the Old and New Testaments into the colloquial speech of China. Unable to use a pen and able to use only one finger of each hand, he typed the entire Bible.

Jonathan Goforth (1859–1936) spent 46 years in China. In 1900 during the Boxer Rebellion he was brutally beaten and hacked on the head, neck, and back with long, broad-blade swords. Miraculously surviving, he continued work despite suffering from many diseases and eventually blindness.

Robert Wilder (1863–1938) helped found in 1886 the Student Volunteer Movement and pursued its aim—The Evangelization of the World in This Generation. Despite chronic health problems, he sacrificially promoted missions on four continents.

Christian and Missionary Alliance missionary Robert Jaffray (1873–1945) had diabetes and heart disease from childhood, but that didn't stop him from ministering in Asia for 59 years.

Lord, thank You that in weakness I can find Your strength.

March 9: A Tract's Message

"For the Word of God is living and active. Sharper than any double-edged sword" (Heb. 4:12 NIV).

The power of the Bible is greater than time, human plans, and distance. It can even travel across the oceans and accomplish something totally unexpected.

Workers at the American Tract Society, an organization dedicated to spreading the word of God throughout America and the world, are used to hearing stories about how the Bible has reached out to individuals in unexpected places and in unexpected ways.

They recently received a letter from a man in Australia. It said: "I recently had the privilege of reading your tract 'How to Become a Christian,' and because of it I finally received Christ as my personal Lord and Savior."

Another letter came from Min-chi Cho, a 22-year-old who discovered a tract in his homeland of Taiwan. Still others from Indonesia, Poland, and Jamaica tell of similar experiences.

What's so amazing about these stories is that they all come from places where the American Tract Society does no direct shipments. God, however, got the tracts where they needed to be to reach the people.

How can you use the Bible to reach out to those around you? Can you distribute Christian tracts and Scripture portions throughout your community?

∼

Omnipresent God, I pray today that Your Word will reach someone who needs so desperately to hear its message.

Stories used with permission from the American Tract Society, Garland, TX.

March 10: An Early Calling

"Happy are those who are strong in the Lord, who want above all else to follow your steps" (Psalm 84:5 TLB).

Did you have a call early in life to pursue your vocation?

Three Southern Baptist missionary nurses did.

Jessie L. Pettigrew grew up in Virginia hearing about Lottie Moon and knew that she wanted to work with her. After completing nursing training in New Orleans and missionary training in Chicago, she headed for China. In 1901 she became the first Southern Baptist missionary nurse. She worked closely with Lottie Moon who called her "my little Virginia girl."

Grace McBride wanted to follow in the steps of her missionary brother who had died in China of typhus. From 1916 to 1918, she served successfully at the Baptist hospital in Hwanghsien, China. In 1918 she volunteered with the American Red Cross to accompany soldiers to Siberia. By Christmas she was dying from typhus. Before she sank into a coma, she said, "Still I love my country. I'm glad I came."

As a child, Ruth Kersey felt called to missions. She enrolled in nursing school because of an appeal by a Nigerian medical missionary. Arriving in Ogbomosho in 1921, she began taking care of sick, starved, and orphaned babies. With the help of Virginia Baptist women, she formed a home for motherless children in 1925. The Kersey Children's Home did much to improve the level of childcare in the African nation.

God, empower Christian nurses around the world to bring Your healing love.

March 11: Hold God's Hand

"But my God shall supply all your needs according to his riches in glory by Jesus Christ" (Phil. 4:19 NIV).

"Daddy, if you'll hold my hand, I won't be afraid."

Little Philip Thurman earnestly said these words to his father, Tom, as they and the rest of their family slept under a table piled high with mattresses. It was 1971, and East Pakistan—where Tom and Gloria Thurman served for nearly three decades as Southern Baptist missionaries—was in a state of chaos as India and East Pakistan fought against the Pakistani military.

Gloria remembers that night as one of the longest and recalls that her husband prayed a similar prayer that evening: "Oh, Lord, if You will hold our hands, we won't be afraid."

From the very beginning, the couple felt a strong call to East Pakistan for their missions work. Tom says of his wife's diligence: "She always found her place, rolled up her sleeves, and went to work."

Gloria affectionately calls one of the places she went to work the Quack Clinic. She began a clinic for nearby residents who couldn't make it to a hospital, despite the fact that she wasn't a doctor or a nurse. "I treated as I would treat my boys," she says.

In all of their experiences, the Thurmans relied on the above verse from Philippians, calling it their family verse.

Do you trust that God will always hold your hand and supply your needs?

Thank You, Everlasting God, for Your protection and love.

March 12: Good News on the Radio

"He was given authority, glory and sovereign power; all peoples, nations and men of every language worshiped him"(Dan. 7:14 NIV).

"I'm so happy to know that Jesus died for me. I thought that His death was for others, but not me."

This message came to Trans World Radio, an interdenominational ministry that airs Christian radio broadcasts in native languages, from a 45-year-old Mozambican widow who speaks Ndau.

The African country of Mozambique gained independence from Portugal in 1975, then embarked on a bloody 17-year civil war. For years, the Ndau people were oppressed and the language ignored. And although many Ndau were Christians, church leaders often felt ignored by Christian missions groups.

TWR-Mozambique's national director Luis Zaqueu heard the cries for radio programs in the Ndau language and, in 1995, traveled more than 1,000 miles over rough terrain to meet with church leaders. "I arrived late at night and slept on a mat in a round hut. In the morning, I expected to discuss the concept under a tree with about 10 pastors. Boy, was I surprised!" he remembers. "The next day, more than 1,000 people gathered in an open field, some of whom had walked all night to attend. They demonstrated to me their thirst for the gospel."

Today, the Ndau people—like the widow who finally realized Jesus died for her—can hear daily Bible programs in their own language.

Lord Jesus, today let me reach those who feel left out of Your plan.

March 13: A Diligent Worker

"Diligent hands will rule" (Prov. 12:24 NIV).

His 1825 diary demonstrates his energy and industry: "I have been absent from home fifty-three days; have travelled through eighteen counties in Illinois and nine in Indiana, rode nine hundred and twenty-six miles, preached regular sermons thirty-one times, . . . enabled to revive three Bible societies, . . . to establish seven new societies."

John Mason Peck had so many ministries that he was nicknamed the Man with 20 Hands. Appointed missionary to the Missouri Territory in 1817, John and his wife, Sally, traveled for 129 days from the East to St. Louis by wagon, boat, and on foot. Upon their arrival, John had to be carried ashore on a stretcher because he was too sick to walk. Soon, though, he began to preach, start a school, do evangelistic work among the black population, and distribute Bibles and tracts.

John laid the foundation for strong Baptist work in the Midwest. He founded Sunday Schools, women's mite societies, and missionary societies. He founded the first Baptist churches west of the Mississippi, published the first newspaper in that area, and founded Alton Seminary (later Shurtleff College), the first college in the West.

He cofounded the American Baptist Home Mission Society in 1832. Active in the Tract Society, he was secretary from 1843 to 1846.

He served two terms in the Illinois state legislature where he is credited with helping keep slavery out of the region.

Are you using your time and energy effectively?

Today, Lord, make me a diligent worker for You.

March 14: A Gift for Teaching

"For wisdom will enter your heart, and knowledge will be pleasant to your soul" (Prov. 2:10 NIV).

When Anne and Chipley Bennett went to Odessa, Ukraine, for a year of missions work through the Presbyterian Churches in America, there was little question as to how they would serve. They would teach.

Both retired educators, the Bennetts had many decades of teaching experience behind them. Anne taught high school English and humanities for 33 years. Chip taught middle school history and geography for just as long. Their combined years of experience came in handy when they got ready for their mission stipend.

Ukraine authorities were surprisingly open to letting the Bennetts and other short-term workers teach religion courses in their schools. During their time in the country, Anne and Chip helped Ukrainian teachers plan and lead Bible classes and also instituted a course in Christian morals and ethics. They also taught the children of full-time missionaries while they waited for their full-time instructors to arrive.

All her years of teaching couldn't prepare Anne for the spiritual rewards she received for her work in Ukraine.

"It was unbelievable seeing people there who had never had a Bible before smile when we gave them one," she says. "There is so much spiritual hunger there."

Do you have a special gift for teaching? Can you use that gift for God's glory?

∽

Dear Lord, bless teachers as they spread Your word throughout the world.

March 15: Empowered for Service

"'Now go; I will help you speak and will teach you what to say'" (Ex. 4:12 NIV).

Have you ever been reluctant to share the gospel because you don't have formal training?

Take heart. Although many missionaries had college and seminary degrees, some did not. A cobbler, a gardener, a mill worker, a parlor maid—these became some of the world's most famous missionaries.

The founder of the modern missionary movement, Baptist William Carey (1761–1834) had little formal education. However, the precocious youth mastered six languages. A cobbler for 14 years before his calling to missions, he served 40 years in India.

Apprenticed as a gardener, Robert Moffat (1795–1883) was accepted reluctantly by the London Missionary Society because of his poor education. He served 53 years in Africa not only exploring and establishing mission stations but also translating the Bible into Bechuna.

Mary Slessor (1848–1915), a Scottish textile mill worker with a meager education, was sent by the Presbyterian Church to Calabar (Nigeria) in 1876. She served there—often alone and in danger—for 39 years as a pioneer explorer and missionary.

A parlor maid, Gladys Aylward (1902–1970) was determined to be a missionary to China. After her rejection by the China Inland Mission, she set out in 1932 on an incredible journey from London to Yangcheng. When the Japanese invaded China, she became famous after leading nearly 100 Chinese children on a hazardous journey to safety.

~

O God, use me as I am to serve You wherever You want me to be.

March 16: I Learned More

"Love bears all things, believes all things, hopes all things, endures all things" (1 Cor. 13:7 RSV).

A little girl's hug taught Kathryn Anderson the importance of love and attention in a child's life.

Kathryn went on a short-term missions trip to the west side of Chicago. Her team worked alongside Uptown Baptist Church members leading Backyard Bible Clubs in two apartment complexes. One of the dwellings was in an area known for gang activity.

On the last day of the trip, a quiet little girl came to the club.

"She was really shy and would only come to me," Kathryn recalls. "She sat in my lap all during the morning and hung around me during playtime."

Kathryn got ready to help take the children back to their apartments when the girl ran into her arms. She gave Kathryn a huge hug and said she'd miss her.

"This really touched me because I realized that these kids only want to be loved," she says.

People involved in missions and ministry often acknowledge that they learn more from their experiences than they could ever teach someone else. Kathryn says this is true—that she went on the trip to help the children, "but the kids were there to help me."

When has God used a child to teach you about Himself or about the world?

Holy Teacher, thank You for what You teach me every day. Help me always to be open to Your lessons.

March 17: Good Triumphs over Evil

"But Joseph said to them, 'Don't be afraid. Am I in the place of God? You intended to harm me, but God intended it for good to accomplish what is now being done, the saving of many lives'" (Gen. 50: 19–20 NIV).

Screaming pirates charged up the slopes at the seaside British villa and captured 16-year-old Magnus Sucatus Patricius and many of his father's servants. Patrick, the son of a nobleman, was taken to Ireland in 405 and sold to a Druid tribal chieftain. After laboring in filth and squalor as a swineherd, Patrick turned to God and experienced a conversion. His captivity became an opportunity to grow close to Christ. After serving his master for 6 years, Patrick escaped when a voice in a dream told him to leave. After traveling 200 miles through hostile country to the coast, he found a boat sailing for Britain.

He became a monk, and 21 years later he was back in Ireland crisscrossing the country in his chariot preaching the gospel to rulers and slaves alike. Thousands of people were converted. St. Patrick later wrote in his *Confessions*, "The only reason I had to return to the people I once barely escaped from was the Gospel and its promises."

Have you ever made a concerted effort to minister to those who have wronged you?

Almighty God, help me today to make the best out of bad situations. Let the love of Christ be my champion.

March 18: A Small Voice

"Your ears will hear a voice behind you saying, 'This is the way; walk in it'" (Isa. 30:21 NIV).

The magazine story should have made her rejoice. It told of a woman who often invited missionaries into her home. Her own children had become preachers and missionaries.

Amy Garner felt bitter thoughts coming to her mind. "I can't invite missionaries into my home," she thought. She felt as if she had nothing to contribute to missions.

That night a missionary couple spoke at her church's prayer meeting about their work with deaf children in Haiti. As she listened, Amy heard a small voice creep into her thoughts: "Ask them if they could use that roll of material."

The day before Amy had found a 50-yard roll of black and white checked material collecting dust in her attic.

Again she heard the voice, but tried to push it aside. "This is crazy," she said to herself. "No one wants that ugly material."

She finally asked the missionaries if they could use it. Together, they said, "We certainly can. We make the children's uniforms out of that type of material."

Amy asked the couple to her family's home for the evening. The two families spent several hours sharing together.

Later that night, the voice said to her, "Who said you couldn't have a missionary in your home?" Amy felt humbled and full of wonder.

Do you ever feel inadequate to help in missions?

~

Thank You, Lord, that all of us can spread Your word.

March 19: A Seeker of Lands, Souls, and Justice

"He will make your righteousness shine like the dawn, the justice of your cause like the noonday sun" (Psalm 37:4–6 NIV).

"19 March [1873]—Thanks to the Almighty Preserver of men for sparing me thus far on the journey of life. . . . Oh my good Lord Jesus!"

Missionary explorer David Livingstone (1813–1873) penned this entry only a few weeks before his death. Suffering from debilitating illnesses for years, he was not strong on his 60th birthday.

Word had reached England in 1870 that David was dead, and expeditions were sent to locate him. Journalist Henry Stanley finally found him in 1871 pronouncing the now famous words: "Dr. Livingstone, I presume." Henry's kindness probably saved him for another 18 months.

David was found dead on May 1, kneeling by his bed. His beloved native helpers, Susi and Chuma, buried his heart under a mvula tree. They preserved his body with salt, sun-dried it for two weeks, and then wrapped it in calico, tree bark, and sailcloth. He was carried 1,500 miles to the coast, a journey that took over eight months to complete and left ten men dead enroute. On April 18, 1874, David Livingstone was buried in Westminster Abbey amidst a huge crowd.

The words on his tombstone seem fitting: "For thirty years his life was spent in an unwearied effort to evangelize the native races, to explore the undiscovered secrets, to abolish the desolating slave trade of Central Africa."

Where can you demonstrate God's love and justice?

∽

Lord, may I work for Your cause all the days You give me.

March 20: God's Social Justice

"'Woe to him who builds his palace by unrighteousness, his upper rooms by injustice, making his countrymen work for nothing, not paying them for their labor'" (Jer. 22:13 NIV).

How do you feel toward the poor? Could you have prejudices against those in social classes different from yours?

When Cathy Butler worked in community ministries in Shelby County, Alabama, she learned that almost everyone has such prejudices.

Part of Cathy's job was to interview people who came for food and clothing assistance. "These were the people that some middle-class and rich people scorned as too lazy or too ignorant to support themselves; but with a few exceptions, I found this was not the case," she remembers.

She found, instead, that most of the people were sick, old, abused, or didn't have the mental and emotional resources to support themselves. Others, she says, were hard workers who had been mistreated or defrauded. The situation reminded her of the above verse from Jeremiah.

"It made me realize," she says, "that our society truly would be different if God's laws for social justice were honored."

Cathy believes that people who are called to missions work among the destitute must analyze their own prejudices because almost everyone has them. "With an open heart and mind, God can show them how they are prejudiced and remove those hard feelings," she says.

∽

Dear Lord, give me an open heart and mind toward those who have less than I do. Help me remember Your laws of justice.

March 21: A Generous Spirit

"Command them to do good, to be rich in good deeds, and to be generous... to share" (1 Tim. 6:18 NIV).

Lizzie Helen Snyder Glide (1852–1941) was one of the most philanthropic women in the Methodist Episcopal Church.

Born into a deeply religious southern Methodist family, she moved at the age of 17 to Sacramento, California. In 1871 she married businessman Joseph Glide and raised five children while working actively in her church.

Following a revival meeting, Lizzie dedicated her life completely to God. She helped establish a mission in Sacramento and gave her testimony at street meetings. "I believe my wife is leading more souls to Christ," her husband once said, "than all the ministers in the city."

When Joseph died in 1906, she took over his business, attributing her success to prayer. After building and furnishing the Mary Elizabeth Inn, a residence for working women in San Francisco, she presented it to the Woman's Missionary Council in 1914.

She provided funds for two college dormitories: one for Epworth Hall at the University of California in Berkeley and another for Glide Hall at Kentucky's Asbury College. In addition, she financed the education of many college students.

She also donated money for a radio station for evangelistic work and two hotels to provide safe housing in San Francisco. Her generosity provided for the Glide Memorial Church in San Francisco and the Glide Foundation.

Are you contributing to church and community needs?

Today, God, bless me with a generous spirit of giving.

March 22: Worldwide Prayer Net

"Devote yourselves to prayer, being watchful and thankful" (Col. 4:2 NIV).

The Internet has revolutionized so much in our society—now it is revolutionizing missions.

Dawne-Marie and Mike Martin founded Ichthus Ministries in 1999 to bring together those who need prayer with those who want to pray for others, all via the Internet. The result came in the form of PrayerNeeds.org, a Web site that catalogs prayer requests and praise reports. In early 2000, the site had already processed 2,750 prayer requests from 42 different countries.

Mike says that one of the purposes of the ministry is "to engage in Christian missionary work through meeting the spiritual and prayer needs of those using the Internet." That has happened in countless ways.

Two prayer requests—one from a man in South Carolina who said he wanted to commit suicide and another from a single mother in Illinois who needed financial help—resulted in tangible help. Mike contacted churches in the two areas, and both individuals received help. Many other requests have been answered, and that, he says, is the best part of it all.

Prayer requests on the site cover a lot of ground. There is a place to post prayers of intercession, prayers concerning finances, physical concerns, and missions-related requests from missionaries around the globe.

Mike says he never imagined his own missions work would stretch so far. "Our missions field is the world," he says.

Do you support other Christians through prayer?

~

I praise You, Lord, for answering prayers everywhere.

March 23: Underground Christians

"'You are the light of the world. A city on a hill cannot be hidden'" (Matt. 5:14 NIV).

What would you do if you could not freely talk about your faith?

Many missionaries live with that restriction as they serve in Last Frontier countries, places where the majority of the population has little or no access to Christianity. Religious beliefs, culture, and governments create this barrier and make it difficult for missionaries to work in traditional ways.

Churches often meet underground, and new Christians must be especially careful with their words and actions.

To gain access in such areas, missionaries serve as medical workers, teachers, business people, or even tourists. They then witness within their circles of influence.

Nancy,* who works with her husband, Joshua,* in a predominantly Muslim area, says that she strives to share her faith in natural circumstances and conversations. "The most freeing thing for me was to adopt their dress," she says. When other women ask if she is Muslim and she says no, they assume that she's married to a Muslim. As conversation continues, they often ask how she prays (since Muslims follow strict prayer guidelines). "I tell them, 'My heavenly Father is my best friend. I was just talking to Him as I walked along.'" Conversations like this free her to share her faith in a nonthreatening way.

～

Thank You, God, for the freedom I have to share my faith with others. May I daily be grateful.

*Not their real names.

March 24: Rescue for the Perishing

"For we are to God the aroma of Christ among those who are being saved and those who are perishing" (2 Cor. 2:15 NIV).

"Rescue the Perishing, Care for the Dying;
Jesus is merciful, Jesus will save."

One of the greatest hymn writers in history, Fanny Crosby (1820–1915), wrote "Rescue the Perishing" while ministering in the Bowery section of New York City.

Born on March 24, 1820, she became blind at six weeks of age. Blindness did not keep her from writing more than 2,000 hymns, being a friend to several Presidents, and speaking before the US Senate (the first woman to do so). "Blindness cannot keep the sunlight of hope from the trusting soul," she once wrote.

Hymns such as "Blessed Assurance," "Safe in the Arms of Jesus"—which was played at President Grant's funeral—and "Pass Me Not, O Gentle Savior"—a favorite of Queen Victoria's—touched countless lives.

Her goal was to bring salvation to people through her hymns. For most of her life she lived among the poor. At the age of 60 she began missions work in one of America's most depressing places, the Bowery, bringing love to alcoholics, prostitutes, and derelicts. She considered missions work her main occupation for many years and wrote hymns urging people to make decisions for Christ and offering hope to the downcast.

Have you ever considered yourself the "aroma of Christ"?

O Lord, help me to reach out today to those who need Your rescuing power.

March 25: Mobilizing for Missions

"I have been constantly on the move. I have been in danger from rivers, in danger from bandits. . . . I have labored and toiled and have often gone without sleep" (2 Cor. 11:26–27 NIV).

He never had a home. He never married. Constantly traveling, he swam rivers, braved snowstorms, slept under the open sky, and detoured to avoid hostile Indians or bandits. He broke John Wesley's record for one day's horseback travel going 93 miles to Wesley's 90.

Luther Rice (1783–1836), the most famous Baptist circuit rider, is known for mobilizing his denomination for missions.

Born in Northborough, Massachusetts, on March 25, 1783, he became a Christian in 1805. He attended Williams College and Andover where he became a member of the Brethren, a group dedicated to foreign missions. As one of America's first foreign missionaries, he sailed with the Judsons on February 19, 1812, for India. The next year he returned to America never to go overseas again.

Traveling to churches throughout Virginia, Kentucky, Tennessee, Georgia, and the Carolinas, he gave compelling missionary messages. Soon local and regional societies agreed to share in foreign missions work.

Luther was at home in crude frontier cabins or fine Boston homes. While staying overnight with a family, he would read the Bible, sing a hymn, pray with the family, and give a missions testimony.

Do you have a gift for mobilizing people for missions?

Lord, thank You for the pioneers who tirelessly paved the way for what we often take for granted today.

March 26: Crowds in Need

"'They do not need to go away. You give them something to eat'" (Matt. 14:16 NIV).

What is your definition of church? Can only certain types of crowds worship God?

Sometimes even the most well-intentioned Christians think that people can worship God only in specific places and ways.

It is just this type of attitude that Betty and Frank Stark fight in their missions work every day. They reach out to race car fans and, in doing so, challenge the notion that worship must always be traditional.

Race car fans themselves, Betty and Frank stood in the stands at a race back in 1975. Looking out at the thousands of fans gathered, Frank said to his wife, "Somebody ought to be doing something."

That started a seed in their minds, and Frank became an Automobile Racing Club of America chaplain. Then he founded Raceway Ministries, a not-for-profit organization whose purpose is to take the gospel of Christ to race fans and teams on the ARCA and NASCAR circuits.

Churches, the Starks say, must reach out to such nontraditional groups. They give as one example a church that prayed for months for a local NASCAR Sunday race to be rained out. It did rain out seven times, but the track kept rescheduling. The church finally decided to start a raceway ministry and reported 21 professions of faith during that first race.

∼

Dear God, give me a heart for the crowds who don't know You. Show me how to reach them in nontraditional ways.

March 27: "Qualified" to Serve

"For our light and momentary troubles are achieving for us an eternal glory that far outweighs them all. So we fix our eyes not on what is seen, but on what is unseen" (2 Cor. 4:17–18 NIV).

He had tuberculosis. His wife and child had just died, and he was in poor emotional as well as physical health. He had been a failure in his pastoral work in the United States. He was at the point of despair.

Do you think a person with these "qualifications" would be chosen today to go to the missions field?

Melville Cox, the first foreign missionary of the Methodist Episcopal Church in America, would probably not have a chance today to be a missionary. However, in 1832 when Melville expressed a desire to go to Liberia representing the Methodist Episcopal Church, he was appointed.

He arrived in Africa in March 1833. After being there only a month, he demonstrated that although physically weak he had a genuine missionary spirit and grasped the importance of training local villagers to evangelize. "I have thought too that through them the gospel might be more readily communicated to the natives around them," he wrote.

His voyage to Africa lasted longer than his missionary career of only four months, but his courage stirred the cause of Methodist missions. Five new missionaries soon followed him.

∼

Thank You, Lord, that we can be used by You. Whatever the length of our service, we know that You will achieve Your eternal purposes.

March 28: Encourage One Another

"May the God who gives endurance and encouragement give you a spirit of unity among yourselves as you follow Christ Jesus" (Rom. 15:5 NIV).

We sat in a circle on the hard concrete floor, taking turns sharing our thoughts about others in the group.

"She is really great with kids and is very loving and kind," I said of one of the other college students.

"She is a fantastic listener and is creative," someone said of me.

This impromptu share time was our way of preparing for the work we'd start in the morning.

During the spring break of 1988, a group of students from the University of Alabama headed to Jamaica on a missions trip.

Jamaica sounded exotic—images of white beaches and sparkling seas filled my mind—but it turned out to be challenging. The people who live outside the tourist areas struggle every day amidst poverty. They, however, are incredibly open and loving. They eagerly listened to our stories of Christ.

The morning after we shared with and shored up one another, we started our work. We held worship services each night, visited in the streets during the day, and gave programs at local churches and orphanages. Everywhere we went smiling faces greeted us.

The experience taught us that God equips each Christian. Everyone has gifts God can use for His glory.

Dear God, thank You for my missions experience. Remind me today of the lessons I learned then.

March 29: Knowing Christ

"I want to know Christ and the power of his resurrection and the fellowship of sharing in his sufferings" (Phil. 3:10 NIV).

One day while on a tour of Europe an Austrian nobleman entered a gallery and stood before a noted painting of Christ which portrayed the agony of His suffering. Underneath the painting were the words, "All this I did for thee; what hast thou done for Me?"

This visit to an art gallery marked a turning point in the life of Count Nicholaus Ludwig Von Zinzendorf (1700–1760). He left ready to give his talents and possessions for the cause of Christ.

In 1722 Nicholaus purchased a large estate near the Bohemian frontier in Saxony. He invited persecuted Christians from all over the world to settle on his land. He called the colony Herrnhut.

In 1731 he met a slave from the Danish West Indies named Anthony and took him to Herrnhut, where Anthony spoke about the plight of the slaves in the West Indies. Some from the colony left to work among them—thus launching the Moravian missions work for which Nicholaus would be known.

He traveled to many other countries establishing settlements modeled after Herrnhut. Ordained as a bishop of the Moravian Church, he went to America in 1741 where he evangelized Indians in Pennsylvania and preached in Reformed and Lutheran churches.

Are you daily seeking a deeper relationship with God?

O Savior, stir in me a yearning to know Christ and the power of His resurrection more fully.

March 30: Building Bridges

"'Give, and it will be given to you'" (Luke 6:38 NIV).

For years Olga Carter tried to reconcile her faith in God with the ideological system of the former Soviet Union. As a teacher at Odessa Economic University, she tried to send the message of God's love "between the lines" of her lectures to Russian students, and then later expanded her witness as more freedom was granted—even though it almost cost her job.

Today Olga works to build bridges between American and Ukrainian churches as an international coordinator for the Missions Our Mission organization. "I see that my mission is to be an ambassador, using all of my personal and professional skills to organize trips of American Christians who are willing to share the good news with the people in Ukraine at a very difficult time in their country," Olga says.

Olga says that the key to being a powerful missionary for Christ is to stand firm in your convictions. "The stronger we are as Christians, the more others will follow Him," she says.

In all of her work—and through the personal journeys she has made—Olga says that God has given the above words from Luke 6 to her. "It's as if I can hear His voice saying, 'Don't be afraid of getting tired. I will recharge your batteries.'"

How can you build bridges between different individuals or different groups?

You are the great bridge builder and destroyer of barriers, Lord. I want to be an agent of Your change.

March 31: A Reluctant Parting

"When he had said this, he knelt down with all of them and prayed. They all wept as they embraced him and kissed him" (Acts 20: 36–37 NIV).

"Grown men cried like children; over the entire room there was a deep heart rending cry as if the heart would break. Many were the prayers that were offered for her safety."

Malla Moe (1863–1953), a pioneer missionary who served in Swaziland for 54 years, had a close affinity with the African people. According to one of her colleagues, their love for her was so strong that many cried when she took her first furlough in 1903.

Working under the Scandinavian Alliance Mission, Malla established the Bethel station in South Africa, which served as her base for several decades.

She closely identified with the Africans accepting their culture and living their lifestyle. Much of her success was largely due to her dependence on native leaders. Johane Gamede, a Zulu and one of her first converts, aided her for decades in bridging language and cultural differences. An African woman named Dorika helped her in evangelism for many years.

Malla was often innovative in her outreach approaches. In 1927, at the age of 65, she traveled from place to place in her "gospel wagon." Aided by Africans, she taught in places the gospel had never been presented.

Do you try to identify with the people you are trying to help?

Today I thank You, Lord, for the love that I receive from others when I reach out to them.

April 1: Believing in the Pierced Hands

"Then he said to Thomas, 'Put your finger here; see my hands. . . . Stop doubting and believe'" (John 20:27 NIV).

One day she was about to put a coin in an offering plate when she noticed that engraved on the bottom of the plate were the pierced hands of Christ. She then emptied her whole purse into it.

Later Isabella Lilias Trotter (1853–1928) emptied her whole life into missions work in Algeria.

Born into a genteel London family, she had a sensitive nature which led her to painting and writing. She developed a friendship with the writer John Ruskin who encouraged her to pursue an art career. Instead, after her conversion under the Plymouth Brethren teaching of Robert and Hanna Whitall Smith, she dedicated herself to North Africa missions. When a mission refused her because of her poor health, she set off independently with two friends.

In 1888, she organized the Algiers Mission Band (AMB), an evangelical, interdenominational agency. The AMB grew from 3 to 30 workers, mainly single women. In 1964 it merged with the North Africa Mission (now the Arab World Ministries).

Isabella made dangerous journeys into Muslim regions, leading Arabs, French, Jews, and Black Africans to become Christians. Her work included translating the New Testament into the common tongue of Algeria and producing tracts in Arabic and French.

Have the pierced hands of Christ made a difference in your life?

∼

Lord, enable me to give up my doubts and hesitations and follow You.

April 2: Neighbors Working Together

"Whatever other commandments there may be, are summed up in this one rule: 'Love your neighbor as yourself'" (Rom. 13:9 NIV).

As a missions leader at First Presbyterian Church, Tupelo, Mississippi, Lori Dickerson prayed for a way to get the church's youth more involved. Her prayers were answered when she heard of a project started by a minister at First Methodist Church, a fellow downtown congregation. Mark Denham had begun HillTOP, an outreach ministry to the city's handicapped and elderly residents.

Lori called Mark and asked if her church could join his church in this ministry. Then more congregations joined them. Five churches worked together that first year. Five years later, 20 churches worked together at 36 different work sites.

The involved youth gather on a Friday night soon after the Easter season. They have a worship service and get their team assignments. On Saturday and Sunday, they get out and work—doing everything from roofing, to plumbing repair, to electrical wiring.

A companion ministry, KidTOP, involves children of adult workers in making crafts such as refrigerator magnets and goody baskets for the people whose homes are being worked on. The children deliver their projects on one of the workdays.

How can you reach out to your community? Can you start a similar ministry in your town?

∼

Dear Lord, give me an understanding of the needs in my own community and then a willingness and motivation to minister.

April 3: Keeping the Faith

"I have fought the good fight, I have finished the race, I have kept the faith" (2 Tim. 4:7 NIV).

In a tribute to his fellow missionary, Samuel Zwemer, using 2 Timothy 4:7 said, "One of the great characteristics of this life we mourn and in which we rejoice is that our friend and brother was a soldier, every inch—a soldier of Jesus Christ."

When news of the death of William Borden (1887–1913) was cabled from Cairo, Egypt, in April 1913, newspapers throughout America carried an account of the young man who had given so much of himself and his wealth to the world.

A graduate of Yale University, William was active in the Student Volunteer Movement and began the Yale Hope Mission, a skid row rescue mission. After his graduation from Princeton Seminary, he became a director of the Moody Bible Institute and wrote its doctrinal charter.

William, who refused to own a car because he thought it wasn't good stewardship, wrote his last will only weeks before he sailed to Cairo to share the gospel with Muslims. Within three months he was dead of cerebral meningitis.

At his death his almost $1 million was given to such ministries as the China Inland Mission, National Bible Institute, and Moody Bible Institute.

Although William was wealthy, it wasn't his money that impressed people. It was his integrity and his faithfulness.

Will you be found faithful?

~

God, help me to be a good steward of my life.

April 4: Help a Neighbor

"And love your neighbor as yourself" (Matt. 19:19 NIV).

This biblical admonition is one of the most familiar to us. But how, specifically, can we love our neighbors as we love ourselves?

One volunteer organization provides its answer to that question: help those neighbors who can't help themselves. Christmas in April works in partnership with communities to rehabilitate the houses of low-income, elderly, and disabled persons. The work culminates in National Rebuilding Day, usually on the last Saturday in April, when volunteers come together to do their work.

The story of Christmas in April began in 1973, when volunteers in Midland, Texas, devoted one day in April to spruce up the homes of their neighbors. One elderly neighbor commented on their work: "Why, this is like Christmas in April." The name stuck.

Since that day, the gratitude in the voices of those helped continues. A homeowner helped recently in Alexandria, Virginia, said: "I am left speechless that so many strangers did so much for me."

Christmas in April renovates approximately 7,700 homes a year and involves almost 240,000 volunteers. It works in more than 700 cities and towns across America.

Many of the volunteers for the program come from churches. They are Christians who understand the value of giving back to their own communities.

Look around your neighborhood and community. Are there ways you can help those who have substandard housing?

~

Dear God, give me the vision to see the needs of my neighbors. Empower me then to help them.

April 5: God's Power

"The voice of the Lord is powerful" (Psalm 29:4 NIV).

Did you know that the first Methodist missionary to the Indians in America was a black man?

John Stewart was an unlikely hero, but his story is a testament to the power of salvation.

One Sunday in 1815 in Marietta, Ohio, an itinerant preacher was speaking to a congregation. John heard the loud, penetrating voice of the minister. Some accounts say that John was drunk at the time. Other stories say that he was on his way to commit suicide in the Ohio River. What is known for sure is that when he heard the preacher's message he was converted. He joined the church the next Sunday and soon resolved to be a missionary to the Indians.

A good reader and singer, John first went to the Delaware tribe where he was often in danger. It was said that his singing soothed the Indians and often saved his life. Among the Wyandott Indians, John found a captive black man who had been stolen as a child in Virginia. That man became John's interpreter. John's work spread until he had a great influence on the Wyandott tribe. He became a local preacher and continued his work until his death in 1823.

John's work with the Indians stimulated interest in Methodist missions which led to the establishment of the Missionary and Bible Society of the Methodist Episcopal Church in America on April 5, 1819.

Help me to hear Your voice today, Mighty God.

April 6: Turning to Christ

"'For my Father's will is that everyone who looks to the Son and believes in Him shall have eternal life'" (John 6:40 NIV).

As the Romanian Easter season approached, Southern Baptist missionaries Cynthia and Ron Gunter prepared for a big event. Cynthia would be directing the Easter pageant, *The Living Cross,* for three days in Bucharest.

They prayed mightily for the presentation and asked Christians in America to do so as well. More than 10,000 people attended the pageant, 537 people prayed to receive Christ, and another 800 dedicated themselves to a deeper Christian walk.

Cynthia rejoiced when she heard the story of a choir member who invited a neighbor mother and daughter to the pageant. They both professed faith in Christ that night. Several days later, a Romanian Christian living in the United States contacted Cynthia to tell her that his mother and sister, for whom he had been praying for years, had become Christians. They were the neighbors invited to the Easter play by the choir member!

Cynthia prays that the choir's presentation can continue to reach people for Christ with the saving message of Easter.

"With God, all things are possible!" she exclaims.

Do you believe that God can work through you to reach others? How can you testify, during this Easter season, to God's salvation?

Use me to further Your kingdom, O God, as we celebrate Your Son's resurrection.

April 7: Martyred for Their Faith

"They were stoned; they were sawed in two; they were put to death by the sword" (Heb. 11:37 NIV).

The first twentieth-century missionary martyr in the Pacific Islands sailed from Britain in 1866 on the *John Williams*, a ship named after the famous martyred missionary.

Scottish James Chalmers (1841–1901) decided as a teen to become a missionary after his pastor read a letter from a missionary in Fiji describing the power that the gospel had over the cannibals. Ordained a Congregational minister, he trained with the London Missionary Society.

After suffering a shipwreck, James and his bride landed on Rarotanga. "What fellow name belong you?" a native asked him. He replied, "Chalmers." Trying to say his name, the native replied, "Tamate," a name the islanders continued to use for him.

In 1877 he traveled to unevangelized areas of New Guinea. An avid explorer, he established a series of mission posts through which entire areas were reached with the gospel. He became well known and respected for his courage and for his concern for the islanders. He founded a training college and supported indigenous churches.

On April 7, 1901, he was going into new territory when cannibals on Goaribari Island killed him, fellow missionary Oliver Tomkins, and some native Christians. The world was shocked by their deaths.

Would you go into a country knowing that your life would be in jeopardy?

~

Thank You, Lord, for the truly committed who paid with their lives.

April 8: A Birthday Prayer

"With man this is impossible, but with God all things are possible" (Matt. 19:26 NIV).

Birthdays usually mean presents, cake, and celebration. For Janice Day, though, her birthday meant an answer to prayer.

Janice and her husband, Fred, who today serve as Southern Baptist missionaries in the Caribbean Basin, worked six years in the South American country of Suriname.

Early in their ministry, they needed a building. They had built benches under a mango tree, but passersby often threw rocks at them while they studied. They finally found a piece of property owned by a man outside the community and hoped he would sell to them.

Requesting prayer from the United States, they learned in February that he was ready to sell. "All of this happened several months after our yearly budgets were planned, and there was simply no money," Janice remembers. They petitioned their mission board for money. March went by, and April approached with no word.

Janice knew that people would be praying for her on her birthday, April 8, and felt that an answer would come that day.

"On my birthday, a man came with a telegram saying, 'Money is available. Go and purchase your land,'" she says. "What an answer to birthday prayers!"

The icing on the cake came later when she learned that the man selling the property shared her birthday. That day was his 50th birthday—the most important day in his culture.

~

Teach me, Lord, that with You all things are possible.

April 9: Your Legacy?

"In all my prayers for all of you, I always pray with joy because of your partnership in the gospel from the first day until now, being confident of this, that he who began a good work in you will carry it on to completion until the day of Christ Jesus" (Phil 1:4–6 NIV).

Can you look back on your life and see how God has blessed your work? Can you see tangible results from your efforts for Christ?

John and Katherine Nielson, former Nazarene missionaries to Denmark and now teachers and administrators in Manila (where John serves as president of Asia Pacific Nazarene Theological Seminary), say their greatest joy comes from seeing the results of their work.

They desire to have students, neighbors, co-workers, and their own family members learn more about Christ because of their efforts.

John says that 90 percent of his university graduates work in full-time ministry, as ministers, missionaries, or other Christian workers. On the home front, their children are both ordained ministers open to missionary service.

"I would like there to be mature, competent Christians in many countries of the world who have been inspired and equipped for effective, varied service that strengthens the kingdom of God long after my death," John says.

What kind of legacy for Christ will you leave behind?

∼

O Creator, thank You for the tools and talents You give each of us to work for You. Help me to make a difference in someone's life today.

April 10: The Salvation Army

"All the ends of the earth will see the salvation of our God" (Isa. 52:10 NIV).

"O Kate, I have found my destiny!" William Booth (1829–1912) told his wife. "These are the people for whose salvation I have been longing all these years.... And there and then in my soul I offered myself and you and the children up to this great work."

William Booth's idea for the Salvation Army began when he was working in London's East End, a place of extreme poverty, prostitution, and drunkenness. On Sunday, July 2, 1865, he started preaching in a tent in an unused Quaker burial ground in Whitechapel. He called his movement the Christian Mission.

Slowly William and Catherine's work grew. It was not until 1878, though, when the name of the organization was changed to the Salvation Army that rapid growth occurred. In addition to evangelizing the lost, William set up a network of agencies of social relief and rehabilitation to help people overcome poverty, intemperance, and unemployment.

Due to the vision and efforts of "General" William and "Mother" Catherine and two of their children who became "generals," the Salvation Army now works in over 100 countries in more than 140 languages. The organization's varied services include hostels for the homeless, food distribution centers, and homes for alcoholics.

Salvation Army Founder's Day is celebrated on April 10, William Booth's birthday.

Thank You, God, for the legacy of the Booths. Bless the work of the Salvation Army today.

April 11: Pray and Don't Stop!

"We were under great pressure, far beyond our ability to endure, so that we despaired even of life" (2 Cor. 1:8 NIV).

Sarah (not her real name) is not ashamed to admit she is often scared.

"I'll be painfully honest," the Southern Baptist missionary serving in an undisclosed Middle Eastern country says. "At times, I feel suffocated by Satan and his demons. Nightmares will consume me." She and her husband will rise and pray fervently for the nightmares to cease, and they will.

In times such as this, Sarah covets the prayers of Christians back in the States and from around the world. She says she wants to raise her hands and shout across the ocean: "Pray harder! Pray and don't stop! My life and lives of those who don't yet know Jesus depend on it!"

Such fervency comes from the hostile and dangerous situations Sarah finds in the country she now calls home. It is an area where religious police call Christians blasphemers and demand them to kneel and renounce their faith. If they don't, they can be killed immediately.

Despite obstacles, Sarah says that there are many loving individuals who don't harbor hate like the authorities. Others are people who hate simply because they don't understand Christianity.

Can you promise today to pray for Sarah and others who live out their faith in a culture where their faith can cost them their lives?

∼

I send my prayers across the oceans this moment, Lord.

April 12: A Loving Defense

"But in your hearts reverence Christ as Lord. Always be prepared to make a defense to anyone who calls you to account for the hope that is in you, yet do it with gentleness and reverence" (1 Peter 3:15 NIV).

"The nearest way to the Muslim heart," he said, "is the way of God's love, the way of the Cross."

For 60 years Samuel Zwemer (1867–1952), the Apostle to Islam, was the greatest missionary statesman to the Muslim world. His evangelistic approach was to directly present the gospel message in a spirit of love.

Born in Michigan on April 12, 1867, he was the 13th of 15 children of a Dutch Reformed Church pastor. He was ordained as a missionary by the Reformed Church in America in 1890.

The next year he started his ministry to Muslims with the founding of the Arabian Mission. Living in Basra, Bahrain, and Cairo, he distributed thousands of Bibles and tracts to introduce Muslims to the Living Word, Jesus.

In 1896 he married Amy Wilkes, a missionary nurse who became his colaborer. From 1912 until 1929, his work as an itinerant missionary to Muslims established his international reputation.

A professor at Princeton Theological Seminary from 1929 to 1936, he had the mind of a scholar and the heart of an evangelist.

Are you confronting those who oppose Christ in a loving manner?

~

Everlasting God, enable me to exhibit the love of Christ as I witness today.

April 13: A Covenant to Serve God

"They entered into a covenant to seek the Lord, the God of their fathers, with all their heart and soul" (2 Chron. 15:12 NIV).

"Today, in the middle of the Indian Ocean, I renew the covenant which I have made with you, my God and Father. . . . Sealed and signed on 13th April 1862," he wrote in his prayer diary.

That day Ludwig Ingwer Nommensen (1834–1918) was renewing the vow he had made at the age of 12. Because of an accident, he had been confined to bed for almost a year. During that time after reading the Bible, he became a Christian and took a vow to become a missionary if he recovered.

Born on the island of Nordstrand (then Danish), he completed studies at the seminary of the Rhenish Missionary Society. In 1861 he was sent to Sumatra (modern Indonesia) to direct the Batak mission. Caring for the physical and spiritual needs of the Batak—an ancient Malayan tribe who believed in nature and spirit worship—he gained their confidence. He instituted the preacher-teacher system which gave the native people leadership in the church.

The Apostle to the Bataks served tirelessly for 56 years. At Ludwig's death, the Batak church had 180,000 members, 510 schools, 32,700 pupils, 788 teacher-preachers, 2,200 elders, and 34 ordained pastors. Today the church has approximately 2.5 million members.

Are you seeking the Lord with all your heart and soul?

∽

My God, today I renew my commitment to serve You diligently.

April 14: Nearer to God

"Come near to God and he will come near to you" (James 4:8 NIV).

He conducted the only religious service aboard the *Titanic* on April 14, 1912, closing the service with his favorite hymn, "Nearer, My God, to Thee." Several hours later he asked the band to play the hymn as the ship sank.

Minister Robert Bateman (1859–1912) was returning to America after visiting his birthplace—Bristol, England—to study methods used there in orphanages founded by George Muller.

Robert came to America as a young man because he was interested in rescue missions work. He founded and directed Jacksonville's Central City Mission located in a notorious red-light district.

Although he had visited England because he wanted to reorganize his mission using Muller's techniques, he was already receiving much praise, being dubbed "the man who distributes more human sunshine than any other in Jacksonville."

A monthly report of his mission demonstrates his impact on the city: "836 men given beds, 1,284 meals furnished . . . 182 men were sent to work . . . five wayward girls were sent to the Rescue Home."

After Robert's death, his nephew received a letter from him, mailed when the *Titanic* had stopped in Ireland. "Tom, if this ship goes to the bottom, I shall not be there, I shall be up yonder. Think of it!"

Are you living your life in useful work but in triumphant hope?

∽

Dear Lord, may my life daily echo the words of the great hymn: "Nearer, my God, to thee, Nearer to thee!"

April 15: Navajo Land

"The mountain of the Lord's temple will be established as chief among the mountains; it will be raised above the hills and all nations will stream to it" (Isa. 2:2 NIV).

When the first European settlers arrived in the Southwest, they recognized the dignity of the Navajo people and called them Lords of the Earth. We can rejoice today that many Navajo know *the* Lord of the earth.

Four Corners Native American Ministry, a mission of the United Methodist Church, works in Shiprock, New Mexico, to establish Navajo churches and reach reservation residents for Christ.

Associate director Rev. Paul West works with Navajo ministers to reach the community with the gospel and says that there is an incredible need by new Christian congregations for support.

The ministry recently added the Rough Side of Mountain Church. "Here in this out-of-the-way place, hidden behind mountain ridges, is a strong group of Christians," says Paul.

A group of 15 Christians, meeting in the bedroom of a small house, established another new church. They poured a concrete floor for a church building, but had no more money. With the ministry's support, they constructed a small church building with a dirt floor. "They wanted a church, even a small one, so they could reach out to their relatives and friends," he says. "It was beautiful how they shared their great desire that all their people be saved."

Isn't it exciting to have Christian brothers and sisters in all cultures?

∼

Give me a fervor to reach others, Lord.

April 16: A Woman of Worth

"And now, my daughter, do not fear, I will do for you all that you ask, for all my fellow townsmen know that you are a woman of worth" (Ruth 3:11 RSV).

"Her death was deeply lamented by those who knew her worth; and many of the Dong-Yahn women came to her funeral, crying, 'The mamma is dead!'" wrote her biographer.

Have you ever considered the worth—the value or importance—that one life can have on a community or the world?

New York native Eleanor Macomber (1801–1840) may have had a short tenure as a missionary, but her legacy continues to inspire people today.

In 1830 she was sent by the Baptist Missionary Board to teach the Ojibwa Indians in Sault Ste. Marie, Michigan. Because of bad health, she left after four years.

In 1836 she joined the Karen mission of Burma. Stationed at Dong-Yahn, she labored alone among a people known for their drunkenness and idolatry. She soon began to see people's lives transformed. At the end of 1838 she wrote to her supporters, "The native Christians here now number 23, twelve of whom have been baptized the present year." Compared to Adoniram Judson who worked in Burma for five years without a convert, Eleanor experienced success quickly.

On April 16, 1840, Eleanor died of jungle fever. Although her ministry was brief, her impact was great.

My God, I want to be a person of worth to those around me.

April 17: Unlikely Angels

"Lord, I have heard of your fame; I stand in awe of your deeds, O Lord" (Hab. 3:2 NIV).

Has a miraculous event ever made you stand in awe of God's power or renewed your reverence for Him?

Andrea Tawney says an experience on a missions trip to Baja, Mexico, reminded her that God is truly awesome and can work in unexpected ways.

Andrea went with a group from her Vineyard church to Baja's Mission La Hai Roi. She and others worked during the day at the mission's medical clinic and cabins. In the evenings, they visited migrant Native American Indian camps for evangelistic services. They also went into the migrants' homes (which were made of either plastic or cardboard) to witness and pray.

On the first night of visitation, six of them headed to the home of Tomas, the group's translator who had been converted during a previous trip but was now involved again in an alcoholic lifestyle. When Andrea and two other women opened the plastic door and peered inside, Tomas fell to his knees crying, "Las angelinas!" He told them that he'd just had a dream that three angels would visit him and tell him that he would be healed. The angels, he said, had their faces.

They all prayed with Tomas, and he renewed his faith. He was delivered from alcohol and today works as an evangelist in central Mexico.

"I'd certainly never expected to be known as an angel," Andrea exclaims. "But God can use anyone, in any fashion, to bring about His purposes."

God, help me to be open to Your miraculous works.

April 18: A Teaching Legacy

"We proclaim him, admonishing and teaching everyone with all wisdom, so that we may present everyone perfect in Christ. To this end I labor, struggling with all his energy, which so powerfully works in me" (Col. 1:28–29 NIV).

She began her school on April 18, 1870, with six little girls and a man with a club outside the door to protect them.

The first missionary of the Woman's Foreign Missionary Society of the Methodist Episcopal Church, Isabella Thoburn (1840–1901) joined her brother, Bishop James Thoburn, in Lucknow, India, in January 1870. Encountering bitter prejudices on the part of Hindus against the education of women, she boldly opened her mission school for girls three months after her arrival. Soon after she purchased a nine-acre estate for a boarding and day school.

In the 1880s Isabella campaigned for a women's college. In a widely distributed leaflet she wrote, "There are over one hundred colleges in India for young men, but only one for young women, and that not Christian." In 1887 she achieved her dream with the establishment of the Isabella Thoburn College, the first Christian college for women in Asia.

Laboring 31 years in India, her strenuous work lowered her resistance which led to her death from cholera. Her last words were in Hindustani, the language of her adopted country.

Is God giving you a vision for a ministry that is needed but may require overcoming deep-seated prejudices?

~

Give me energy, Mighty God, to do Your work even when I encounter opposition.

April 19: Homes Built of Love

"The builder of a house has greater honor than the house itself" (Heb. 3:3 NIV).

The work of Habitat for Humanity embodies the meaning of this Scripture—that the building of a house is more important than the structure itself. Builders, in helping others, learn the meaning of love and generosity.

Viola Allen, a Habitat for Humanity homeowner in Pickens, South Carolina, says of the builders who constructed her home: "If it hadn't been for these people, I don't know where I'd be. I just love 'em all. They just don't come any better than these Habitat people."

Eighty-year-old Viola moved into her elderly mother's home when her mother suffered a stroke. That house, says construction supervisor Everett Gladden, "was more like a chicken coop. No hot water. No toilet. And she was trying to care for an invalid there." Part of the house had only a dirt floor. She cooked on an old woodstove.

Viola learned of Habitat for Humanity when the organization built a house in her neighborhood. Soon volunteers were building a home for her. She contributed to the project (as all homeowners are required to do) by cleaning the work site and cooking for the volunteers. She now works on other sites and tells of Habitat's work as often as she can.

How often do you reach out and help others in a tangible way—like building a home? Since April is National Volunteer Month, what better time to do so!

～

Help me realize, Lord, that the act of helping is more important than the work itself.

April 20: A Special Gift

"Whatever you have learned or received or heard from me, or seen in me—put it into practice. And the God of peace will be with you" (Phil. 4:9 NIV).

The pink stuffed bunny stands as a reminder of the special way I learned about missions as a young child. It bore the name of Duncan, an elderly man my family visited regularly through the benevolence work of my childhood Baptist church. Mr. Duncan gave the toy to me for Christmas when I was 12 years old.

My parents told me to appreciate the gift, reminding me that Mr. Duncan lived in a tiny, one-bedroom apartment and relied on our church for help with utility bills and food. It must have been a sacrifice for him to buy it.

Mr. Duncan was just one of the people I met through my parents' volunteerism at church. Every Sunday after church, my brother and I would help my parents pack up bags of food from our church's food pantry. We would deliver food to Mr. Duncan and several other families on our way home from church. It was a simple act—one I sometimes saw as a bother when I wanted to get home to play—but it taught me a great truth about reaching out to those in our own communities.

What memories of reaching out to others do you have from childhood? If you have none, why not begin now?

Dear God, bless those in my community who have so little.

April 21: Sharing Afflictions

"Turn thou to me, and be gracious to me; for I am lonely and afflicted. Relieve the troubles of my heart, and bring me out of my distresses. Consider my affliction and my trouble" (Psalm 25:16–18 RSV).

As he stood on the pier in 1885 ready to board the ship to his native Belgium, he looked down at his hands. The white spots could mean only one thing—leprosy. He turned and walked back to the leper colony.

In 1873 Father Joseph Damien (1840–1889), a Catholic missionary, volunteered to work among the lepers on the Hawaiian island of Molokai. On his arrival, he found the lepers without a permanent nurse, counselor, or grave digger. Gradually, he assumed those duties laboring for 12 years to alleviate their sufferings. He became discouraged, though, when his chapel remained empty week after week and the lepers never really accepted him. He decided to quit.

After he left the pier that day in 1885, word spread quickly that he was now one of them. His chapel now overflowed.

Worn-out, the now world-renowned missionary died in April 1889. A likeness of Father Damien has stood in the Statuary Hall of the US Capitol building since 1965 as a reminder of a man who gave his life for others.

Cancer, stroke, depression—these are troubles that you may have encountered. Can you now be a mentor to others?

∽

God of comfort, help me today to touch someone who needs encouragement and understanding.

April 22: The First Commandment

"You shall have no other gods before me" (Ex. 20:3 NIV).

You are familiar with the first of the Ten Commandments, and you can easily understand it. Only God, it says, is worthy of worship.

In many parts of the world, however, people worship idols—not unlike the way the Israelites bowed before a golden calf. In many African countries people practice the rituals of animism, creating a major obstacle for Christian missionaries.

Animism is a religious practice involving the worship of inanimate objects such as rocks, trees, and statues. Worshipers even offer human sacrifices to appease the religion's deities.

Bob and Caroline (not their real names) work in a West African country where animism rituals are common. They try to learn more about the rituals and the belief systems behind them so that missions work can be more productive and effective.

They recently experienced the horrors firsthand, as they learned of a young man who had been missing for several days. Authorities found him dead, his throat slit and internal organs cut out. He had been offered as an animist sacrifice.

Bob and Caroline say that several things could help this situation: a better understanding of the religion, more missionary and medical personnel to meet the practical needs of the people, and an outpouring of the Holy Spirit on entire West African families.

Do you ever worship something or someone other than God?

∼

Holy Lord, I know that You are the one, true God. I acknowledge Your worthiness today.

April 23: A Man of Humility

"Be sympathetic, love as brothers, be compassionate and humble"
(1 Peter 3:8 NIV).

Would you like to be known for your love and humility?

After his death, a friend described him as "affectionate and beaming with love.... Character outshone everything.... He was the humblest of men."

Anglican missionary Henry Martyn (1781–1812) was a much-loved man in life and in death.

Born in Cornwall, England, he was educated at St. John's College, Cambridge. He felt called to be a missionary after reading the life of David Brainerd, missionary to the Native American Indians.

Upon arrival in Calcutta in April 1806 as an East India Company chaplain, he said, "Now let me burn out for God!" Henry preached to Hindus and Muslims as well as the British. After studying Hindustani, he translated the New Testament into that language.

Beginning to have signs of consumption that had killed his two sisters in England, he went to Cawnpore in 1809 where he endured a long illness. There he worked on a Persian translation of the New Testament. Because of his health, he went to Persia and there perfected his translation.

Leaving for England where he hoped to marry his love, Lydia Grenfell, he fell ill. He died at Tokat several hundred miles from Constantinople and was buried in the Armenian cemetery with honors usually reserved for archbishops. Through his *Journals and Letters* (1837), the humble missionary who "burned out for God," had a profound impact.

Give me a humble and loving spirit, Holy God.

April 24: Away from Home

"If they had been thinking of the country they had left, they would have had opportunity to return. Instead, they were longing for a better country—a heavenly one" (Heb. 11:15–16 NIV).

Is it worth it to follow God's call, knowing our family can't depend on us in a crisis and knowing that the people we love may be gone the next time we come home?

Carrie and Lance Borden felt burdened by such thoughts after finding out that Lance's mother was seriously ill. The couple, Southern Baptist missionaries to Austria, were in Spain at the time and unable to return home. They wrestled with the fact that their commitment to missions meant they must be separated from family during times of crisis.

When Lance told his father of their concerns, he told them: "We would never want you to come home because of us. No matter what the situation, we want you where God has called you. That is where you belong."

Carrie says that the call to missions truly involves an entire extended family. "Our families are called to release us into God's care in foreign places," she says. "It is heartwrenching each time we part, but it is worth it to part for His sake."

The above verses in Hebrews have lifted up Carrie many times, giving her peace that their call is of God and reassuring her during times of homesickness.

Has service to God ever separated you from your family?

∼

Thank You for Christian families, Lord.

April 25: A Persevering Spirit

"Let us not become weary in doing good, for at the proper time we will reap a harvest if we do not give up" (Gal. 6:9 NIV).

Do you have a persevering spirit?

Many missionaries certainly did.

After six years in Mudnabatty, India, Baptist missionary William Carey still had no converts. He then relocated to Serampore, and on December 29, 1800, he baptized the first native Indian convert. At Carey's death in 1834, thousands of Christians mourned.

Baptist missionaries Adoniram and Ann Judson began their missions work in Burma in 1814. Five years later in May 1819, they reported their first convert. By the summer of 1820, their church had ten baptized members.

Samuel Pollard (1864–1915), missionary of the Bible Christian Church (now known as United Methodist Church) to China, had no converts for five years. A mass movement developed, and after ten years, there were 10,000 Christians.

Ludwig Ingwer Nommensen of the Rhenish Missionary Society arrived in Sumatra in 1861. It was not until 1865 that he baptized his first converts. At his death in 1918, the church had 180,000 members.

Maybe James Gilmour (1843–1891) best exemplifies perseverance. The Scottish missionary wrote in his diary after being in China for 16 years: "Preached to 24,000 people, treated more than 5,700 patients, distributed 10,000 books and tracts . . . and out of all this there are only two men who have openly confessed Christ."

∽

Dear God, help me not to be discouraged by obstacles but by courage and patience persevere.

April 26: Unity in Christ

"For ye are all the children of God by faith in Christ Jesus. For as many of you as have been baptized into Christ have put on Christ" (Gal. 3:26 KJV).

In Baton Rouge, Louisiana, six different churches work together to operate a food pantry and provide financial help to struggling families in their area. The churches are of different denominations—Baptist, Disciples of Christ, Episcopalian, Methodist, and Presbyterian—and their work together exemplifies the unity God asks of all Christians.

Broadmoor United Methodist Church began Southeast Ministries in 1995. Two years later, the other churches joined the ministry.

In 1998, the ministry distributed 73,000 pounds of food to more than 3,000 individuals, and helped more than 700 with financial aid. It also provided personal and job counseling workshops, as well as breakfast, through Cafe Hope.

Pam Williams of Broadmoor Baptist Church says: "Among the program's goals are to encourage spiritual growth by offering prayer cards during each client's visit, and to provide an environment of care and concern and help restore dignity."

Does your church work with other churches in your community? How does unity between churches and denominations increase the work of God?

Lord of us all, help me remember today that I must be unified with other Christians. Working together we can do great things for You.

April 27: Far from Home

"And immediately they left the boat and their father and followed him" (Matt. 4:22 NIV).

In the past I had heard of missionaries whose names had to be disguised because they worked in places hostile to the Christian gospel. I had casually thought about how difficult it must be to work so far from family.

The reality of such a situation hit home, though, when one of my best friends from my youth moved to Russia as a missionary. Not long before she left for overseas, she told me the little she could about her plans—she'd be in Russia teaching English classes. Her faith, even in unsure circumstances, shone through strong.

Later other friends, fellow church members, and I began to rely on the updates she'd send in letters from Russia. She told us to be careful when writing and emailing her. She and other missionaries felt as if the government was checking their correspondences. She told us of the difficulty in sharing the gospel without the safety of proclaiming that it was her official work. She told us, though, of the excitement in seeing that she could reach others through her teaching and her lifestyle.

In the years my friend has been gone, I've often wondered how she does it. Could I live thousands of miles away from my parents? How could I survive without daily telephone calls? Would my faith be strong enough to endure such separation and isolation?

∽

Thank You, O Lord, for missionaries willing to serve You far from home.

April 28: A Worthy Speaker

"I will give you thanks in the great assembly; among throngs of people I will praise you" (Psalm 35:18 NIV).

She was the first woman to address a public meeting in South Carolina.

Maria Davies Wightman (1833–1912) had that honor when she spoke following her election as the president of the South Carolina Woman's Foreign Missionary Society of the Methodist Episcopal Church.

Maria Davies, a native of Sparta, Georgia, moved to Alabama during the Civil War. After graduating with honors from Centenary Institute in Summerfield, Alabama, she married in 1863. Three years after their marriage, her husband, William, became bishop in the Methodist Episcopal Church.

They moved to Charleston, South Carolina, where she became the heart of missions in the women's societies of the state. She served as president of the South Carolina Foreign Mission Society for 34 years. She also was national president of the Woman's Foreign Missionary Society from 1894 to 1906.

Maria labored for many missions causes in America and abroad. Wightman Chapel at Scarritt College in Nashville, Tennessee, was named for her after she worked for the original funding of the school. The Wightman-Hambert Chapel, a religious building at Holston Institute in Songdo, Korea, was named for her and another leader. In 1899 she solicited funds for a school in Cienfuegoes, Cuba, which opened the next year.

Are you using your "voice" as a forum for missions?

Equip me daily, God, to be a worthy spokesperson for You.

April 29: A Witch!

"Test the spirits to see whether they are from God, because many false prophets have gone out into the world" (1 John 4:1 NIV).

"This is the neighborhood witch."

On a 1998 trip to care for victims of a hurricane in the Dominican Republic, Health Care Ministries' Jim Wood sat in his makeshift clinic and greeted those hurt in the natural disaster.

An interpreter announced to the doctor that his next patient was the village witch.

Jim began to look at the woman's wounds, simultaneously praying that the Holy Spirit would reach her heart. He understood that this woman would not immediately see her need for Christ. He knew he would be praying for her deliverance many times in the future.

He finished his examination, then told her about Christ, and asked if he could pray with her. To his astonishment, the woman calmly asked Jesus into her life.

The woman then visited other spiritual counselors; later HCM, a ministry arm of the Assemblies of God denomination, visited her on a follow-up trip. Missionaries and health-care workers found that she had led her entire extended family and others to Christianity.

Looking back at the moment when the woman first prayed to God, Jim remembers: "I looked upon a countenance absolutely transformed, radiating with complete joy. I felt like weeping. What a privilege to bring her to Jesus!"

Has Jesus made a transformation in your life?

O Redeemer, continue to transform me today.

April 30: Serving God

"'Whoever serves me must follow me; and where I am, my servant also will be. My Father will honor the one who serves me'" (John 12:26 NIV).

At the end of her life she reflected upon her service to God: "It has been an adventure—and a toil. But to be allowed to wear oneself out serving God, that is the greatest happiness."

Missionary nurse Annie Skau Bernsten (1911–1992)—Sister Annie—was a devoted servant of God. She received the Norwegian King's St. Olaf's Orden, the Florence Nightingale Medal, and was named a Member of the British Empire.

Sister Annie, a native of Oslo, Norway, was a leader in her Karl Marx youth club. While attending nursing school, her life changed—the Marxist became a Christian.

After participating in the China Inland Mission training program, she arrived in China in 1938 and worked there until 1951. She labored from 1953 to 1955 at the Rennie's Mill refugee camp in Hong Kong. In 1955 she founded the Hope of Heaven Hospital which has treated thousands of refuges from mainland China. Today the hospital is one of the main rehabilitation institutions in Hong Kong.

At the end of her life, Sister Annie welcomed death. "Now I just look forward to meeting Jesus," she said. "The most magnificent thing which can happen to me is to be allowed to serve Him day and night."

Does serving God bring you happiness?

∼

God, may I joyfully serve You all the days of my life.

May 1: Sewing for God

"We have different gifts, according to the grace given us" (Rom. 12:6 NIV).

Preaching, teaching, witnessing, ministering—these are the gifts we often imagine missionaries having.

Heather Rehn, a Southern Baptist missionary in Guinea, West Africa, is a wonderful example of how God gives many different gifts and talents to all Christians. One of her talents is sewing.

Heather learned to sew as an eight-year-old child of missionaries in Brazil. She later studied fashion design in college, where she also felt God's call to missions.

She asked God for guidance. "I surrendered my life and my talents to Him, trusting that if I made myself available, He would equip me for His service," Heather remembers.

God's answer was for Heather to go to Guinea, along with husband, Paulo. There, she learned that God could utilize her unique gifts.

She began by teaching sewing at the Baptist Community Center in the town of Forecariah. In 1997 she opened a downtown sewing center.

"The people here in Guinea are very poor, and have no marketable skills," she says. "Sewing is a very useful skill. Some want to learn how to sew in order to work as a tailor or seamstress. Others wish to sew for their families."

Heather never imagined that God could use her sewing skills in such a mighty way. Have you ever—like Heather—wondered how God could use your talents?

Dear God, show me where my gifts and talents lie and teach me how to use them for You.

May 2: A Nation's Glory

"All the nations you have made will come and worship before you, O Lord; they will bring glory to your name" (Psalm 86:9 NIV).

Did you know that missionaries had a great influence on the religious, educational, and political life of Hawaii?

The first Protestant missionaries from New England arrived there in 1820. In only 20 years Hawaii was officially a Christian nation.

One of the first missionaries to Hawaii, Hiram Bingham (1789–1869) was a Congregationalist from Bennington, Vermont, sent by the American Board of Commissioners for Foreign Missions. He set up mission stations and was pastor of Honolulu's Old Stone church (1820–1840). On preaching tours he was accompanied by the Hawaiian queen, an advocate for Christianity.

He served as an advisor to the king and chiefs in their dealings with foreigners. He created a written language for the people and founded schools. Aided by colleagues, he completed the translation of the entire Bible in 1839.

William Richards (1793–1847), missionary from Massachusetts, went to Hawaii in 1823 and served as government advisor from 1838 until his death. He was the leader behind the first Hawaiian constitution (1840) and for the system of public education.

Medical missionary Gerrit Parmele Judd (1803–1873) arrived in Hawaii in 1828. He served as translator, interpreter, foreign minister, and minister of finance under King Kamehameha III. From 1842 to 1853 he was the most influential man in Hawaii.

Thank You, Lord, for missionaries who have made far-reaching contributions.

May 3: Friends in Need

"During the night Paul had a vision of a man in Macedonia standing and begging him, 'Come over . . . and help us'" (Acts 16:9 NIV).

In times of tragedy, friendship is often the key to getting through the hard times.

On May 3, 1999, a tornado ripped through Moore, Oklahoma, killing more than 40 and destroying or damaging more than 8,000 homes.

Pastor Alan Cox of Moore's First Baptist Church immediately called his congregation to action. After serving more than 40,000 meals to more than 2,000 families, however, he knew that the task was too big just for them. He called on old friends in North Carolina's Buncombe Association, where he once served as pastor of a church.

Soon 200 teenagers and adult chaperons from 17 different congregations headed to Moore on a quickly arranged missions trip.

The youth from North Carolina joined approximately 1,100 teenagers who came to Oklahoma from around the country. They helped rebuild homes, assisted in cleanup, and aided in food distribution.

The missions work touched the many people whose lives were altered by the tornado, but it also touched those who served in volunteer capacities.

Alison Hardison, a high schooler from Woodhaven, North Carolina, says the experience deeply affected her.

"This one really touched me. The people had hardly anything left," she says. "It was still a disaster situation three months after the tornado."

When have Christian friends reached out to you in a time of need?

God of love, today show me how to help a Christian brother or sister.

May 4: Fighting for Justice

"But let justice roll on like a river, righteousness like a never-failing stream!" (Amos 5:24 NIV).

Missionaries throughout history have been committed to social reform. Suttee, slavery, temple prostitution, killing of twins—these were social practices that four famous missionaries battled.

English Baptist missionary William Carey campaigned vigorously against suttee, the Hindu custom of widow burning. After examining sacred Sanskrit texts to determine the status of suttee in Hinduism, he discovered the custom was not part of Hindu law but that the sacred texts only approved the practice. Finally, in 1829 suttee was declared a homicide.

In over three decades in Africa, David Livingstone worked to abolish slavery. Once he told a tribal chief, "I can't follow the slave route. The slave traders know I am against slavery. That route is too dangerous for me now." Livingstone hoped that his explorations would not only open up Africa for missions work but also would open it up for commerce, which would be a blow against the slave trade.

Presbyterian missionary to India for 56 years, Amy Carmichael began her work rescuing young Hindu temple prostitutes in 1901. She founded the Dohnavur Fellowship in 1926 which cared for over 1,000 children.

Mary Slessor, Presbyterian missionary for 38 years in West Africa, worked against the barbarous practice of killing twins at birth. Rescuing castaway babies, she raised dozens of sets of twins in her home.

What would Jesus do?

∽

Righteous Lord, give me a boldness to speak up about social concerns.

May 5: Take His Cross

"Anyone who does not take his cross and follow me is not worthy of me" (Matt. 10:38 NIV).

"I want to evangelize."

This was the powerful sentence a North Korean seminary student spoke to a United Methodist bishop on a relief tour through the country.

Following a deadly drought in North Korea in 1998, missionaries and church leaders worked throughout the country, providing practical relief through donations of blankets, medical supplies, and food. They also gave spiritual encouragement to the many fledgling congregations and emerging church leaders.

In visiting a church in Pyongyang, Bishop Solomon met a young woman who asked for something simple. Solomon always carries a supply of small crosses with him. The woman asked for some of them, explaining that they would help her evangelize. He gave her all the crosses he had.

This young student was determined to evangelize and then disciple her friends in her very non-Christian community and nation. Her zeal for witnessing demonstrated the true meaning of taking up Christ's cross daily. And it was a humbling experience for the bishop, as he was reminded anew of Jesus' call to all of us to work daily for Him.

Does the Cross have the same power for you? Or do you need to be reminded of it?

Dear Savior, thank You for what You did on the Cross for me. Help me to remember that sacrifice today and every day.

May 6: A Liberator of Widows

"Religion that God our Father accepts as pure and faultless is this: to look after orphans and widows in their distress and to keep oneself from being polluted by the world" (James 1:27 NIV).

"There is no shelter for the unhappy creatures, clothed as they were in dripping rags, suffering intense pangs of hunger along with the bitter cold of the wind," she wrote of the thousands of dying widows cast out during a famine.

A native of southern India, Pandita Ramabai (1858–1922) was a great liberator to thousands of widows and orphans who suffered under Hinduism.

His peers excommunicated her Brahmin father after he taught his wife Sanskrit. Growing up in poverty, Pandita was also taught the Hindu Scriptures. Recognized for her remarkable knowledge, she received the title of Pandita (Mistress of Learning), a designation never before given to a woman.

She married in 1880, had a daughter, and was widowed after 19 months. Having become disillusioned with Hinduism, she studied Christianity and embraced it after religious training in England.

In 1889 she opened Sarada Sadan (Home of Wisdom) to teach and provide for widows. Relying on God to supply all of her needs, she later established Mukti Sadan (Place of Salvation) for widows, orphans, and other girls of the lower caste. From her homes and schools came thousands of Christian women who served as evangelists, teachers, and godly mothers.

Are you reaching out to the downcast?

Lord, give me a burden for widows.

May 7: Darkness Defeated

"The demon threw him to the ground in a convulsion. But Jesus rebuked the evil spirit, healed the boy and gave him back to his father" (Luke 9:42 NIV).

Other missionaries thought Deborah and Robert Nichols were crazy to venture into Nueva Palmira, a city in southwestern Uruguay. The Southern Baptist missionaries had been warned that the area was dominated by witches (called *brujas*) and spiritist religions (called *umbanda*).

The couple soon came face-to-face with this reality when they started a Bible study with two families. One of the mothers told of being washed in goat's blood and honey to cure an illness. The other mother said she believed her family experienced problems because of a curse put on them by a witch. The Nicholses saw that it was true what the other missionaries had said—a spirit of darkness did seem to have a stranglehold on the area.

Deborah rejoices, though, that opportunities for preaching the gospel are available. She and her husband told the two families of Jesus' sacrifice and gave them Bibles. They have continued coming to a weekly Bible study.

Deborah says that the answer for the people caught in spiritism in Uruguay is for them to realize that Jesus "holds power over darkness."

Do you believe that spirits of darkness exist? How can you combat them?

∽

Give me strength today, Lord, to have victory over evil. I believe that You have the ultimate power in this world.

May 8: God Is Your Companion

"'Be strong and of good courage; be not frightened, neither be dismayed; for the Lord your God is with you wherever you go'" (Josh. 1:9 RSV).

Opium addicts and witch doctors—the very people she so heroically ministered to—were the same people who were responsible for her death. Missionary doctors are rightly lauded for their service to others, but missionary nurses are often equally heroic. One such nurse was Lilian Hammer, a former mill worker from Lancashire, England, who served in remote Thailand.

A member of the China Inland Mission, Lilian worked under primitive conditions to help the Lisu tribespeople. As her reputation for bringing relief to opium addicts spread from one village to another, the tribe built a hut for her on a mountain ridge. There she often worked alone in a region where marauders sometimes plundered innocent travelers. She once wrote, "For twelve months I have been alone. . . . However, whether alone or with a companion, the Lord is able to work."

In April 1959 while traveling alone through jungle trails, she was killed by an opium addict who had accepted a bribe from a witch doctor and a Chinese quack who were losing their power over the tribe.

Today a small bamboo and grass church 200 yards from where Lilian died is a testament to her work.

Are you willing to go—even alone and amidst danger—where the Lord sends you?

～

Lord, today give me courage to go where I am needed to bring physical or spiritual healing.

May 9: Safe Haven

"The Lord is a refuge for His people" (Joel 3:16 RSV).

Have you ever been forced out of your home? Do you know how it feels to be separated from the place you love?

Refugees do. They want to be in their home country, but for some reason—usually war—they can't. They come from nations all around the world.

Lisa Dye, an International Service Corps missionary, often meets refugees in her work in the Netherlands, since the country is considered a peaceful haven. More than 120 refugee camps operate in the Netherlands for people from various countries.

She recently met a group of Albanian refugees in one camp. When a young Albanian woman heard one of Lisa's team members speak her native language, she invited them into her makeshift home for tea. They spent the rest of the evening in the home—which consisted of a sink, four metal lockers, and four steel-framed beds—hearing about her family's plight. Thankful for the refuge, she still yearned for her homeland.

Lisa shared an Albanian Bible with the woman, who is Muslim, and left the door open for spiritual conversations. She prays that their friendship (the woman calls Lisa her best American friend, and Lisa calls the woman her best Albanian friend) will give the woman an understanding of Christ's love. Hopefully, she can take that love home with her someday.

Dear God, be with those who have no home. Let them know that Your love offers the perfect haven and refuge.

May 10: Truth in Parables

"Jesus spoke all these things to the crowd in parables" (Matt. 13:34 NIV).

She used parables in sharing truths to a hard-to-reach group in India.

Charlotte Maria Tucker (1821–1893) was a popular author known by her pen name, ALOE (A Lady of England), before she made a career change. Writing captivating stories for young people, ALOE was loved by thousands of readers.

At the age of 54, Charlotte decided to become a missionary. After studying Urdu, one of the languages spoken in India, she went there representing the Church of England Zenana Missionary Society. She stayed until her death 18 years later.

Working in Batala, she went to the zenanas—the secluded chambers reserved for women who were not permitted to be seen in public—and sitting on the floor she told them stories. Then she taught some truths to the women. Charlotte wrote her stories in the form of parables. She also had a series of stories printed in tracts which explained the parables of Jesus.

Zenana work was not easy. A biographer wrote of her, "There were houses where she was spit upon, or even rudely turned away by the master; but there were others where the women welcomed her as a friend and learned eagerly to anticipate her coming."

Can you incorporate parables or other creative methods in your missions efforts?

Dear Lord, show me daily the best way to share Your love with others.

May 11: A Universal Language

"The heavens declare the glory of God. . . . There is no speech or language where their voice is not heard" (Psalm 19:1,3 NIV).

How could a bunch of "gringos" make a difference in the lives of Peruvians, when they couldn't even speak Spanish?

That's the question Bonnie Harvey asked herself as she and other members of Chapel Woods Presbyterian Church in Decatur, Georgia, prepared to spend a week in the mountains of Peru. Looking back, she knows that God can truly work wonders even when it may seem impossible by human standards.

She and other members of her group ventured into Peru's mountains one afternoon to invite the natives—Quechua Indians—to an evangelistic meeting at a nearby town's soccer field. They took it as an opportunity also to witness. But how could they speak to people so different from themselves?

"We shared our faith in very limited Spanish," Bonnie says. "And, luckily, we had the four spiritual laws written in Spanish."

The response? Bonnie says the people greeted the American visitors with open minds and ears.

"We were gringos, so they looked at us in wonder," she remembers, laughing. "But the people were so open! It was just such a warm, wonderful time as we shared what we could of Christ's love."

There truly is, Bonnie's experience shows, no speech or language barrier to God's love.

∽

Eternal God, when I doubt that You can reach others through me, give me faith in Your awesome power.

May 12: Losing Children

"'Rachel weeping for her children and refusing to be comforted, because her children are no more'" (Jer. 31:15 NIV)

Have you ever considered the grief that missionary mothers and fathers experience when they lose their children?

William and Dorothy Carey, J. Hudson and Maria Taylor, David and Mary Livingstone—they are a few of the many couples who experienced the death of children on the missions fields.

Mary Williams, whose husband, John, was a pioneer missionary in the South Sea Islands, suffered much. She wrote in 1831 about her pregnancy that she hoped to be "spared the distress of consigning a seventh sweet babe to a premature grave." The baby was stillborn. Several years later Mary would lose John to cannibals.

Jonathan and Rosalind Goforth developed a highly effective ministry in their 46 years in China. They paid, though, a high cost, losing 5 of their 11 children in infancy or early childhood. Once after the loss of 4 children, Jonathan proposed going into the interior villages. Rosalind at first opposed her husband writing, "My one and only reason was because it seemed a risking of the children's lives."

William and Anne Bagby lost 4 children during their six decades in Brazil. Their strong faith got the Southern Baptist couple through the deaths of 2 babies to fevers, a son who drowned saving the life of another man, and a son who mysteriously disappeared while in college in Galveston.

∼

Today, Loving God, protect the children of missionaries around the world.

May 13: God Will Save

"The Lord your God is with you, he is mighty to save. He will take great delight in you, he will quiet you with his love" (Zeph. 3:17 NIV).

Helen and Gerald Haynes gathered by the sea in Malaysia with fellow missionaries for a time of spiritual and physical refreshment. One morning, Helen rededicated her life to do "whatever the Lord has called upon me to do." Soon came the first challenge to her dedication.

The couple's four-year-old daughter, Marcia, had been playing in the surf with other missionaries' children but now lay unconscious on the beach, stung by a rare Portuguese man-of-war. A missionary nurse (who had packed a needle of adrenaline for the first time in her medical bag) worked to revive Marcia. "We don't know if it was the adrenaline or the prayers of faith going on nearby. We suspect it was both," remembers Helen. "I do know that our little girl's cry was the most beautiful I had heard since her birth. In the end my trial of faith strengthened my faith to rely on God's presence and planning."

Helen and Gerald worked for 43 years through the China Inland Mission in such places as Hong Kong, Singapore, and Malaysia. Retired, they still work with Chinese individuals living in America.

And little Marcia? She grew up to become, with her husband, a linguist missionary in Papua New Guinea.

When has your dedication to God been challenged? Did God quiet you with His love?

~

Give me strength, Lord, even in the difficult times.

May 14: A Consecrated Life

"Now who is willing to consecrate himself today to the Lord?" (1 Chron. 29:5 NIV).

Her years of missionary service were cut short because of her premature death. The memory of her dedicated life, though, was not forgotten.

The Bulape station in the Congo in 1915 was established in the name of Annie Katherine Taylor Rochester "who died at Mutoto on May 14, 1914, after eight years of efficient and consecrated service."

Annie was the last of five black missionary women to go to the Congo at the beginning of the twentieth century representing the Southern Presbyterian Church.

Born in Tuscaloosa, Alabama, and educated at Scotia College in Concord, North Carolina, she sailed to Luebo in 1906. She worked in the Pantops Home for Girls before being transferred to Ibanche where she became superintendent of the Marie Carey Home and taught in the day school there.

Annie married Reverend A. A. Rochester, a Jamaican missionary in the Congo in 1911. The next year they were sent to the new mission station at Mutoto. Her various responsibilities included being a teacher and girls home superintendent.

In February 1914, Annie's illness was diagnosed as appendicitis. Suffering another attack in April, she died in May. She was the first missionary buried at Mutoto.

One of her colleagues recalled that she had four important virtues that made a successful missionary: efficiency, consecration, temperament, and industry.

Are you willing to give yourself completely to God?

∼

Today, Lord, give me a consecrated spirit.

May 15: Exalt the Home

"Blessed is the nation whose God is the Lord" (Psalm 33:12 NIV).

"Elevate woman, and you lift up the home; exalt the home and you lift up the nation," she said while First Lady.

Lucy Webb Hayes (1831–1889) was perhaps one of our nation's most spiritual First Ladies. The only First Lady to ever head a missionary society, she had a strong sense of duty to family, church, and nation.

She was a nurse during the Civil War working in hospitals and camps while her husband served in the Union Army.

A highly principled woman, she refused to serve alcoholic beverages while in the White House (1877–1881). Dubbed Lemonade Lucy, she said the reason she took the stand was as an example to her children.

The first college-educated First Lady was mother to eight children (five of whom lived to adulthood). Sunday evenings were joyful ones at the White House with invited guests joining the family for hymn singing.

In 1880 when the Woman's Home Missionary Society of the Methodist Episcopal Church was organized, Lucy became its first president. She held the position until her death. The Lucy Webb Hayes Training School for Deaconesses in Washington was named in her honor. Today the undergraduate and graduate schools of nursing at American University are named for her.

Do you "exalt the home" in your personal and professional life?

Guide me, Holy God, in making my home a place to honor You and an example for the community around me.

May 16: Taking Tests

"'If you remain in me and my words remain in you, ask whatever you wish, and it will be given you'" (John 15:7 NIV).

Think back to when you were in high school or college and were preparing for a test. You would read your material and memorize as much information as possible.

Missionaries take tests too. Missionary Melinda Kyzar felt nervous as she prepared for her fifth-level competency exams in the Russian language. The test required her to give her testimony and relevant Bible verses in Russian; she also had to be able to carry on a Russian conversation about religious topics.

The night before the test, Melinda got some real-world practice for the exam. She left choir practice and, on her way home, tripped on a railroad track; a man stopped to help her and then noticed her Bible and sheet music from choir. He asked questions about the items and also about where she was from.

"I had the opportunity to practice most of what I studied for my language exam," she says. "I was even able to throw in a few Bible verses and share Jesus Christ."

Melinda says the experience showed her God's sense of humor and His perfect timing: "After that, I didn't care how I did on my language exam. I passed the real test by the railroad tracks."

Do you get nervous about sharing your faith?

Empower me, God, to speak boldly for You.

May 17: A Bishop Finds His Mother

"Hannah conceived and gave birth to a son. She named him Samuel, saying, 'Because I asked the Lord for him'" (1 Sam. 1:20 NIV).

Have you heard the nineteenth-century story of Hannah and her son Samuel?

The young boy was separated from his mother when slave traders seized him. He didn't see her again until he was a bishop. One day a woman came to Samuel Adjai Crowther (c. 1806–1891) for baptism. After asking her questions to see if she was ready for baptism, he discovered that she was not only a Christian but also his mother. He called her Hannah, the mother of Samuel.

The British Navy rescued Samuel, one of the most famous African missionaries, from a slave ship in 1822. He was taken to Sierra Leone where he became a Christian and was educated by missionaries of the Church Missionary Society.

In 1843 he was ordained a priest and went to Yorubaland (Nigeria) as a missionary. He planted many mission stations along the banks of the Niger River.

Consecrated as bishop of the Niger Territories at Canterbury Cathedral in 1864, Samuel spent the rest of his life building up the Anglican Church in Nigeria. He translated parts of the Bible and the prayer book into the Yoruba language. He fought evils such as the liquor trade, practices such as the murder of newborn twin babies, and cannibalism.

∼

Thank You, Lord, for the love that binds together a mother and a child.

May 18: Joy Borne of Sacrifice

"Therefore, brothers, in all our distress and persecution we were encouraged about you because of your faith. . . . How can we thank God enough for you in return for all the joy we have in the presence of our God because of you?" (1 Thess. 3:7,9 NIV).

Have you ever been so overcome by joy that you wept?

Rowland Bingham (1872–1942) did in 1914 when he found 1,500 believers in an area of Nigeria.

"He was overcome with sheer joy. The fountains of the deep were literally opened within his heart as tears of joy flowed down his cheeks," a fellow missionary said.

After 21 years of sacrifices and losses, the founder of the Sudan Interior Mission, now known as SIM (Society for International Ministries), was finally beginning to see the fruit of his work.

It all started when a Scottish Canadian widow, Mrs. Gowans, started praying for people in the Sudan. Her son Walter, Thomas Kent, and Rowland arrived in Nigeria in 1893. Rowland contracted malaria and wasn't able to go into the interior known as the Sudan. Thomas and Walter went, but died of malaria within a year.

In 1897 Rowland organized the Sudan Interior Mission board. In 1900, when he attempted again to enter the Sudan, he was stricken with malaria. Finally, in 1901 a station was established.

From a mother's prayers has come an organization that works in 23 countries with 1,900 missionaries.

Thank You, God, for the joy borne of sacrifice.

May 19: Always Thankful

"Give thanks in all circumstances, for this is God's will for you in Christ Jesus" (1 Thess. 5:18 NIV).

"Have I ever thanked God for the paint on my walls?"

That's the question Faithe Finley, a missionary who worked in Africa with the Society for International Ministries, once asked herself.

Monica, a young woman who worked for Faithe, had just lost both her brother and father. Faithe went to comfort Monica and her mother.

Monica's house consisted of a 10-by-12-foot room for 15 family members. Two chairs, a bench, and grass mats made up the room's furnishings. The room's only window had just a small opening, making ventilation almost impossible. As the sweat trickled down her face, Faithe noticed the room's freshly painted walls and clean floors.

Faith told the two women how sorry she was for their losses. Then the mother began to tell Faithe: "If it were not for you hiring my daughter, we would not have paint on the walls. Thank you for the paint. If it were not for you, we would be fighting mosquitoes through the night. But you helped us get a screen door and screen for the window."

Faithe was humbled. "I had gone to minister to this woman, to share the hope we have in Christ," she says. "I went away ministered to and convicted of my own ungratefulness."

Are you thankful for the paint on your walls?

∼

Holy God, thank You for the blessings, both big and small, You have brought into my life.

May 20: Equipped for Service

"Then the Lord said, 'Rise and anoint him; he is the one.' So Samuel took the horn of oil and anointed him, . . . and from that day on the Spirit of the Lord came upon David in power" (1 Sam. 16:12–13 NIV).

One day in 1820 King Frederick William III of Prussia visited Stettin to review his troops. When the king received an emotional poem written for him by a 17-year-old boy, he ordered that the boy be found. After questioning him, he learned that the precocious youth had left school and worked as an apprentice to a girdlemaker. The king then decreed that the boy should receive a scholarship to further his education.

That boy was Karl Gützlaff (1803–1851), a pioneer missionary to China.

Karl used his scholarship for two years at Johannes Jänicke's missionary seminary in Berlin before sailing for Indonesia in 1826. Working among the Chinese in Siam (Thailand) in 1828, he severed himself from the Dutch Missionary Society and became a freelance missionary. He translated the Bible into Siamese within three years. Doing itinerant evangelism, he worked in Malacca, Canton, Singapore, and Hong Kong. He founded the Society for the Diffusion of Useful Knowledge and the Chinese Union. Attracting to China a large number of German missionaries, he influenced many missionaries, including J. Hudson Taylor.

Have you found the ministry God has chosen for you?

Daily equip me, O Lord, for the work You would have me to do.

May 21: Reaching Internationals

"'I am coming to gather all nations and tongues; and they shall come and shall see my glory'" (Isa. 66:18 RSV).

Hispanics. Cambodians. Koreans. Chinese. Vietnamese. Arabs. Laotians.

You might expect a ministry that reaches out to these and other people groups to be found in a major international city—maybe London or New York. You might be surprised, then, to find that a dynamic ministry to internationals is alive and well in Mobile, Alabama.

Aias and Gecina de Souza came from Brazil to the United States for additional education. They planned to return to their home country and teach in a seminary. God put another plan on their hearts, though, and they decided to serve at Mobile's International Center.

The center provides Bible studies, recreation, chapel services, children's activities, language classes, and counseling services every month for more than 1,200 people from 125 countries. In addition, a person from the center visits Mobile's harbor every day and invites sailors from around the world to visit the center.

Gecina also makes her home a welcoming place for sharing the gospel with international groups and individuals coming through Mobile.

Aias says that much of the work depends on local churches. Sixty-five volunteers work regularly, and every night a different church helps at the center. "Seeing the churches plug into the International Center brings great joy," Aias says.

How can you help internationals in your community?

∽

God of all, today I praise You for drawing people to You from all nations.

May 22: Intrepid Evangelists

"But as servants of God we commend ourselves in every way: through great endurance, in afflictions, hardships, calamities" (2 Cor. 6:4 NIV).

They crossed the great Gobi Desert five times taking the gospel to remote places. China's Great Northwest was opened to the gospel because of the amazing feats of three single women—Mildred Cable and sisters Evangeline and Francesca French.

After two decades of conducting successful, but routine, schoolwork with the China Inland Mission in Hochow, China, they shocked the missionary community in 1922 when they announced that God was calling them to evangelize the vast regions beyond them. They refused to allow their critics to deter them.

The great Gobi Desert, inner Mongolia, and the far western outposts of Kansu, Sinkiang, and Chinese Turkestan were their missions fields. Setting up their base of operations at the City of the Prodigals, or Suchow—the last city inside the Great Wall—they established a church. Here they ministered during the snowbound winters. The remaining eight months they traveled.

Braving muddy mountain roads and dangerous criminals, they taught, witnessed, doctored, and distributed Scriptures in the remote villages. Traveling by camel or mule cart, the middle-aged women lived in tents and ate poor food. Despite being captured by both brigands (bandits) and Communist bands, the intrepid women labored on until 1936 when deteriorating political conditions stopped their work.

Do you allow hardships to deter you from accomplishing what God has called you to do?

∽

Today, Lord, help me to be Your intrepid disciple.

May 23: Living in the Voodoo Capital

"Yet I reserve seven thousand in Israel—all whose knees have not bowed down to Baal and all whose mouths have not kissed him" (1 Kings 19:18 NIV).

Elijah felt discouraged and alone. After preaching to the Israelites, he felt that they were all rejecting him and turning to false gods. God lifted him up, however, and told him that there were still 7,000 in the land who gave their allegiance to him. Elijah felt bolstered by the support and went out to continue God's work.

Ted York, a Southern Baptist missionary in the West African country of Benin, serves in a place overrun by non-Christian influences. Like Elijah, he is tempted sometimes to get discouraged. But the number of people coming to Christ encourages him and his wife, Frances.

Benin is known as the world capital of voodoo. In such an environment Ted works as a mission administrator, supporting those who are trying to establish churches for all people in Benin.

Of God's call to them Ted says, "We believe that God has called us to lift up the name of Jesus Christ here in Benin. In spite of the fact that Benin is considered the cradle of voodoo and there is a strong Muslim influence in the country, many people are coming to know Jesus Christ as Savior and Lord."

When do you feel discouraged or alienated?

∽

I praise You today, God, for the power of Your message that reaches past the barriers others set up against it.

May 24: Supporter of Missions

"In Galilee these women had followed him and cared for his needs. Many other women who had come up with him to Jerusalem were also there" (Mark 15:41 NIV).

"Jesus Christ is the great Emancipator of women," wrote one of the most important female missions leaders of the women's missionary movement.

Helen Barrett Montgomery (1861–1934) was the first American woman to lead a major denomination and the first woman to translate the New Testament. Her missions work, though, was her passion.

Helen grew up in Rochester, New York, the daughter of a Baptist minister. She received degrees from Wellesley College and Brown University. After a brief time as a school administrator, she married industrialist William A. Montgomery, who built a company that became the General Motors Corporation. Her wealth enabled her to support missions work—she gave away half a million dollars to causes.

She organized and taught a women's Sunday School class for 44 years at Lake Avenue Baptist Church in Rochester. A leader with Lucy Peabody in the support of foreign missions, she was the first president of the Women's American Baptist Foreign Mission Society (1914) and remained as president for a decade. Also president of the National Federation of Women's Boards of Foreign Missions (1917–18), she made history as the president of the Northern Baptist Convention (1921).

Is God leading you into some support work for missions?

Lord, thank You for women of vision who promote missions.

May 25: Truly Changed Lives

"A bruised reed he will not break, . . . he will faithfully bring forth justice" (Isa. 42:3 RSV).

First impressions can definitely be wrong.

Nelly de Arbañil learned this lesson when she first felt the nudge to work with prisoners.

Looking back at her initial attitude, Nelly says, "I told the Lord I would work for Him anywhere except in the prisons. I was afraid and thought that prisoners should putrefy in prison and deserved nothing."

Today, Nelly serves as a Prison Fellowship volunteer in Peru. She began by attending special services for Christmas and other holidays. Then she started teaching seminars. She soon found that she had a heart for prisoners and wanted them to have the chance to find Christ.

"I am motivated when I see, even if society doesn't believe it, prisoners who have changed their lives and have continued to follow Christ when they're released," Nelly says.

Prison Fellowship International was founded by Charles Colson, a Watergate conspirator who became a Christian while incarcerated. He decided to start an organization that would reach out to prisoners, prisoners' families, released prisoners, prison employees, and victims' families. It now has ministries in 81 different countries around the world.

Of the work, Nelly says she is "a witness of how the Holy Spirit is moving among prisoners."

What are your impressions of prisoners?

~

My Rescuer, be with both victims of crime and those who victimize. Give them both knowledge of Your love.

May 26: A Dream Fulfilled

"There were no needy persons among them. For from time to time those who owned lands or houses sold them, brought the money from the sales and put it at the apostles' feet" (Acts 4:34–35 NIV).

She sold her house to finance her missionary journey to Africa.

Because of her age, Maria Fearing (1838–1937) was not accepted as a missionary by the Southern Presbyterian Church's Executive Committee of Foreign Missions. At 56, though, she was not deterred. After selling her home and combining her life's savings with $100 pledged by the women of the Congregational Church in Talladega, Alabama, she petitioned the committee again. This time they backed her.

Born in 1838 in Gainesville, Alabama, to bond servants, Maria had a childhood dream of going to Africa. She was 27 when slavery was abolished, but 30 years passed before she sailed to the Congo on May 26, 1894.

Her dedication to raising orphaned and kidnapped girls led her to manage the Pantops Home for Girls at Luebo until 1915. Mother Fearing instructed her girls in religion and taught them life skills such as cooking and managing a household.

Have you ever been stopped from fulfilling a dream because of your age? Whether you are a college student or a senior adult, don't let age become a barrier to ministry.

Show me, Lord, that You can provide the means for me to accomplish what You want me to do.

May 27: Assisting Older Adults

"When I am old and grayheaded, O God, forsake me not" (Psalm 71:18 KJV).

When Ann began attending the Older Adult Day Care Center in Birmingham, Alabama, she was in the beginning stages of Alzheimer's disease. Not much later she stayed in the fetal position while there. She had tried other care, but always came back to the center, for she knew the staff and volunteers cared deeply for her.

Beulah's 95-year-old mother stayed in the center while Beulah took care of a sick daughter and other concerns. "I don't know what I would do without this care," she says.

Beulah's mother and Ann are just two of those whom director Betty Lee has encountered over the years. She, as well as other staff members and volunteers, provide a variety of ministries such as lunches and snacks, weekly health screenings, supervised educational and recreational activities, and companionship with other older adults. The services are open to those who can't remain at home without assistance, those who need care during the day while their caregivers are at work, those who suffer from isolation, and others. Many of them have Alzheimer's disease and other debilitating illnesses.

Betty says that the center, a United Methodist Church mission, has changed her life. "There is something so special about this place," she says.

May is Older Americans Month. Can you volunteer this month at an adult day-care center, assisted-care facility, or nursing home that reaches out to older adults?

∽

Bless those, God, who suffer from Alzheimer's disease and other age-related illnesses.

May 28: No Age Limits for Missions

"They will still bear fruit in old age, they will stay fresh and green" (Psalm 92:14 NIV).

Although most missionaries begin their work early in life, some are called to the missions field when they are older. The career change proved very successful for many missionaries.

Thomas Mayhew (1587–1680) began work among the Native American Indians when he was 70. His son, Rev. Thomas Mayhew Jr., was a missionary who started the first school for Native American Indians in New England in 1651. His son was lost at sea while traveling to England to raise money for his mission. Thomas, governor of Martha's Vineyard and adjacent islands, took up his son's work. After studying the Native American Indian language, he walked sometimes 20 miles to meet his congregations. In 1670 he organized the first Native American Indian church with a native pastor. He labored until his death at 93. His grandson and his great-grandson continued the family legacy.

At age 53, Anne Norton (1846–1926) received her license to practice medicine and surgery in New York and Ohio. Representing the Methodist Episcopal Church, she was sent to the Philippines in 1900. In 1905 she received her license to practice there. As the first medical missionary to the Philippines, she traveled thousands of miles living and working among the island people for 26 years.

Are you letting your age be a hindrance today to your getting involved in missions?

∼

Lord, thank You that there are no age limits when working for You.

May 29: Facing Hardships with Faith

"Three times I was shipwrecked, I spent a night and a day in the open sea" (2 Cor. 11:25 NIV).

When hardships come, how do you face them?

Alexander Duff (1806–1878) shared some of the same adversities the Apostle Paul experienced, but, like Paul, was undaunted.

Sent as a missionary to India from the Church of Scotland when he was 23, he and his wife arrived in Calcutta in May 1830 after a perilous voyage. Twice they nearly lost their lives in shipwrecks. First, on a rocky reef when rounding the Cape of Good Hope they lost everything including their precious books, plans, and manuscripts. The second time was on the coast of Ceylon. Alexander's third shipwreck years later occurred near the mouth of the Ganges River when he barely escaped with his life.

Undiscouraged because of his shipwreck losses, Alexander founded an English-speaking college where the Bible was the main textbook. His aim was to train Indians to oppose Hinduism and superstition with the Bible and European culture. Some of his pupils became Christians and leaders in the Indian church.

He helped found the University of Calcutta and opened a school for high-caste girls. Witnessing the Sepoy Rebellion (1857), the beginning of India's struggle for independence from British rule, he publicly condemned some British government policies toward India. His health—always poor—finally failed him, and he returned to Scotland, an honored man.

Today, Lord, help me to face adversities with a strong faith.

May 30: A "World" Vision

"If a brother or sister is ill-clad and in lack of daily food, and one of you says to them, 'Go in peace, be warmed and filled,' without giving them the things needed for the body, what does it profit? So faith by itself, if it has no works, is dead" (James 3:14–17 NIV).

"What are you going to do about it?"

A nun asked Bob Pierce (1914–1976) this penetrating question after he inquired why an undernourished little girl wasn't being fed. It was at the end of World War II, and Pierce was visiting an orphanage run by German sisters near the Tibetan border.

The nun told Pierce that the orphanage had stretched its food as far as it could and could not help one more person. He refused to accept her answer and asked, "Why isn't something being done?" The nun then carried the girl to his arms and responded, "What are you going to do about it?"

His immediate answer was to buy the girl a bowl of rice. Pierce, whose life slogan became Let My Heart Be Broken with the Things That Break the Heart of God, then answered the nun by founding World Vision in 1950 and later Food for the World, which he rebuilt as Samaritan's Purse.

"What are you going to do about it?"

Dear Lord, let my heart be broken today with the needs I see and then show me how to go beyond lamenting conditions to finding solutions.

May 31: Homeless Isn't Hopeless

"Even the sparrow has found a home, and the swallow a nest for herself" (Psalm 84:3 NIV).

As Shirley walked the early morning streets near New Orleans's French Quarter, a businessman stood outside his store hosing down the sidewalk. Glancing up at Shirley, he turned the water on her and said, "I'm washing the trash off the sidewalk."

Shirley, one of more than 15,000 homeless people in New Orleans, spends most of her nights at Brantley Baptist Center. After the incident on the sidewalk, she went back to the center and told Southern Baptist missionary Ginger Smith about it.

Ginger, who is a case manager at the center, encounters people like Shirley every day. They are people caught in a lifestyle summed up in a phrase they often use themselves: "Homeless is hopeless."

The Brantley Center provides shelter and meals for up to 230 homeless people, as well as a free live-in substance abuse treatment program. Nine chapel services throughout the week provide worship opportunities, and workers like Ginger offer individual spiritual counseling.

Ginger says that most of the people are eager to hear the message of the gospel. In a world where they often feel ashamed and out of place, Jesus offers them real hope.

How do you view homeless people in your community?

∼

My Sheltering Lord, help me feel empathy toward the homeless and give them hope through You.

June 1: A Godly Romance

"For this reason a man will leave his father and mother and will be united to his wife" (Gen. 2:24 NIV).

"It is as clear as the morning sky, as bright as the sun—and I know that you are the one I'll walk through time with. Wherever He leads, I'll be by your side."

On the day Todd Lafferty asked Susan Ingouf to marry him, she had her response prepared. She sang the above words to him to say, "Yes, I will marry you." At their wedding a few months later, she sang the song again.

God had guided Todd and Susan toward each other for years. The paths that led them to one another were too amazing to call coincidences. They were truly part of a divine plan.

Susan grew up as a missionaries' kid in Indonesia. Todd worked in the summers as a short-term missionary in Scotland. Susan signed a commitment card to foreign missions on New Year's Eve 1979. Todd did the same thing just 24 hours later, on the other side of the country. They both went to Southwestern Baptist Theological Seminary, where they started dating. Three weeks later, they both knew they wanted to spend their lives together.

After marrying, they felt called to Pakistan and began work there in 1991. They presently live in and serve from Bangladesh.

God of love, thank You for Your divine and perfect plans.

June 2: A Trustworthy Partner

"The heart of her husband trusts in her, and he will have no lack of gain" (Prov. 31:11 RSV).

She is known as the third wife of Adoniram Judson.

Before her marriage to Adoniram, Emily Chubbock Judson (1817–1854) was an accomplished author writing under the pen name of Fanny Forrester.

A native of Eaton, New York, she learned the discipline of work early in life. At the age of 11 she was already working 12 hours a day in a woolen factory. Later she became a schoolteacher. It was then that she started writing for newspapers and magazines and publishing fiction.

Adoniram was introduced to Emily as a suitable writer to pen a biography of his late second wife, Sarah. Their friendship grew into romance even though he was almost 30 years her senior. They were married on June 2, 1846, and left soon for Burma.

After arriving there, she completed *The Memoir of Sarah B. Judson, Member of the Mission to Burma.* In a letter she wrote home, Emily said, "Dr. Judson is pleased, and I care little whether anyone else likes it or not." Other people did like it—the book published in 1848 sold 28,000 copies.

Their first child, Emily Frances, was born in 1847. Adoniram died in 1850, and ten days after his death, Emily lost their second child, Charles.

Returning to New York, she cared for her daughter and three of Sarah's children. She died on June 1, 1854, of tuberculosis.

Do others have confidence in you?

~

Lord, may I always be found trustworthy.

June 3: Committed Couples

"Then he [Paul] left the brothers and sailed for Syria, accompanied by Priscilla and Aquila" (Acts 18:18 NIV).

A successful missionary couple truly takes two. Both husband and wife must be committed to their calling.

Barbara and David Branstetter, missionaries to Bonaire for Trans World Radio, felt called to service in different ways and at different times.

Barbara still remembers the visits of missionaries to her church when she was a little girl. She attended a Bible college and participated in a two-month missions trip to Uruguay. Years later and married to David, she felt a tug at her heart to be a missionary. She prayed, "God, if this is what you want, You're going to have to talk to David about it."

David, on the other hand, never gave missions much thought. "In fact," he says, "I was in my 20s before I even met a missionary."

David's career aspirations took him in different directions—he worked as an electrician and a telecommunications specialist. He says, though, that "God gave me a godly wife who had a heart for missions."

Soon after Barbara felt God calling her, David came to her and said, "You know, Barb, I think God wants us to be missionaries."

They soon learned about Trans World Radio, a ministry that reaches out to native people in their own languages, and moved to Bonaire in January 2000.

If you are married, how can you serve God with your spouse?

∽

Thank You, Eternal God, for godly husbands and wives.

June 4: An Effective Partner

"She opens her arms to the poor and extends her hands to the needy" (Prov. 31:20 NIV).

Because she was not considered a "real" missionary, only a missionary wife, she was unable to raise funds through her husband's mission board.

Not deterred, Lillian Dickson formed her own organization—Mustard Seed, Inc.—to help the impoverished mountain people of Taiwan. Through her relief efforts, she distributed food and clothing and founded a medical clinic that monthly served approximately 7,000 patients.

Newly married pioneer missionaries Jim and Lillian Dickson arrived in Taiwan in 1927 representing the Board of Foreign Missions of the Canadian Presbyterian Church. Although the couple had not come to minister to tribal people, they were drawn into the work after meeting the first believer of the head-hunting Tyal tribe named Chi-oang who went on to lead 1,000 of her people to Christ.

As principal of a theological seminary, Jim didn't have the time to devote to the churches. He handed over to Lillian the responsibility of Bible teaching and overseeing the churches. Once she was away for four months visiting 70 mountain churches. As Lillian's church work and humanitarian efforts grew, she had the opportunity to tell her story on television with Bob Pierce, the founder of World Vision. Her book *These My People* further captured the remarkable story of an effective husband-wife partnership.

What need is God calling you to fulfill?

Lord, I praise You for husband-wife partnerships that have had an impact on the world.

June 5: A Steadfast Heart

"He will have no fear of bad news; his heart is steadfast, trusting in the Lord" (Psalm 112:7 NIV).

When she arrived in Siam (now Thailand) in 1865 to join her fiancé, she learned that he had died seven months earlier. Although his death was a devastating blow, she determined to take up his work.

Adele Fielde (1839–1916), a New York native, grew up as a Universalist. Following her whirlwind courtship with Cyrus Chilcot, a Baptist missionary candidate, she became a Baptist.

After Cyrus's death, Adele proved a committed but spirited and independent missionary. The only single woman with her group, she strongly protested that her salary was half of her single male colleague's. Her social activities, which included card playing and dancing, led to her dismissal by the Baptist mission board.

On her return trip to America while in a China port city, she caught a vision for women's work. The mission board reinstated her, and in 1872 she was back in China training native women. Using the Bible-women plan, she revolutionized missionary service in the Far East. For 21 years she trained 500 women to evangelize and train their own people.

Ten years after her death, the Baptist Foreign Missionary Society eulogized her as the "mother of our Bible women and also the mother of our Bible schools."

Do you have a steadfast faith that will guide you through difficult times?

∽

God of hope, help me to turn my adversities into opportunities for service.

June 6: Friendship Evangelism

"A man of many companions may come to ruin, but there is a friend who sticks closer than a brother" (Prov. 18:24 NIV).

The poet Robert Browning once eloquently wrote: "Hand grasps at hand, eye lights eye in good friendship, and great hearts expand and grow."

The Bible also extols the virtue of friendship. Jesus Himself developed relationships with people first and then told them of His divine plan.

Many missionaries develop friendships both out of their own desire and of necessity. Friendship, for many, is the only way to reach others when they work in a hostile environment.

Donna Hills, a Southern Baptist missionary to Senegal, is often a target of speculation and judgment. The unreached people groups she works with don't know that Christians love God and are good people. It's a challenge sometimes for her and her husband, Ken, to get the message across.

The answer, for Donna, is to reach out in friendship and love, and to stand firm in her commitment and convictions to Christ.

"Every action I take either proves or disproves what they've been taught," she says. "My ministry is mostly of friendship and loving people."

Although you may not live in an environment openly hostile to Christianity, you are still called to be a witness by being a friend. How can you use friendship as a springboard to witnessing in your own life?

Help me be a better friend, Jesus, to the unbelievers around me.

June 7: Seeking Meekness

"Blessed are the meek, for they will inherit the earth" (Matt. 5:5 NIV).

On her 30th birthday, she chose a motto: Seek Meekness, prompted partly because her fiancé desired a humble wife.

Independent-minded Maude Cary (1878–1967) was often accused of having pride. She recognized her weakness and prayed daily to overcome the sin. As a single woman missionary, she often didn't conform to what was expected of her. After 2 years of service, the Gospel Missionary Union wanted to terminate her. Her plea to remain, though, was granted.

Maude longed to be married. Her fiancé, George Reed, kept her in a state of uncertainty about wedding plans for several years before he finally left Morocco for another missions field.

Arriving in 1901, Maude served over 50 years in Morocco as a single missionary in a difficult Muslim society. She was a tireless worker who went on her first furlough after 23 years.

During World War II she and three other single women were the only missionaries who stayed in Morocco. They kept work going with three stations open.

A spunky 77-year old, she was forced to retire in 1955. GMU terminated its 75-year outreach to Morocco in 1967. Ironically, Maude died that year. A small handful of people attended her funeral. Perhaps the two sprays of flowers were fitting for a woman who sought meekness.

Are you seeking meekness in your life?

Teach me, Lord, that meekness can be a strength.

June 8: Does God Love Me?

"Praise the Lord, O my soul, and forget not all his benefits—he who forgives all your sins and heals all your diseases" (Psalm 103:2–3 NIV).

The young woman, racked with pain caused by the advanced stage of AIDS, asked the questions in a faltering voice: "Does God still love me? Will anybody ever love me again? Will I ever get another hug?"

Malcolm Marler, chaplain for the ecumenical Care Team Network, knew the answers without thinking twice. He leaned over and gave the 34-year-old single mother a hug. He then went on to explain God's grace, telling the woman that nothing could cause God to stop loving her.

Malcolm and the thousands of others involved in the Care Team Network experience moments like this regularly. Originally founded to teach church groups how to provide compassionate care to people with AIDS, today the Care Team Network also gives care to people with cancer, Parkinson's disease, Alzheimer's, and other illnesses.

Malcolm says the mission of the organization is to exemplify Christ's love. "It gives people the opportunity to put their faith into action and show their concern for the very ones that Christ spent the most time ministering to, the sick," he says. "For those receiving care, it is a demonstration that the body of Christ cares in very practical, emotional, and spiritual ways."

How can you compassionately reach out to sick people around you?

~

Dear God, guide me as I minister to the sick in my family, church, and community.

June 9: Diligence for the Lord

"Whatever you do, work at it with all your heart, as working for the Lord, not for men, since you know that you will receive an inheritance from the Lord as a reward. It is the Lord Christ you are serving" (Col. 3:23–24 NIV).

Can you plod?

William Carey could. The father of modern missions saw himself as a plodder.

"I can plod," he once said. "I can persevere in any definite pursuit. To this I owe everything."

Considered an exceptional plodder by any standards, he was a man of vigorous intellect who even as a teen could read the Bible in six languages.

William labored more than 40 years in India. Working with William Ward and Joshua Marshman, the three became known as the Serampore Trio. They were responsible for translating the Scripture into 44 languages and for founding 26 churches and 126 schools. They organized India's first medical mission, savings bank, seminary, Indian girls school, and vernacular newspaper.

William translated the Bible into Sanskrit, baptized the first Hindu Protestant convert in 1800, and campaigned vigorously for the eradication of suttee (burning a widow on her husband's funeral pyre). His efforts also led to India's first organized printing operation, paper mill, and steam engine.

When Carey died on June 9, 1834, tens of thousands mourned him.

~

Lord, help me today to truly be Your worker. Give me wisdom to know where I should work for Your kingdom and then help me invest in the work with all of my heart.

June 10: Seeking the Lord

"Those who seek the Lord lack no good thing" (Psalm 34:10 NIV).

The missionary monk loved the Psalms and loved to copy them. In June 597 he died after copying Psalm 34:10.

Columba (521–597), known as missionary to the Scots, diligently sought the Lord.

Born in Donegal, Ireland, he was educated in monastic schools. For 20 years in Ireland his work as an evangelist and founder of churches and monasteries gained him a reputation as a godly and scholarly Christian.

In 561 he became involved in a 2-year controversy concerning a book he had copied without permission. Civil war ensued. Columba and his allies were victorious at the bloody battle of Culdrevney where 3,000 men were killed. Columba felt such remorse over the carnage that he decided to leave Ireland and become a missionary. On a self-imposed exile, he set out for Scotland with 12 companions.

They arrived on the island of Iona in 563. Overcoming the Druids, he helped secure the independence of the Scots from the Picts, brought civilization to the people, improved their agriculture, and introduced them to Christianity.

Iona became a center of missionary activity. Monks were trained and sent out to preach the gospel in Scotland and northern England. When Columba died, he had made an immeasurable impact on Scotland and the entire Celtic Christian world.

Are you seeking the Lord with all of your being?

Holy God, may I love You with all of my heart, soul, and mind.

June 11: Truth in Numbers

"For God so loved the world that He gave his only begotten son, that whosoever believeth in him should not perish, but have everlasting life. For God sent not his son into the world to condemn the world; but that the world through him might be saved" (John 3:16–17 KJV).

Numbers surround us—on our television sets, from our computers, in newspapers, in advertising. And even though numbers can be confusing and hard to understand, they are important.

In missions they are important because they put things in a global perspective. They help us realize who "the world" truly is.

Consider the following numbers from mission statistician David Barrett.

Approximately 2 billion of the earth's 6.1 billion people (or 33 percent) consider themselves Christian, at least in name.

Church members total 1.9 billion, with 1.3 billion attending services.

Second in numbers to Christians are Muslims, who number approximately 1.2 billion. There are approximately 790 million Hindus, 360 million Buddhists, 225 million members of tribal religions, and 100 million members of "new religions."

Many unbelievers populate the world as well, with 770 million calling themselves nonbelievers and 150 million atheists.

There are 24,000 missions organizations worldwide, and they collect $120 billion a year.

Think about these numbers and consider where you fit in. Can you do anything in response to these numbers?

∽

I want a better understanding, Lord, of the world You sent Your Son to die for. Give me a love and concern for the world.

June 12: The Awesome Power of Prayer

"And pray in the Spirit on all occasions with all kinds of prayers and requests. With this in mind, be alert and always keep on praying for all the saints" (Eph. 6:18 NIV).

Do you believe in the power of prayer?

The following stories remind us that the power of prayer is extended to people all over the world.

Lance and Carrie Borden, Southern Baptist missionaries to Austria, joined with two other couples for a four-hour evening of prayer. One request concerned another couple who seemed to be getting "colder rather than warmer" to the gospel. Two days after the prayer vigil, the couple asked to come to Bible study and have been attending regularly ever since. "They were not interested in Him, but He started drawing them to Himself, and we are confident that it is only a matter of time before they give their lives to Jesus. We believe the prayer evening was the key to this progress, so we're planning regular prayer evenings now!"

Ken and Donna Hills, Southern Baptist missionaries to Senegal, faced a difficult situation. A fellow Christian had been called in front of Muslim authorities to answer for his activities. Donna immediately called for prayer from friends in America. At least 1,000 prayed for the man. The result? The man stood firmly in his commitment and says that he had peace knowing that people were praying for him.

∼

Today give me a new appreciation for prayer, God.

June 13: For the Glory of God

"So whether you eat or drink or whatever you do, do it all for the glory of God" (1 Cor. 10:31 NIV).

"It makes but little difference after all where we spend these few fleeting years, if they are only spent for the glory of God. Be assured there is nothing else worth living for," she wrote to her niece who wanted to be a missionary.

These words exemplify the spirit of sacrifice that permeated the life of Elizabeth Freeman and that would characterize her death.

In 1851, after only five weeks of marriage to veteran missionary and widower John Freeman, Elizabeth began the sea voyage to northwest India. Representing the Presbyterian Board of Foreign Missions, Elizabeth undertook language study on the voyage. Soon after she arrived at the Futtehgurh Mission she began work in women's and children's ministries. Although she found life in India full of hardships, she was convinced that difficulties on the missions field were well worth the cost.

On June 2, 1858, Elizabeth wrote that two Muslim regiments from Lucknow had mutinied and were headed to Futtehgurh. On June 13, 1858, at 7:00 in the morning, the Freemans, along with several other missionary families, were marched to the town's parade ground and ruthlessly massacred.

Do your thoughts, words, and actions demonstrate that you are doing all for the glory of God?

∽

Lord, help me today to give myself completely to You. Use me for Your service.

June 14: Love Is the Answer

"I am come that they might have life, and that they might have it more abundantly" (John 10:10 KJV).

A popular song of the late 1960s proclaimed that "what the world needs now is love."

It may sound like a simple solution, but it's true.

In their work as Assemblies of God missionaries to Native American Indians near Mobridge, South Dakota, Eric and Cathie Gebhart see children literally dying from lack of attention and love. Without love, the children lose the will to live.

"Last winter, there were over 40 suicide attempts with 6 deaths—all with children and teens," Cathie says.

One of the young girls who attempted suicide attended the Gebharts' Kids Club program, one of their outreach ministries to people living at Standing Rock reservation. She told Cathie: "The hospital was really nice; I even had my own bed. They brought me food all the time. I want to go back there." The girl received more attention and love at the hospital than she did at home or in the community.

"There is a medical condition often associated with infants called failure to thrive, where there is no will to live," Cathie says. "I believe I see that condition in many of our reservation children."

The answer? Show them love, and show them that God loves them.

Do others see God's love through you?

∼

Gracious God, bless the children in the world who feel unloved. Use me and others to show them Your love.

June 15: Brothers and Sisters Around the World

"A time is coming and has now come when the true worshipers will worship the Father in spirit and truth, for they are the kind of worshipers the Father seeks" (John 4:23 NIV).

On their trip they discovered cultural differences and language barriers. They also found that people had a spiritual thirst.

The moments, however, that seemed most powerfully to affect Nona Crowder, Rosalind Holloman, and others who traveled on a missions trip from Tuscaloosa, Alabama, to the Ukraine were the ones spent with fellow Christians. They gained new understanding of and appreciation for their brothers and sisters in Christ who live on the other side of the globe.

Nona and her group of three worked in Balta with a new church and held evangelistic services in various villages. Some of her most precious memories come from worshiping with the Ukrainian Christians. "Their faith in God and love for Christ was a challenge to me personally," she says. "They wanted to know all about America and our church."

Rosalind taught Bible school for children and worshiped, along with her three-member team, in a small church in Belgorod-Dnevestrosky. She also learned much from worshiping with fellow Christians. "To assemble with the believers is a real inspiration," she says. "The light that shines from their eyes lets us know that the Spirit is moving in their congregation."

∼

God, bless Christians who live in my own community and those who live on the other side of the globe. Help us be united in spirit.

June 16: Joyful Living

"May the God of hope fill you with all joy and peace as you trust in him" (Rom. 15:13 NIV).

"All through her invalid's year there sounded out these two full, clear notes—hope and joy," wrote her biographer.

Fannie Exile Scudder Heck (1862–1915), president of Woman's Missionary Union for a record 15 years, spent the last year of her life in a hospital. Despite much suffering, she discovered what she had always found in life—joy.

In her book *Everyday Gladness* she recorded her thoughts: "God's great purpose in the world is the joy of man whom he made in his image." Fannie also wrote about joy as an ideal she wished to strive for: "To find joy in little and everyday things."

Ironically, Fannie's birth on June 16, 1862, in Buffalo Lithia Springs, Virginia, was not during a joyful period. Her pregnant mother had been "exiled" because of the fighting in Richmond—thus, Fannie's middle name Exile. She spent happy years, though, growing up in Raleigh, North Carolina.

After Fannie dedicated her life to the cause of missions, she added Scudder to her name. She was proud to be descended from the famous Scudder missionary family.

As WMU leader, she was responsible for a magazine, organizations for young women and girls, a missionary training school for women, and a Christian social action program. She worked full time for missions for 27 years with only one vacation—all voluntarily.

How do you daily confront life?

∾

Lord, help me to embrace life—and death—with joy.

June 17: A Devoted Follower

"'Worthy is the Lamb, who was slain, to receive power and wealth and wisdom and strength and honor and glory and praise!'" (Rev. 5:12 NIV).

Kathleen Mallory (1879–1954) read from Revelation 5:6–14 at Woman's Missionary Union's 25th anniversary meeting in St. Louis in 1913. She quoted her favorite Bible verses again at the 50th commemoration.

Elected executive secretary of WMU in 1912, Kathleen had the longest tenure of any Southern Baptist agency executive, serving tirelessly for 36 years.

After her death, it was said of the Selma, Alabama, native: "Under her administration Woman's Missionary Union became the important auxiliary, the vital missionary ally to the denomination which it is today."

Kathleen lived a spartan lifestyle. She always traveled the cheapest way and dressed beautifully in remodeled old clothes. Living in a tiny room, her diet consisted of crackers, boiled eggs, and cafeteria food. Never owning an automobile, she sold her few luxuries to contribute to missions.

Greatly admired, she has been honored with a scholarship fund in Japan; a hospital in Pingtu, China; the Good Will Center in Baltimore; and a missions offering in Alabama. For her interracial leadership, she was given an honorary degree from Selma University.

At her death her Selma pastor said, "I think Miss Mallory was the most completely devoted person to Jesus Christ I have ever known."

Does your devotion to Christ include giving to missions?

Faithful God, today help me to give up luxuries for Your kingdom.

June 18: The Two Herberts

"Always be prepared to give an answer to everyone who asks you to give the reason for the hope that you have" (1 Peter 3:15 NIV).

Herbert Behrens went to Malawi in the 1980s as one of the first missionaries to the Yao tribe. When he arrived, he was told to speak to Chief Chauke, a leader who could give him permission to preach.

When the chief asked him his intentions, he replied, "My name is Herbert, and I have come to preach the gospel of Jesus Christ." As he spoke, pandemonium broke out, and all the elders spoke at the same time. The chief finally answered, giving him permission to preach.

Herbert later learned what had caused the commotion: "Over 20 years before, an African Christian had visited the same village. He had dropped his African name, changing it to Herbert, which is very unusual for an African. The first Herbert also went to Chief Chauke and said, 'My name is Herbert, and I have come to preach the gospel of Jesus Christ.' The chief gave him permission to preach in the village square. Six people decided to become Christians and were immediately killed by the villagers, along with the first Herbert."

When the second Herbert arrived, villagers believed the first had come back to avenge himself. He went on to preach and help plant 12 churches in the region.

∽

We give You praise, Lord, for the seemingly mysterious ways in which You work.

Story ©DAWN Europe.

June 19: Working Despite Conflicts

"They had such a sharp disagreement that they parted company. Barnabas took Mark and sailed for Cyprus, but Paul chose Silas and left" (Acts 15:39 NIV).

While many effective missions and marriage partnerships have existed, not all were ideal.

Martha Crawford, Baptist missionary to China, had such a marriage.

When Alabama native Martha Foster felt God calling her to missions work, she knew that as a Baptist she could not go as a single woman to the missions field. When she sought a husband, she found missionary T. P. Crawford looking for a wife. In 1852 they met, soon married, and sailed for China.

Martha carved out a women's ministry there before Lottie Moon arrived and later became one of Lottie's mentors. Martha also taught the Chinese language to new missionary appointees, established a school, and worked in evangelism.

T. P. resented Martha's success. He desired that she work more in evangelism. He also didn't get along well with the Chinese and other missionaries. Suffering from emotional and mental instability, he left her twice to travel in America.

Because T. P. believed that missionaries should be sent out directly from churches instead of mission boards, he started his own missionary organization called Gospel Mission Movement. Martha resigned reluctantly from the Baptist board.

Inside the Tenchow Baptist Church in the Shantung Province a plaque memorializes the pioneer work of Martha Foster Crawford—but not her husband.

Lord, teach me how to deal with difficult circumstances.

June 20: A Heroic Saint

"To those who by persistence in doing good seek glory, honor and immortality, he will give eternal life" (Rom. 2:7 NIV).

Do you know about the heroic exploits of Boniface?

"Cease, my children, from conflict.... Fear not those who kill the body but cannot kill the immortal soul.... Receive with constancy this momentary blow of death, that you may live and reign with Christ forever," he said.

On Pentecost Sunday 755 at Dackum, Germany, Boniface (680–755) stood near the Borne River preparing to confirm some new believers. A band of barbarians rushed upon him. He died with the Gospels in his hand.

Born Winfred in Wessex, the Apostle of Germany was trained in a Benedictine monastery and ordained at 30. In 716 he went to Frisia, Germany. Because Radbod, the Frisian king, opposed Christianity, Winfred soon returned to England. In 718 he received a commission from the pope to evangelize Germany.

Winfred journeyed to Thuringia, and because Radbod was dead, he returned to Frisia and then traveled to Hesse. In 723 he was consecrated a bishop and given a new name—Boniface.

Returning to Hesse, legend says that he struck the Thundering Tree, a pagan landmark, with an axe, and it fell to the ground. Christianity then became a strong force in Germany.

In 747 he was named archbishop of Mainz and spiritual leader of all Germany. In 753 he resigned. With his burial cloak he returned to Frisia.

Almighty Powerful God, thank You for courageous saints.

June 21: The Name of Jesus

"Salvation is found in no one else, for there is no other name under heaven given to men by which we must be saved" (Acts 4:12 NIV).

The Bosnian teenager grew up confused about religion.

With a Muslim father and a Catholic mother, Sanela Sljivo considered herself Muslim. "Growing up, I believed there was a God, but I didn't know His name," she says of her early beliefs.

Confusion grew when she saw Serbian soldiers, most of them Orthodox Christians, doing horrendous things in God's name. They committed rapes and murders. Her own aunt was abducted by the soldiers and never heard from again.

Sanela still wanted to find the good in people. She soon learned—from a Baptist missionary—that peace and love could come through the name of Jesus.

"I searched for goodness and love in people, but at that time I didn't realize that those things can truly come from knowing Jesus Christ," she remembers.

After giving Jesus control of her life in 1997, Sanela began serving with International Mission Board missionaries throughout Bosnia.

"My dream for the country is that all the people can know God and His Son Jesus Christ. He is the only One Who can give them the peace and love they are looking for after those terrible years of war."

How does knowing the name of Jesus bring peace and love to your life today?

My Savior, I praise Your name and the name of Your Son.

June 22: Advocate for the Neglected

"Learn to do right! Seek justice, encourage the oppressed. Defend the cause of the fatherless" (Isa. 1:17 NIV).

"The woman who creates and sustains a home and under whose hand children grow up to be strong and pure men and women is a creator second only to God."

This quote by Helen Hunt Jackson sounds as if she may have had Elizabeth Reaves Wiley (1844-1921) in mind.

Elizabeth became "mother" to over 3,000 children who lived in the Orphans' Industrial Home and School at Greeneville, Tennessee. She founded the orphans home in 1895. Today the home is known as the Holston United Methodist Home for Children, Inc. It serves as a refuge for neglected, troubled, and rejected children.

A native of Jonesborough, Tennessee, Elizabeth was a schoolteacher, minister's wife, and mother of three who helped organize the Woman's Board of Home Missions of the Methodist Episcopal Church, South. From 1890 to 1896 she was president of the Woman's Parsonage and Home Mission Society and Woman's Home Mission Society.

Traveling around her conference, she challenged women to help her in providing a place for homeless children. After her retirement as superintendent of the home in 1913, she maintained ties by praying for and supporting its needs.

Are you praying for the welfare of the troubled youth of your community, state, and nation? Are you supporting homes that minister to neglected children?

∼

Today, Lord, help me express my love for the children around me who need guidance and understanding.

June 23: A Life-Changing Trip

"How beautiful on the mountains are the feet of those who bring good news" (Isa. 52:7 NIV).

When did you first understand God's grace and love?

For Lori Barstow, the time is very clear, even though it happened almost two decades ago. "I became a Christian while on a missions trip to Cherokee, North Carolina, when I was 13," Lori says.

Lori traveled to the Smoky Mountains with family friends for four years. They taught Vacation Bible School at Rock Hill Baptist Church, a one-room church of Cherokee members. They were welcomed to the church by Mr. Junaluska, an influential man in the community who sang "Amazing Grace" in his native Cherokee language.

To invite children to VBS, the team scoured the mountains knocking on doors. In doing so, Lori learned about a lifestyle very different from her own—one of poverty and social struggles.

Lori taught kindergartners and first-graders at the nightly school. She still wonders if the lessons affected any of the children.

"All I know is that my summers there changed my life," she remembers. "How would I have learned about these people and their lives? How would I have gained compassion for people different from myself? How would I have understood the depth and breadth of God's grace in my life?"

~

Today remind me, Lord, of the moment when I first learned of Your grace. Thank You for Your gifts of grace and love.

June 24: Our Lady of the Potatoes

"You believe in Him and are filled with an inexpressible and glorious joy" (1 Peter 1:8 NIV).

Barbara Joiner has learned to find joy in all situations—even as she's picking potatoes with migrant workers.

Barbara took a group of Acteens®, a group of missions-minded teenaged girls in her Baptist church, to Mobile, Alabama, to teach Vacation Bible School and minister to migrant workers and their children. When they arrived, however, no one had time to do anything but work. Benito, the crew chief, worked everyone extremely hard and discouraged workers from participating with the Acteens.

One day, she visited Benito to tell him they were moving on to another camp. He stomped toward her and scowled.

"You think you understand my people! But you won't understand them until you work beside them in the field."

Barbara took that as a challenge and joined the workers for a hot, exhausting day of potato picking. She wanted to fall to her knees, but the growing camaraderie with the other workers and Benito's slight signs of approval spurred her on.

By the end of the day, she found herself joking with Benito.

"Benito's mother gave me the name that has lingered on in migrant circles: Our Lady of the Potatoes," Barbara laughs. "The God I serve is Lord of the mountains, and Lord of the sea, and surely He is Lord of the potato fields. I'm living proof."

Do you take time to laugh, even in trying circumstances?

~

O God, give me a joyful spirit.

June 25: Complete Dependence on God

"Do not be anxious about anything, but in everything, by prayer and petition, with thanksgiving, present your requests to God" (Phil. 4:6 NIV).

Displaying his unwavering faith in God, he once wrote, "I am no longer anxious about anything . . . for he, I know, is able to carry out his will, and his will is mine. It makes no matter where he places me, or how."

J. Hudson Taylor (1832–1905), one of the greatest missionary statesmen the world has ever known, founded the China Inland Mission (now called Overseas Missionary Fellowship) which became the model for interdenominational "faith" missions.

Hudson left Liverpool, England, on September 19, 1853, and arrived at Woosung, China, on March 1, 1854. The next six years found him journeying inland preaching and depending totally upon God to meet his needs. One of the lessons he learned he later taught others—"Depend upon it. God's work, done in God's way, will never lack for supplies."

He and wife, Maria, whom he married in 1858, returned to England in 1860. During the next five years he translated the Bible into the Ningpo dialect and completed his medical training. On June 25, 1865, the idea of CIM was born. On May 26, 1866, the Taylors sailed for China with 17 missionary recruits.

At Hudson's death, CIM had 205 mission stations, 849 missionaries, and an estimated 125,000 Chinese Christians.

Are you depending on God completely to meet all needs?

∽

Sustaining Lord, when my faith wavers, help me to rely on Your promises.

June 26: Songs of Faith

"With singing lips my mouth will praise you" (Psalm 63:5 NIV).

In a country once part of the Communist Soviet regime—where religion of any kind was once condemned—more than 700 people showed up to listen to a Christian choir.

The music was provided by the Musica Sacra Globale, a collegiate missions choir made up of singers from 22 different United Methodist-related universities across the United States. The mission was designed to encourage the emerging churches in the former Soviet bloc.

Methodism and many other Protestant groups were banned in Lithuania in 1944. After the country declared independence from the Soviet Union in 1991, remnants of churches were reorganized.

From June 1 to July 20, 1998, the choir traveled throughout the region, performing in Lithuania, Latvia, Estonia, and Russia. Everywhere they went, members felt awed by the experience.

Carrie Ann Smith, a participant from North Carolina, said that the faith of the people she met encouraged her own spiritual journey. "No wars have been fought on our land, and my family members were not imprisoned in concentration camps," she said. "Nor have we been told how we must worship. Through all such adversities, these people stood close to God and remained steadfast. We set out to share our faith, but they taught us much about faith and love."

Am I thankful for my freedom to worship God?

Thank You, God of praise, for the freedoms I have today. Bless those who don't have such freedoms.

June 27: Faithful Beginnings

"These all died in faith, not having received what was promised, but having seen it and greeted it from afar" (Heb. 11:13 RSV).

Did you know that a haystack was the site of the birth of the foreign missions movement in America?

Early in the nineteenth century several students at Williams College, a Congregational school in Massachusetts, regularly met together for prayer. Led by Samuel Mills (1783–1818), the group had formed the Society of the Brethren whose purpose was to take the gospel to the ends of the earth. One day the men were caught in a sudden thunderstorm and took refuge under a nearby haystack to continue their prayer.

After the Haystack Prayer Meeting, Samuel went to Andover Seminary. Joined by Adoniram Judson from Brown and two other men, they offered themselves in 1810 as missionaries to the General Assembly of the Congregational Church. This step led to the formation of the American Board of Commissioners for Foreign Missions which in 1812 sent the first American missionaries to India.

Samuel's health prevented him from going overseas. Instead, his touring the western US led to the formation of the American Home Missionary Society. He also founded the American Colonization Society whose purpose was to repatriate slaves to Africa. He died at sea in June 1818. Although he never fulfilled his dream of becoming a missionary, he was instrumental in starting both foreign and home mission societies.

Lord, help me plant seeds for those on the front lines of missions.

June 28: Real Christianity

"Those who live according to the sinful nature have their minds set on what that nature desires; but those who live in accordance with the Spirit have their minds set on what the Spirit desires" (Rom. 8:5 NIV).

Is it harder to reach a non-Christian who has never heard of God's love, or someone who considers himself a Christian because he lives in a "Christian" land?

For Fran Wakefield, a Southern Baptist missionary to the island country of Fiji, that question typifies the struggle she faces almost daily.

She and her husband, Mark, live and work in a country evangelized by Methodist missionaries in the 1800s. They turned Fijians away from pagan worship and cannibalism and set the foundation for a Christian country—a land with knowledge of the Bible and plenty of churches.

The challenge is double-edged. People are knowledgeable of Christ, but many of them don't know Him personally.

The good news, Fran says, is that "the indigenous Fijian is already predisposed to believing that the Bible is the Word of God and is interested in knowing more." The bad news? "Many call themselves Christians without having a personal walk with the Lord," she says.

Fran and her husband work out of Suva, a city on the largest of the 100 inhabited islands in the Fiji chain.

Fran's experiences teach us that we are not Christians because of our heritage or our location. We are Christians by our faith.

~

Forgive me, God, when I don't live a genuine faith.

June 29: "Identifying" in Love

"I have become all things to all men so that by all possible means I might save some" (1 Cor. 9:22 NIV).

"Demonstrate a Chinese-style Christian life," Lottie Moon said. "We must go out and live among them, manifesting the gentle, loving spirit of our Lord."

The Baptist missionary discovered that identifying with the Chinese people made a difference in her ministry. The first time she wore the padded robe worn by Chinese women she was accepted by them and no longer called Devil Woman.

Mary Slessor dressed in the Calabar national costume. She ate the same food and drank unpurified water. Although her health was impaired, she felt that the people would listen to her teachings if she lived as they lived. She built her own hut out of sticks and mud. Her bed was a mat on the floor. She made tables and chairs out of mud molded into shape and dried. She wrote of her home in West Africa: "It is an exhilaration of constant joy—I cannot fancy anything to surpass it on earth."

Missionary Karl Gützlaff adopted the Chinese lifestyle wearing the indigenous clothing—a purple garment with a blue sash. Three years after Karl's death in 1851, J. Hudson Taylor arrived in China. He shaved the front of his head, dyed his hair black, attached a pigtail, and bought teacher's robes.

Are you "identifying" with people and their needs?

∽

Dear Lord, help me to relate to people in a Christlike manner.

June 30: God's Healing Touch

"Praise the Lord, O my soul, and forget not all his benefits—who forgives all your sins, and who heals all your diseases" (Psalm 103:2–3 NIV).

When was the last time you got a Bible verse with a doctor's prescription?

For Larry Pepper's patients, it's a regular occurrence. The Southern Baptist medical missionary mixes physical healing with spiritual encouragement.

"As part of the prescriptions for medicine, I write out Scriptures," he explains. "When they come back the next week, I ask them if they read it."

Larry works in southwestern Uganda at the Mbarara University Teaching Hospital. He helps Ugandans suffering from a variety of ailments and also mentors other Christian doctors.

"My job is to teach them by example how to be a Christian physician versus just a physician," he says. "Death is in evidence every day, so it's easy for them just to say, 'Oh well, it's just another sick person.'"

Death is, indeed, a daily reality in Uganda. The devastation from AIDS is especially evident in the area. Larry works with an AIDS outreach, a new mission of the hospital, and encounters many dying people there.

"You just experience a reality in life and death in Uganda. I lost more patients in the first month here than in my whole career."

The answer? To give hope to the patients he encounters.

∽

Help me today, God, to reach out to people in my own workplace.

July 1: God's Security

"You will be secure, because there is hope; you will look about you and take your rest in safety. You will lie down, with no one to make you afraid" (Job 11:18–19 NIV).

She became a celebrity when Ingrid Bergman played her in the film, *The Inn of the Sixth Happiness*.

The year was 1940. The Japanese had invaded Shanghai Province in north China where missionary Gladys Aylward (1902–1970) had served since 1933. One hundred children were housed at a compound near the enemy lines. Since their lives were in danger, Gladys agreed to guide them from Yangcheng over the mountains to Sian where Madame Chiang Kai-shek had an orphanage. Biographer Alan Burgess wrote of the historic trek: "Keeping a hundred children out of sight and earshot of enemy soldiers who were often in the region was the most strenuous aspect of the long journey."

God protected them and met all of their needs. After five and a half weeks of traveling through mountainous terrain, they reached their destination safely—except for Gladys who collapsed, near death. After recovering in the Baptist Hospital at Sian, she stayed in the city working with refugees. Later her poor health led her back to England. Years later she returned to the Orient opening an orphanage in Taiwan where she died.

Are you secure in the knowledge that God will take care of you?

∽

Thank You, Lord, that You are our place of safety during times of upheaval.

July 2: Spiritual Rebirth

"'No one can see the kingdom of God unless he is born again'" (John 3:3 NIV).

How important could spiritual rebirth be to an entire country?

Timothy Richard (1845-1919) thought it was of utmost importance.

Arriving in China in 1870 under the Baptist Missionary Society of London (BMS), Timothy found himself in the Shansi Province in 1877 in a great famine in which millions died. He felt certain that Western science could raise the standard of living for the peasants. He proposed to the BMS that Christian colleges be created in all 18 provinces of China to educate Christian leaders who could transform China. Not convincing the BMS, he resigned and joined the new Christian Literature Society.

In 1895, 10,000 young Chinese scholars presented a petition to the emperor for reforming China. The emperor asked, "Where did you get the ideas for these demands?"

The scholars told him they had copied them from Timothy's writings. The emperor then sent his prime minister to Timothy to ask how China could become a great nation. Timothy recommended educational reform, economic reform, peace, and spiritual rebirth. He was then asked to become advisor to the emperor.

He refused saying, "If I did, I should not have time to be a missionary, and the greatest of those four reforms is spiritual rebirth."

Timothy later was involved in the founding of a state university in China that taught Western ideas.

Lord, thank You for the power spiritual rebirth brings.

July 3: Secret Code

"In fact, everyone who wants to live a godly life in Christ Jesus will be persecuted" (2 Tim. 3:12 NIV).

I used to love to do code-breaker puzzles when I was young. Remember them? You'd have to decipher a Bible verse or a secret sentence by decoding words.

Many missionaries today must use a secret code as well. Because they live in places where authorities track the activities of Christians and non-nationals, they must communicate in code form.

I recently realized, after emailing a missionary in one of these areas, that my ignorance about the need for coded communication could have put the missionary's work and life in danger.

One missionary told me: "We live in a very Christian-unfriendly world. We are in a very sensitive situation here, and such a publication would cause any of us to have to leave." Concerning the way he must communicate with friends around the world, he said that "emails are like postcards, easily read by those who wish to read them. In certain situations, we are monitored rigorously, and certain words could spell the demise of the work or even the worker." He ended his message by saying he would be "yarping" (the coded word for "praying") for me.

Shouldn't we be grateful for the freedoms we have and can exercise? Many Christians around the world are not so fortunate.

∼

Sometimes I take communication for granted, Lord. Be with those Christians throughout the world who cannot speak freely about You.

July 4: Ambassadors for Christ

"Jesus answered, 'I am the way and the truth and the life'" (John 14:6 NIV).

Country singer Lee Greenwood sang in the 1980s: "I'm proud to be an American where at least I know I'm free." Most Americans take pride in the sentiment of that popular song.

Aren't you prouder, though, to be a Christian? You should be.

Leona Choy has worked in missions in Hong Kong, Singapore, and China. As the cofounder with her husband, Ted, of Ambassadors for Christ, Inc., she has traveled to China 14 times. There she learned the value of being first, a Christian, and, secondly, an American. She learned also to appreciate the Chinese for the one-of-a-kind, precious people they are.

Leona says we are "world Christians" who have a message for the entire world, and we should act accordingly. The problem is that when we travel overseas or visit with people from another country, we carry the baggage of our culture, background, and history.

The solution to this is clear: We must remember that we don't represent a particular country. We represent God.

"No 'ism' can provide ultimate satisfaction," Leona says. "We have an authentic kingdom message to share. We have eternal life, the true light, and genuine freedom in Christ."

We, therefore, are ambassadors not for America, but for Christ.

~

I know You are the only truth, Eternal God. Help me to remember that Your truth is better than any I could come up with on my own.

July 5: Help from God

"The woman came and knelt before him. 'Lord, help me!' she said" (Matt. 15:25 NIV).

When the Mexican War ended in 1848, returning American soldiers told about the needs of the Mexican people. Melinda Rankin (1812–1888) heard these stories and tried to arouse interest in churches and missionary societies. After being unsuccessful, she finally exclaimed, "God helping me, I will go myself."

Since Protestants weren't allowed in Mexico at that time, the spunky New Englander settled in Brownsville, Texas. She rented two rooms—one for a bedroom and one for a schoolroom. Although she had no furnishings, her needs were met as she later wrote: "A Mexican woman brought me a cot, an American sent me a pillow, and a German woman said she would cook my meals." Immediately Melinda opened her school to many students.

Because a woman asked her for Bibles, Melinda began sending hundreds of Bibles and hundreds of thousands of tracts to Mexico. She also carried Bibles herself as an agent for the American and Foreign Christian Union. During this time Melinda almost died of yellow fever.

Because of the Civil War, Melinda entered Mexico. She founded the first Protestant mission under extreme difficulties. Never deterred, she said, "The word *discouragement* is not in the dictionary of the kingdom of heaven." When she left in 1872, she turned over a church of 170 Mexicans to the Presbyterian Board of Missions.

Is God calling you to meet an urgent need?

God, remind me daily that with Your help I can answer pleas for help.

July 6: You Are Free

"Trust in the Lord with all your heart and lean not on your own understanding; in all your ways acknowledge him, and he will make your paths straight" (Prov. 3:5–6 NIV).

How can a servant be free? Do you realize that, as God's servant, you are free?

Mark Lozuk, a Southern Baptist missionary in Bolivia with his wife, Carolyn, puts it this way: "As God's servants, we are the freest people on Earth. Our responsibility is simply to be obedient and let God do the rest."

Mark and Carolyn's work is based out of Santa Cruz; they start churches, targeting the Quechua Indians, the largest native group in Bolivia and a largely unreached people.

"When God calls us to a task, our job is to answer," he says. "God's job is to get the task completed."

A recent conversion reminded them of God's awesome plans. Martha came to their first Bible study, adamantly standing against the need for a personal Savior. Two weeks later she confessed Christ and her life changed. She sells lunches out of her house; no one gets a meal without also hearing about Jesus. She brings to church people she has led to become Christians, prays earnestly, and teaches a Sunday School class.

Martha is a wonderful example for us. "When God asks you to do something, you should not take it as a suggestion," Mark says.

Dear Lord, I acknowledge Your will in my life. I know You have wonderful plans for me.

July 7: Protecting Hands of God

"Thou wilt show me the path of life. In thy presence is fullness of joy; at thy right hand there are pleasures for evermore" (Psalm 16:11 KJV).

Throughout the operation, she didn't complain but kept affirming: "God's left hand is underneath my head. His right hand sustains and embraces me. I am willing to suffer."

In 1855 Hawaiian missionary Lucy G. Thurston (1795–1876) bravely endured breast cancer surgery without any anesthetic. Her doctors had advised her to do so because her exposure to tuberculosis had partially paralyzed her. The 60-year-old experienced intense pain and was so weak for days after the surgery that she had to be fed with a spoon.

Thirty-five years before her cancer surgery the new bride had arrived in Hawaii with her husband, Asa. They found the native Hawaiians worshiping volcanoes, sharks, wood, and stone; and possessing no written language and no organized government. They soon built schools and churches and printed books. They taught the people to read, write, sing, and print.

Mother of six children, she assisted her husband for 48 years until his death.

The mother of American missions in Hawaii lived 21 years after the surgery, surviving all of the original missionaries with whom she had gone there.

Are you relying on the peace and joy of God to sustain you through difficult times?

∼

Precious Lord, thank You today for Your hands of protection that encircle me when I encounter suffering.

July 8: Window Screens and Thankfulness

"Give thanks in all circumstances, for this is God's will for you in Christ Jesus" (1 Thess. 5:18 NIV).

When Larry Williams and his youth group of World Changers first arrived at the Marks, Mississippi, home where they would work for a week, he wondered about their assignment. They were supposed to fix windows and repair the house's siding, but he immediately learned that the roof leaked and that the owner had no place to bathe inside the house. She bathed in a washtub behind the house.

By Wednesday the group had fixed and put screens on the windows. The next morning, the homeowner greeted them outside her house. "I had the best sleep last night in years," she announced. They soon learned that in the summer, mosquitoes overran this Mississippi Delta area. The woman had two choices—shut the windows and burn up during the night, or open the windows and be attacked by mosquitoes. Larry then realized why the window repairs were so important.

"I went home from that trip realizing that I was so ungrateful," Larry says. "When was the last time I thanked God for my window screens?"

Larry serves as a service project coordinator for World Changers, an organization that started in 1991 with around 1,000 participants at 7 work sites. In 2000, around 14,000 people were involved at 75 work sites.

Are you thankful for life's simple things?

Faithful God, thank You for all of life's blessings, and thank You for Your Son.

July 9: Proclaim Freedom

"The Lord has anointed me to preach good news to the poor. He has sent me to bind up the brokenhearted, to proclaim freedom for the captives and release from darkness for the prisoners" (Isa. 61:1 NIV).

Both the Old and New Testament are clear in their instructions—we are to minister to prisoners. Why, then, do Christians often ignore this group in our society?

Fear, misunderstanding, discomfort. All of these may help explain why Christians often neglect prisoners.

Many churches and organizations, however, have a heart for captives. Perhaps today you can consider becoming involved with one.

Cliff Rawley, supervisory chaplain at the Federal Prison Camp in Duluth, Minnesota, says that prison ministry is challenging but can be an immense blessing.

"[Jesus'] parables teach us that God reaches out in His infinite mercy to those people others might see as lost causes," he says. "Both chaplains and volunteers tell inmates there is hope for forgiveness, building a new life, and being the person God created them to be."

Some of the ways Christians can minister to prisoners include leading worship services, teaching small-group Bible studies, building mentoring relationships, leading addiction support groups, and providing aftercare once the prisoner is back in society. "We should remember the Lord's concern for those who were lost and fallen," Cliff says.

Could God be calling you to participate some way in a ministry to prisoners?

Dear Lord, send Your message of love to prisoners around our world today.

July 10: Faith in God

"I live by faith in the Son of God, who loved me and gave himself for me" (Gal. 2:20 NIV).

He took as his motto—Have Faith in God.

William Quarrier (1829–1903), founder of the Orphan Homes of Scotland, relied on God to meet all of his needs. Like George Muller who started his orphanages four decades before him in England, William never appealed for money. Toward the end of his life he spoke of God's faithfulness: "He gave me the utmost of my asking, and I felt that I would need to give Him the utmost of the power I pledged."

William lost his father when he was 3. Going to work at the age of 6, he experienced poverty in the Glasgow slums. He became a shoemaker and prospered in the business, eventually becoming one of the first multiple storeowners in Glasgow.

At 17 he was converted and began leading others to Christ, including his own mother.

In 1864 he started work among destitute and orphan children in Glasgow. Opening his Orphan Homes of Scotland at Bridge of Weir in 1878, he nurtured thousands of children in its school and church. He also set up a base in Canada where many Scottish orphans were settled with families.

In addition to orphanages, he established Scotland's first tuberculosis sanitarium and built an evangelistic center and a large night shelter in Glasgow.

Do you have an abiding faith in God?

~

Today, Lord, make me Your faithful servant.

July 11: A Practical Visionary

"When the righteous are in authority, the people rejoice" (Prov. 29:2 KJV).

"Miss Annie was a dreamer—a dreamer in action," said a minister after her death. "She was a woman of remarkable vision, not visionary but practical, one who dreamed her dreams and then made her dreams come true."

Annie Armstrong (1850–1938) was one of the most powerful church women of the late nineteenth and early twentieth century. As cofounder and first executive director (then called corresponding secretary) of Woman's Missionary Union, Auxiliary to Southern Baptist Convention, she was known as an "organizational genius—highly skilled, able to manage large affairs."

Born into a wealthy Baltimore family on July 11, 1850, she first became interested in missions when confronted with the needs of Native American Indian schools. As her commitment to missions increased, she was in demand for her abilities. From 1888 until 1906, she served faithfully and tirelessly without salary as WMU's executive director. She spearheaded home missions among the Native American Indians, the disabled, immigrants, and African Americans.

Ahead of her time in her cooperation with African American women, she helped them form an auxiliary to the National Baptist Convention and often spoke at their meetings. After helping Cincinnati African American women organize, a leader said of her: "Miss Annie W. Armstrong—the trailblazer in Christian cooperation between white and Negro Baptist women. . . . No woman in America has ever done more to encourage Negro Baptist women."

Do you work diligently to make your dreams come true?

∾

Heavenly God, may Annie's vision continue through the Annie Armstrong Easter Offering for North American Missions®.

July 12: Teenagers Are Special

"Let no one despise your youth, but set the believers an example in speech and conduct, in love, in faith, in purity" (1 Tim. 4:12 RSV).

Some of the best missionaries I've ever met just happened to be teenagers. Christian teens have a unique capacity for love, generosity, and service.

As a college student, I served as a chaperon on a youth missions trip to New Orleans. The missions team members held Vacation Bible School in an inner-city park, not far from drug areas. They also worked in a Christian activity center, playing basketball with the local kids and making friends with youth much like themselves. They also participated in Bible studies, devotional times, and worship.

With each passing moment—as they saw the poverty around them, as they hugged a child they were growing to love—I saw them learn an important missions lesson: missions can be contagious. The teenagers fed on the things God kept teaching them and on the things they saw and felt. They wanted to do more and more and more. And they cried genuine tears when they had to leave at the end of the week.

We often forget that young people have a huge heart for others and for God. We need to encourage the young people in our lives to reach out in God's name. Can you do that today?

Thank You, Lord, for youthful exuberance and faith. Help me appreciate the teens in my life and help me learn from them.

July 13: Making a Home

"She watches over the affairs of her household and does not eat the bread of idleness" (Prov. 31:27 NIV).

She scrubbed her floors with cow dung mixed with water. Although she at first found the cleaning custom repulsive, she learned to appreciate it saying that "it lays dust better than anything, and kills the fleas which would otherwise breed abundantly."

Missionary Mary Moffat (1795–1870) not only had to clean the floors of her mud hut with cow dung but also had to wash her clothes in a cold river, make soap from sheep's fat, grind wheat for bread, and smoke and salt her meat to keep the moths out.

Serving as a pioneer missionary with the London Missionary Society, Mary labored with her husband, Robert, for more than 50 years in South Africa. Their son-in-law, missionary David Livingstone, described their home in Kuruman as an "oasis in the desert." Other visitors described the mission station as a "beautifully ordered household."

The mother of ten children, Mary took pride in her home and its landscaping. She once rejoiced after a rain: "The willow tree is majestic; the syringas have been one sheet of blooms, and the perfume delicious, and now the orange trees are sending forth their still more grateful scent."

Have you ever considered what dedication it took for our missionary pioneers to make a home for their families?

∽

Help me today, Lord, to diligently carry out any task, however unpleasant it may be.

July 14: Pointing Others to God

"And how can they believe in the one of whom they have not heard? And how can they hear without someone preaching to them?" (Rom. 10:14 NIV).

You could say that Stevan Manley is a traveler for Christ. As the director of Evangelistic Faith Missions, an interdenominational missions organization, he has traveled to Honduras 11 times; Guatemala 5 times; Egypt and South Korea 4 times each; Bolivia 3 times; Eritrea 2 times; and Ethiopia 1 time. On his trips he visits the organization's missions and encourages missionaries. He also gets a chance to preach and teach.

Stevan says that his greatest blessings as a Christian come from the knowledge that he can point others to God.

"In 1996 in Eritrea, God helped me while I was preaching and perhaps more than 100 people sought God at the close of the service," he remembers.

"These are times," he says, "I will never forget."

Evangelistic Faith Missions has missions in these various countries and also produces a radio ministry heard on more than 40 stations.

All Christians can be like missionaries in their own spheres of influence. All Christians also can be teachers of the good news. We all can point others to God—through the words we say in front of a group of people or the actions we do in love for one person.

~

Holy God, I pray today that I can point someone to Christ.

July 15: The Secret of Spiritual Power

"'Not by might nor by power, but by my Spirit,' says the Lord Almighty" (Zech. 4:6 NIV)

Early in his ministry he learned that the secret of spiritual power was the Holy Spirit. Canadian Jonathan Goforth (1859–1936) truly lived his life according to Zechariah 4:6.

His dependence on the Holy Spirit together with his evangelistic zeal, childlike faith, and genuine love for others led to a successful 46-year ministry.

Jonathan and his partner-wife, Rosalind, arrived in China in 1888, settling in Honan Province where they established a Canadian Presbyterian mission in central China. They crisscrossed China with their preaching and teaching.

Enduring incredible hardships, they lost 5 of their 11 children. In 1900 during the Boxer Rebellion they were driven from their home. Brutally beaten with swords, Jonathan miraculously survived. Never robust, he also suffered from many diseases.

They spent their last eight years in Manchuria where they experienced great success. In 1934 Jonathan's blindness and Rosalind's ill health forced them to return home. They left 61 full-time Chinese evangelists and Bible teachers and thousands of disciplined converts.

Back in Canada, Jonathan—ever resilient—spoke at 481 meetings in 18 months. His book *By My Spirit* inspired many to dedicate their lives to missions.

Are you relying on the Holy Spirit to guide you in your work?

Enable me to walk daily, Lord, relying not on my power but on Yours alone.

July 16: Fishers of People

"As Jesus was walking along the shore of Lake Galilee, he saw Simon and his brother Andrew. They were fishermen and were casting their nets into the lake. Jesus said to them, 'Come with me! I will teach you how to bring in people instead of fish.'" (Mark 1:16–17 CEV).

Jesus often taught from a fishing boat. He counted fishermen among His best friends and told His followers that they should be fishers of people.

With that in mind, Glenn Chappelear's ministry may not be as unique as it seems when you first hear of it.

Glenn and his wife, Donna, serve as missionaries among the professional fishing community in the United States. Glenn, a former youth pastor and now a professional fisherman, fishes with the Bassmaster and Forrest Wood/Everstart tours and ministers in the process.

Glenn began considering a professional fishing career while a youth minister in Atlanta. He wondered, though, how to serve God if he changed careers. His answer came when he learned of Mission Service Corps, a mobilization effort of the Southern Baptist North American Mission Board to place self-supporting missionaries and chaplains on the missions field.

Today, he leads evangelistic fishing clinics, speaks at wild game dinners, and witnesses to fellow fisherman and fishing spectators.

"I get to stand in my boat and tell them about Christ," Glenn says. "I tell them, 'You've seen what I fish with, but this is what I live by,' and I hold up my Bible and tell them my testimony."

What hobbies or talents do you have that you can cultivate for Christian ministry?

~

Lord, show me how my talent can make me a fisher of people.

July 17: A Calling from God

"We constantly pray for you, that our God may count you worthy of his calling" (2 Thess. 1:11 NIV).

Have you ever felt a clear calling from God?

Amanda Smith (1837–1915) did. In 1870 she felt a call to be a missionary in India. Two years later she sensed a call to Africa.

Years would pass, though, before she was able to fulfill her convictions.

Despite racial and sexist biases against her, Amanda became a respected world evangelist because she depended completely on God.

After two difficult marriages and the deaths of her five children, she felt God's call as an evangelist and began speaking in camp meetings. In 1878 friends persuaded her to go to England on a three-month trip. She stayed two years speaking and attending revival meetings. An English friend convinced her to go to India with her and raised money for her support. Arriving in Bombay in 1879, she stayed and taught and worked at an orphanage.

In 1882 she realized her dream to go to Africa (Liberia) when again supported by British friends. She stayed there eight years, speaking and organizing the Gospel Temperance Band.

Moving to Harvey near Chicago, she lived in a temperance community and wrote her autobiography. In 1899 she opened the Amanda Smith Orphans Home, the first orphanage for African American children in Illinois.

Dear Lord, thank You that through prayer I can sense Your calling today.

July 18: I Believe in You

"Beloved, we feel sure of better things that belong to salvation" (Heb. 6:9 RSV).

Has someone ever believed in you when no one else did? Were you surprised when they did?

If you've ever been through rough times and had someone believe in you despite the circumstances, you know how important it is to have a personal "cheerleader." One aspect of the Christian Women's Job Corps® is building up the self-confidence of women who may feel hopeless because of circumstances.

This is evident in a life Linda Gwathmey saw changed through her work at the CWJC℠ in San Antonio, Texas. The ministry offers a Project Forward class that teaches life skills such as reading, writing, money management, nutrition, and speaking to women who have never worked or who are returning to the job market after years of not working. It also offers mentors who give advice and believe in the women's ability to succeed.

One woman who came to class was the epitome of hopelessness. Shy and disheveled, she never looked anyone in the eyes. The state had taken away her four children, and her marriage had fallen apart.

As the classes progressed, though, Linda saw a marked change in the woman. She began to take seriously the things she learned in Bible study. Her husband came home, and, one by one, so did her children. She finished classes and became a nurse's aide.

∼

Mighty Counselor, reveal to me how to build up someone's confidence.

July 19: This Cup . . .

"After the supper he took the cup, saying, 'This cup is the new covenant in my blood, which is poured out for you'" (Luke 22:20 NIV).

Her job as water bearer on a missions trip to Mexico became a profound experience for Carol Padgett.

Carol, and other adults and youth from her United Methodist church, traveled to Mexico as part of a Constructors para Cristo (Builders for Christ) group. The group built a concrete block home in five days. The family moving into the home had waited for five years for this home, having lived in a shack next door.

Each adult had a specific job, and as a medical caregiver, Carol gladly took the job of nurse. The job, though, became primarily one of water bearer.

"My job was to keep the group from becoming dehydrated by distributing a special drink to each person," she says. "I also refreshed everyone with sprays of water. This job was important because we worked in 102°F temperatures."

Her task became profound when she realized how the little things—space, shelter, water—had such importance to both the workers and residents. "There was a heightened sense of importance to everything," Carol recalls.

Each time she took cups to the team members the act became more powerful, reminding Carol of Christ's love for each of them. "Each time I served them it seemed like I was serving Communion," she says. "This had a deep impact on me."

When participating in Communion, how do you feel? When serving others, how do you feel?

∽

Precious Lord, let me serve others with gladness.

July 20: A Heart for the Sick

"'I was sick and you looked after me'" (Matt. 25:36 NIV).

In 1733 she opened her home to care for the victims of a smallpox epidemic. She nursed them in her own bedroom. She helped bury the dead.

Giertrud Rask's gestures of kindness endeared her to the people of Greenland.

Her compassion, though, bore a heavy price. Her husband wrote: "My beloved wife after that time suffered greatly in strength and health." He went on to say that her "superhuman efforts . . . had undermined her constitution." After 2 more years of reaching out in kindness to the Greenlanders, she died.

Giertrud had been reluctant to leave her home in northern Norway to travel to Greenland in 1718 with her husband, Hans Egede (1686–1758). She had four children, the youngest not a year old. Also, she was not a young woman; she was 45—13 years older than Hans.

Although at first a hesitant missionary, she became an effective partner with Hans and a strong woman of faith. The Lutheran Pietests served as the first evangelical missionaries among the Eskimos.

Two of their children —Paul and Hans—were also involved in the ministry. Many Eskimos became Christians because of Paul's preaching. After Giertrud's death, Hans directed the work from Norway, with his sons carrying on the work in Greenland.

Have you had opportunities to minister to someone who was chronically ill? How did that person's illness affect you?

Gracious God, give me a compassionate heart to minister to the sick.

July 21: Surf's Up!

"How can a mortal be righteous before God? . . . He alone stretches out the heavens and treads on the waves of the sea" (Job 9:2,8 NIV).

The sun is shining brightly and the waves are gathering speed. It's a perfect morning for surfing.

The 22 surfers riding the waves are not your typical surfers, though. They are members of the San Diego chapter of Christian Surfers United States (CSUS).

John Lindsley, the CSUS's western administrator, has surfed for more than two decades off the California coast and tries now to reach other surfers with the Gospel message. CSUS chapters around the country try to do the same thing.

The groups sponsor Bible studies, surf contests, and weekend surf trips; nationally CSUS holds leadership training, national conferences, and the annual Surf Fest.

John says that the effects of this ministry can be far-reaching. One teen showed up at a chapter meeting because there was free food, but soon found that the meetings weren't "churchy" and began attending regularly. "Eventually God got a hold of his heart and transformed a foul-mouthed kid who was once committed entirely to the stereotypical sex, drugs, and rock-and-roll lifestyle to a young man who radiates the loves of Jesus," says John. "He and another surfer started a Christian Club on their high school campus. It's become a huge success."

How can you reach the unchurched masses with Christ's message?

∽

Mighty Creator, empower me to reach out to those who don't know You. Give me the vision to make Your message accessible to them.

July 22: Doing Good

"Do not forget to do good and to share with others, for with such sacrifices God is pleased" (Heb. 13:16 NIV).

Her children called her Chicago brownstone house "a Christian halfway house between the Orient and the West." For 40 years it was a center of international Christianity. Missionaries were always coming and going.

Nettie Fowler McCormick (1835–1923) was one of the most generous Christian philanthropists of her time.

In 1859 she married Cyrus H. McCormick, the inventor of the grain reaper, who was 26 years her senior. When he died, he left her a large estate which she used for good.

The McCormick Theological Seminary and the Woman's Board of the Presbyterian Mission of the Northwest were both dear to her. She and her family gave $4 million to the seminary. She also endowed a library named for her mentally ill daughter. For 34 years she served as vice-president of the Woman's Board.

Although a Presbyterian, she extended her giving to many denominations and causes. She helped John R. Mott reach youth through the World's Student Christian Federation. Working with Southern mountain schools, she improved the daily lives of people through domestic science training. She provided for a college in Teheran, hospitals in Siam and Persia, theological education in Korea, a language school in Nanking for missionaries, and agricultural machinery and land in India.

Do you stay alert to needs at home and abroad?

My God, may I daily and sacrificially share with others.

July 23: Past the Headlines

"How long must I wrestle with my thoughts and every day have sorrow in my heart? How long will my enemy triumph over me?" (Psalm 13:2 NIV).

The images barraged television viewers in 1999. Tens of thousands of Kosovars fled and were pushed out of their homeland by the Serbians. The expressions on the faces of the refugees were ones of extreme sorrow.

Monte and Janet Erwin, Southern Baptist missionaries to Latvia, experienced the reality behind the news stories as they joined other missions groups in ministering to the refugees.

In visiting refugee camps and distributing relief supplies, the Erwins saw a lot of sadness. "They would spend most of their time talking about their beloved homeland and how much they loved their lives there," Monte remembers.

They listened to the stories, prayed with the individuals, and tried to share their testimonies.

Following a service in which several Kosovars were baptized, the missions team's Albanian bus driver came to Monte with questions about Jesus. Monte explained how he could become a Christian. The next morning at breakfast the man whispered to him, "I did it. I knelt down next to my bed last night and asked Lord Jesus to come into my life."

Individual changes such as these may be the ultimate answer for the bigger struggles in the area. Only God can heal such sorrow.

When have you felt overwhelmed by sorrow?

∼

Holy God, I praise You today for Your victory over sorrow and hatred. Bless those who struggle with it around the world.

July 24: Exalting

"I eagerly expect and hope that I will in no way be ashamed, but will have sufficient courage so that now as always Christ will be exalted in my body, whether by life or by death" (Phil. 1: 20 NIV).

"It's all right," the medical missionary said, whispering his last words: "I pray God will be glorified whether by my life or by death."

The risk of deadly disease didn't stop young W. G. R. Jotcham from going to Africa. A Canadian Baptist with the Sudan Interior Mission, he arrived in Nigeria in January 1937 with striking credentials. At the age of 22, he was the youngest to receive a doctorate of medicine at Montreal's McGill University.

After six months studying the Hausa language, he was placed in charge of the Katsina leper colony of 200 lepers. He worked sacrificially with lepers ravaged by mangled hands and stump legs. A letter home indicated his enthusiasm toward his mission: "These cold lives had never warmed themselves before the fire of God's eternal love, nor upon these aching ears had the sweet story of the Gospel ever fallen."

Barely a year after his arrival, an epidemic of spinal meningitis struck the colony. As hundreds died, Jotcham labored until he also fell victim to the disease.

Are you willing to sacrificially give yourself to a cause in which you believe?

Precious Lord, thank You for all the medical missionaries who gave their lives to bring healing to others.

July 25: Fellowship with Jesus Christ

"Our fellowship is with the Father and with his Son, Jesus Christ" (1 John 1:3 NIV).

His lifelong motto was Constant Conscious Fellowship with Jesus.

Fredrik Franson's enthusiasm for missions led him to personally evangelize around the world. He either founded or significantly influenced 15 missionary societies and church denominations in nine countries on three continents.

At the age of 17, Fredrik (1852–1908) arrived in America as a Swedish immigrant. When he was 20, he became a Christian after long hours of prayer and faithful counseling by his mother. In January 1874, a year and a half after his conversion, a woman from the Swedish Baptist Church in their Nebraska settlement asked him about his spiritual condition. He suddenly realized that no one knew he was a believer. He then gave his testimony at church and became an active layman. After serving an apprenticeship with D. L. Moody, he became an interdenominational evangelist on the American frontier in 1877. This began his 31 years of public ministry.

In 1881 he moved to Europe where he evangelized in many countries. Returning to America in 1890, he set up the Scandinavian Alliance Mission of North America (today called TEAM—The Evangelical Alliance Mission). For the rest of his life he tirelessly traveled the globe doing missionary work.

When he died at the age of 56, he was totally expended for the Lord.

Is your fellowship with Jesus bringing results?

∞

Almighty God, help me daily to focus on a close fellowship with You.

July 26: God Is First

"Have I not commanded you? . . . Be not frightened, neither be dismayed; for the Lord your God is with you wherever you go" (Josh. 1:9 RSV).

Who is the CEO (chief executive officer) of your life?

Southern Baptist missionaries Ben and Judy Armacost say that God is their boss and that prayer is the only way they know that He is with them at all times.

"God is the One in charge, and prayer is the crucial link with the CEO of our organization," Ben says. "Everything we do needs to be preceded by and fully bathed in prayer. It is the first step to success as far as God's work is concerned."

Ben and Judy are church planters in Tasmania, a small island off the southeastern coast of Australia. The island is the smallest of Australia's states, with just under half a million residents. They reach out especially to nonbelievers who have a hostile view of the church.

Prayer is the vital tool in their work. Their prayers, and those of friends and supporters back in America, helped them reach 7 percent of their town's population when they celebrated their church's second anniversary. Around 30 people attend their church regularly, but 150 came for the event. "We had a great opportunity to share Christ with a multitude," Ben remembers.

Judy's life verse is Joshua 1:9. It gives her strength and reminds her of "God's presence wherever we go and in whatever we do."

My Redeemer, lead me today wherever I go.

July 27: A Devoted People

"We ourselves boast of you in the churches of God for your steadfastness and faith in all of your persecutions and in the afflictions which you are enduring" (2 Thess. 1:4 RSV).

One country stands out in the mind of missions volunteer Claudia Hucks.

Claudia has participated in numerous home and international missions trips through the Volunteers in Missions program, but she says: "The believers in Romania are the most devoted and ardent people I have ever met in my work."

A trip to Brasov, Romania, in the summer of 1999 taught Claudia much about persecution and perseverance. The Romanian Christians she met had endured many trials under Communist rule. No one under 18 could be baptized or join a church. If a church came into disrepair, it usually fell apart because members couldn't get a permit to fix it. Pastors were interrogated. Some Christians were tortured and killed.

The scars of persecution are still evident in the lives of many Christians there. "Even today, 12 years after their freedom was declared, they still find it hard to laugh and act spontaneously," Claudia says. "It has left a mark on the older generation of believers which is easily seen."

Still, she says, there is much hope and faith in the churches. "They are faithful in attendance, giving, and serving," she says. "Our hearts and lives were entwined as we shared together with them in worship, Bible study, and testimony."

Have you ever felt persecuted for your faith?

Be with Christians today, dear God, who are persecuted.

July 28: Devoted to Christ

"Grace to all who love our Lord Jesus Christ with an undying love" (Eph. 6:24 NIV).

After his death, he was called "a man so filled with the love and grace of God that his whole being—body, soul, and spirit—was devoted utterly to Christ and His service."

Although he had diabetes and heart disease from childhood, Robert Jaffray (1873–1945) never stopped working. He even designed a desk to hang over his bed so that he could work while resting.

He gave up the opportunity to succeed his wealthy father as a newspaper publisher. Instead, after going through missionary training, he joined the Christian and Missionary Alliance (C&MA) and in the late 1800s moved to Wuchow, South China. Opening up country after country, he evangelized in China, Vietnam, Cambodia, and Indonesia.

A versatile missionary, Robert founded Bible schools, edited magazines, and established the Chinese Foreign Missionary Union. As founder and director of the South China Alliance press, he wrote numerous articles and booklets in Cantonese.

After a furlough home in 1941, he refused retirement and returned to Celebes (Indonesia) in December, a day before the bombing of Pearl Harbor. Two months later the Japanese invaded, and he and his wife, Minnie, were interned along with other missionaries in a concentration camp. He died of starvation two weeks before the war ended.

Are you completely devoted to Christ?

∼

Today, Lord, fill my whole being with Your love and grace.

July 29: The Heart of Appalachia

"He raises the poor from the dust and lifts the needy from the ash heap; he seats them with princes and has them inherit a throne of honor" (1 Sam. 2:8 NIV).

The most comprehensive United Methodist mission in the United States defines its purpose quite simply. It is to be "a witness for Christ in the heart of Appalachia."

Appalachia is a land of contrasts: some of the country's poorest people live in some of its most beautiful, serene natural surroundings. Red Bird Missionary Conference reaches out to these Appalachian residents with a wealth of ministries, including a medical and dental clinic, a pharmacy, ambulance services, Red Bird Mission School, senior adult programs, work camp programs, Appalachian Local Pastors School, agricultural ministries, clothing ministries, and other community services.

One of the mission's most unique projects is the Red Bird Mission Craft Program, which offers a way for Appalachian craftspeople to make, market, and sell their creations. The Craft Store in Beverly, Kentucky, is open five days a week to the general public, and the craft program visits approximately 60 churches a year to provide Appalachian Craft Fairs for congregations.

All of these ministries serve to uplift the lives of the needy in Appalachia and, in turn, share with them the saving love of Jesus Christ.

Won't you pray today for the needs of the Appalachian people?

∽

Your graciousness is overwhelming, Lord, for You lift up the needy and poor and give them honor.

July 30: Amazing Faith

"Without faith it is impossible to please God" (Heb. 11:6 NIV).

Years after the experiences Ryan Goodman still remembers how two missions trips to Kentucky taught him great lessons about faith and miracles.

Ryan spent time with the Appalachian Service Project (ASP) building outhouses. The first outhouse project was for an elderly woman and her alcoholic son whose outhouse had been destroyed by moonshiners because the son owed them money.

On the day slated for construction, team members discovered that waist-high weeds covered the spot. It would take at least two days to clear it with their swingblades. Moments later, they heard a loud noise and turned to find a government grass cutter clearing the side of the road. They asked the driver for help, and, within five minutes, the area was cleared.

"I realized then that the word *miracle* did not necessarily have to be something of a supernatural nature," Ryan says. "For us, it meant the right people were in the right place at the right time."

Ryan's lessons in faith continued the next summer when he worked on an outhouse for an extremely needy family. The family had incredible faith.

"It surpasses all I've ever seen," he remembers. "For us it should be easy to have faith. We have nice houses, drive cars, go to work every day. We don't worry about where our next meal is coming from. These people literally had nothing."

Does your faith please God?

O God, I want to have more faith.

July 31: God's Strength

"It is God who arms me with strength and makes my way perfect"
(2 Sam. 22:33 NIV).

Sandy and Jerry Cole looked at the devastation around them in amazement. The ground around the fault line buckled up 15 feet above its normal elevation. Homes and businesses were either completely destroyed or damaged beyond use.

They learned later of the official damage: more than 2,000 people killed and more than 100,000 people left homeless. Sandy and Jerry, Southern Baptist missionaries headquartered in Pingtung, Taiwan, helped with relief efforts as soon as the quake struck.

"We were in Taipei when the initial quake occurred. I was actually awake at 1:45 A.M.," Jerry remembers. "The electricity went off, and then within just a few seconds, the quake started being very evident. I woke Sandy, and we talked about how strong the shock seemed. However, we did not even get out of bed and eventually went back to sleep."

The next day they saw the extent of the damage and traveled back to Pingtung to help victims. They worked with other Christian groups to deliver food, water, tents, and sleeping bags. While delivering goods, they found themselves trapped by two landslides in one village. "But God has given us a great sense of His presence and strength during these days," they say.

When have you felt God's presence and strength?

∽

Give me strength, Lord, when I face situations beyond my control.

August 1: A Cheerful Christian

"A happy heart makes the face cheerful" (Prov. 15: 13 NIV).

She was known as the bicycling American who was always smiling.

Mabel Francis, a member of the Christian and Missionary Alliance, served in Japan for 56 years.

As a teenager, Mabel spoke at revivals throughout her native New Hampshire. At the age of 20, she began a city missions ministry working for 2 years before attending Nyack Missionary College.

She began her work in Japan in 1909. After her brother joined her in 1913, they established 20 Alliance churches. In 1922 Anne, her widowed sister, joined her. For 40 years, with Mabel as evangelist and Anne as teacher, they conducted a very successful ministry. One young convert, Mitsuko Ninomiyo—who later became a missionary in Brazil—was intrigued with Mabel, who was always smiling as she bicycled around Hiroshima.

Her brother Tom left in the 1930s when Japan became more militaristic. After Pearl Harbor, Mabel was placed under house arrest. Then she was sent to Tokyo and interned in a Catholic monastery. Sharing her faith there, she led the man in charge of her internment to Christ.

She suffered through the devastation of the war with the Japanese people and earned their respect. In 1962 the emperor honored her with Japan's highest civilian honor—membership in the exclusive Fifth Order of Sacred Treasure.

Are you known for your cheerful spirit?

∼

Lord, help me daily to share Your love with a glad heart even in times of crisis.

August 2: Island Paradise

"For the sun rises with scorching heat and withers the plant; its blossom falls and its beauty is destroyed. In the same way, the rich man will fade away even while he goes about his business" (James 1:11 NIV).

Where can I take a luxurious island vacation?

If you walk into a travel agency and ask that question, chances are you'll hear Sint Maarten cited as a wonderful possibility.

Sint Maarten, an island in the Caribbean's Netherlands Antilles, is the ultimate vacation destination. White beaches and clear blue water attract tourists from around the world.

Southern Baptist missionaries Patti and Tom Higginbotham find both benefits and downsides to serving in such a beautiful location.

The positive aspect of ministry there is that islanders already have a respect for Christianity. The couple doesn't have to fight persecution or barriers to witnessing and teaching. Patti leads a women's Bible study and volunteer teaches at her daughter's school, while Tom preaches and ministers to church members and nonmembers.

However, negative aspects abound.

"Most people in the international community to whom we minister have little or no time for God," says Patti. "Many of them live in a vacation setting as if escaping everything, especially God."

The materialism created by such an environment results in people who feel they have no practical need for Christ. Patti says the churches, then, are filled with "good listeners."

If you lived on such a beautiful island, would you still need God?

∼

Lord, help me realize I need You always—despite material wealth.

August 3: Courageous Faith

"Be watchful, stand firm in your faith, be courageous, be strong" (1 Cor. 16:13 RSV).

Can you imagine the courage it took for missionaries to work among cannibals?

One of the first tasks English Wesleyan missionary James Calvert (1813–1892) did when he arrived in the Fiji Islands was to bury the bones of 80 victims of a cannibal feast.

James was educated at Hoxton Theological Institution and then apprenticed to a printer and bookbinder for seven years. He married Mary Fowler in 1838, the same year they sailed for Fiji.

The couple mastered the language quickly and showed great courage and tact working with the islanders. James was responsible for 13 towns that had no roads connecting them and for 24 surrounding islands—some spread 100 miles apart. Using a canoe, he carried his printing press from one island to another training Fijian converts in printing and bookbinding.

James earned a reputation as an arbitrator among chiefs and cannibals. He did much to abolish the pagan custom of strangling the women of the household when a king died. He offered to have one of his own fingers cut off if King Thakombau would promise not to strangle any women when the old king died.

In addition to his printing work, James revised the Fijian translation of the Old Testament and revised the New Testament translation twice.

Give me strength, Holy God, to stand firm when witnessing to those whose customs may be so contrary to the Christian faith.

August 4: On Vacation, on Mission

"The mountain peaks belong to him. The sea is his, for he made it, and his hands formed the dry land" (Psalm 95:4–5 NIV).

Vacations take us away from the everyday troubles of life and give us a well-deserved break. How often, though, do we also take a break from God when we're on vacation?

Martha and Winford Haynes decided years ago to give their vacations to God; today, as the national coordinators for Campers on Mission, they encourage others to do so too.

Looking back at the beginnings of their mission, Martha says, "As the Lord blessed us with more weeks of vacation, we would give two, three, four weeks to the Lord. We did Vacation Bible Schools, Backyard Bible Clubs, revivals, and construction work. It's given our family time together to be on mission with Him and to see God's beautiful world."

Campers on Mission is a national fellowship open free to Christian campers of all denominations. It encourages them to carry the gospel wherever they go and promotes ministries not only in campgrounds, but also at parades, fairs, rest stops, truck stops, and raceways. Activities include everything from leading Bible studies and worship services to distributing Bibles and performing puppet shows.

Martha says the missions work has expanded her world. One summer she and her husband went to Alaska, Maine, Colorado, and Nevada ministering to campers and vacationers.

∼

As I go on vacation this summer, Lord, I want You to go with me.

August 5: Prayers Upheld Her

"On him we have set our hope that he will continue to deliver us, as you help us by your prayers" (2 Cor. 1:10–11 NIV).

"My life is one long, daily, hourly, record of answered prayer.... I can testify with a full and often wonder-stricken awe that I believe God answers prayer.... It is the very atmosphere in which I live and breathe and have my being," she wrote.

A mighty woman of prayer, Mary Slessor (1848–1915) was always convinced that it was the prayers of the people in Scotland that sustained her and made her work possible in West Africa.

Representing the United Presbyterian Church, she sailed for Calabar in 1876. During her almost 40 years there she faced chronic illness, loneliness, and fear. Opposing warring tribes, witchcraft, drunkenness, and superstition, the dauntless missionary finally won the respect of the tribes.

Mary continually experienced the power of prayer. For example, she was extremely fearful of riding in a canoe, the only long-distance transportation available in Calabar. Once she was traveling with a group of baby twins she had rescued. As 33 men paddled the huge canoe, a hippopotamus attacked. The men dived overboard, but she stayed with her babies. As the hippo tried to destroy the canoe, she grabbed a tin dishpan and pounded the hippo on the head. Startled, it swam away.

Are you participating in intercessory prayer?

∼

My God of hope, thank You for the opportunity of lifting up others to You in prayer.

August 6: Are You Willing to Serve?

"Last year you were the first not only to give but also to have the desire to do so. Now finish the work, so that your eager willingness to do it may be matched by your completion of it, according to your means" (2 Cor. 8:10–11 NIV).

A lesson we all need to learn about missions is evidenced in the words of Michelle Mullis: "I was quickly shown that God desires nothing but a willing heart and a desire for his glory and gospel in the lives of a lost world."

Michelle learned her lesson in willingness during a three-month trip to Belo Horizonte, Brazil. She and 20 other college students participated in a trip sponsored by Campus Outreach of Birmingham, Alabama's, Briarwood Presbyterian Church (a group that involves college students from a variety of denominations). Group members worked at assigned locations on a college campus in the Brazilian town.

Michelle met with students and tried to build relationships every day at the law building. The team also reached out with activities such as karaoke and soccer games. She especially remembers Carolina, a girl who "over time and from conversations with the team, understood her sin and became overwhelmed by God's grace."

God wants us to be willing to serve Him—no matter what. "I saw that He is able to conquer my insecurities," Michelle recalls. "And He can break barriers of language and culture."

Are you willing to serve Christ today?

~

I am willing to do whatever You call me to do, Lord.

August 7: A Sea Ministry

"Some went down to the sea in ships, doing business on the great waters; they saw the deeds of the Lord, his wondrous works in the deep" (Psalm 107:23-24 RSV).

He fell in love with the sea at an early age. It is fitting then that Wilfred Thomason Grenfell (1865-1940) became one of the most famous missionaries to work with seamen.

Born in Parkgate, England, he grew up near the Irish Sea. After receiving his medical training at London Hospital and degree from Oxford University, Wilfred became a Christian at a D. L. Moody revival meeting.

In 1889 he joined the Royal National Mission to Deep Sea Fishermen and served on a hospital and mercy ship that sailed with the fishing fleet into the North Sea. In 1892 he started a pioneer medical service to fishermen of Labrador and to onshore patients along the coast of Newfoundland.

He spent more than 40 years working with a neglected group of people spreading the gospel and establishing churches, schools, orphanages, and hospitals.

He met his future wife, Anne MacClanahan, aboard a ship. Wed in 1909, she was a significant helpmate in his work.

Wilfred opened the King George V Seamen's Institute in St. Johns, Newfoundland, in 1912. Honored by many universities, he was knighted by the king in 1927.

Is God calling you to a special ministry to a neglected group of people?

∼

Lord, today help me to respond to the needs of those people around me who may be overlooked.

August 8: Happy in Their Work

"Suppose you are very rich and able to enjoy everything you own. Then go ahead and enjoy working hard—this is God's gift to you." (Eccl. 5:19 CEV).

Many women around the world have no marketable job skills. They struggle day by day to provide for their families.

Missionaries often find a solution to this problem by starting crafts ministries.

Thai Country Trim (TCT), a crafts ministry started in Thailand by missionary Betty Butcher, has taught hundreds of women to make items like embroidered Bible covers. The ministry also reaches out to women by holding Bible studies and health clinics.

WorldCrafts, a ministry of WMU, unites TCT and other crafts ministries by providing for the sale of crafts items in the United States. The Baptist organization imports crafts from 14 areas of the world and markets them in the States. The money goes back to the women making the crafts, providing them with some income and the satisfaction of a job well done.

WorldCrafts recently received words of gratitude from a missionary who said: "Half of this order will be made by 23 Muslim women we recruited and trained. Your orders are helping us develop a relationship with them. They trust us now, and we have earned the right to tell them about Jesus."

Are you happy in your work? Could you teach work skills to other women?

Dear Lord, thank You for the work I have been given to do.

August 9: Helping Children

"'Let the little children come to me, and do not hinder them, for the kingdom of God belongs to such as these'" (Mark 10:14 NIV).

A person helped by the counseling services offered by the Alabama Baptist Children's Homes and Family Ministries says: "After my mother died, I wanted to die too. But you gave me a reason to live. You showed me that God loves me and you do too."

A man raised through the organization's foster care ministries says: "Thanks for being there for me and my sister. I am forever grateful to you, for the godly influence you have had on my life."

Founded in 1891 to make a positive difference in the lives of children, the organization has grown to include group homes, emergency shelters, foster homes, a maternity home, a crisis pregnancy hot line, counseling services, and the Madison Project (a service for families coping with the death of a parent).

Executive director Paul Miller says that the ministry challenges all Christians to reach out to children and teenagers. "Our Lord calls us to be a friend to those who so desperately need to experience the love of Jesus," he says. "Together, let us bring into our circle of care children who have been abused, neglected, and abandoned. Every life is worth the sacrifice."

How can you reach out today to the young people around you?

∼

Precious Lord, place Your hands of protection and care upon all the neglected and troubled children.

August 10: Reclaiming the Past

"The Spirit himself testifies with our spirit that we are God's children. Now if we are children, then we are heirs—heirs of God and co-heirs with Christ" (Rom. 8:16–17 NIV).

What would you experience if you worshiped in a church that had once been shut down?

Christians in Ukraine recently learned the answer to that question when they moved into a house of worship that had been used for other purposes during Communist control.

Dee and David Smith are missionaries there with Mission to the World, the foreign missions-sending agency for the Presbyterian Church of America. The first church they helped start met initially in a park, then in a local gymnasium which had no heat and just one electrical outlet. They then moved to a meeting room where local medical workers meet. Finally, the congregation moved back to a building that had been a Reformed church before the Communist Revolution.

"During Soviet times this church was used as a puppet theater, then it became home to a local actor's guild," says Dee. "When the Evangelical Presbyterian Church of Ukraine was able to establish historical ties to this church, the government gave the building back to be used as a place of worship."

The Christians praised God for allowing them to find a new home, and also for being able to reconnect with their Christian ancestors.

∼

Thank You for our Christian ancestors, Eternal Lord. And thank You for making me an heir of Your grace.

August 11: Transforming Power

"Do not conform any longer to the pattern of this world, but be transformed by the renewing of your mind. Then you will be able to test and approve what God's will is—his good, pleasing and perfect will" (Rom. 12:2 NIV).

"When he came to this island in 1848 there was not a single Christian; when he left in 1872 there was not a single heathen," one islander wrote.

The work of Presbyterian missionary John Geddie (1815–1872) transformed the people of Aneityum (New Hebrides).

A native of Scotland, John was brought as an infant to Nova Scotia. During his first pastorate he formed a "missionary society" as an annual overseas project. Soon other Presbyterian churches joined him in missions work. After encouraging his denomination to establish its own mission, one was planned in western Polynesia. Because no one else volunteered, John agreed to go.

He arrived on the island with his wife, three children, a printing press, and a medicine chest. He learned the local language, did translation work, and printed instructional and devotional materials. In spite of attempts on his life, his labor paid off as the islanders embraced Christianity and then as converts went as missionaries to other islands. His journals are an important source for the study of nineteenth-century missions.

Does your life reflect the transforming power of God?

Daily, Lord, give me a vision of Your power to change lives. Help me to reach out to those who need to hear the gospel.

August 12: Building Homes and God's Kingdom

"To prepare God's people for works of service, so that the body of Christ may be built up" (Eph. 4:12 NIV).

"We came together this week to build two houses, but we've also built up the kingdom of God."

That's what Rebecca Williams, president of Mississippi's WMU®, said after helping build two Habitat for Humanity homes in Jackson. The summer 1999 project operated in conjunction with a nationwide blitz—to build a total of seven homes in Jackson; Albuquerque, New Mexico; Cleveland, Ohio; Franklin, West Virginia; Pine Ridge, South Dakota; and Portland, Oregon.

At each WMU-Habitat for Humanity location, volunteers did more than lay foundations and hammer in nails. They also witnessed, held Backyard Bible Clubs, sponsored sports clinics, and held health fairs.

Many of the women involved were motivated to go back to their own communities and do similar work.

Wanda Lee, then national WMU president (now executive director), worked at the Cleveland site and saw lives and attitudes changed. "We wanted the partnership to be one more way to challenge our women to allow Christ to minister through them with something as basic as providing a house for a family in need," she says.

How can you reach a family in need? How might your work build up God's kingdom?

God, thank You for letting me part of building up Your kingdom. Empower me to do my part today.

August 13: Writing It Down

"Of making many books there is no end" (Eccl. 12:12 NIV).

Did you know that many missionaries were widely read authors?

Missionary to Burma, Ann Judson was the leading female missionary author in the beginning of the nineteenth century. In her letters and journal she wrote gripping accounts of the problems of Burmese women and made appeals for women's work.

In her classic *Through Gates of Splendor*, Elisabeth Elliott wrote of the 1956 deaths of the Auca Five—which included her husband, Jim—in Ecuador. Her books also include the autobiographical account of her years as a single missionary, *These Strange Ashes*.

A woman of great literary talent, Amy Carmichael wrote 35 books while a missionary to India for 56 years. Some of the books were written during the last 20 years of her life that she spent as an invalid.

Isobel Kuhn, missionary in China and Thailand for 29 years, wrote eight books. Her story of pioneering missions work in Thailand is told in *Assent to the Tribes*. She wrote until her death of breast cancer in 1957.

William Owen Carver, head of the missions department at Southern Baptist Theological Seminary from 1900 until 1943, was an authority on missions. One of the founders of the WMU Training School in 1907, he wrote 19 books. Seven were about missions.

A. B. Simpson, founder of the Christian and Missionary Alliance, wrote over 70 books. They include *The Gospel of Healing* and *The Life of Prayer*.

~

Lord, thank You for the power of the written word.

August 14: Being a Friend

"Offer hospitality to one another without grumbling. Each one should use whatever gift he has received to serve others" (1 Peter 4:9 NIV).

Friendship evangelism—making friends and developing relationships as a route to witnessing—is the method Southern Baptist missionaries Nancy and John Norton use.

In their work in Japan, which they started in 1978, Nancy and John use their home to reach out in Christ's name. They invite neighbors to an American-style tea party during the Christmas season and during the summer. They also teach Bible and conversational English classes in their home. This approach—becoming friends with their neighbors in the natural setting of their own home—makes it easier to tell the Japanese about Jesus later on.

John describes it this way: "As our neighbors have learned who we are, more and more come to our house to visit and learn." They then have the privilege of sharing Jesus' salvation with them.

The Nortons now pray that the relationships they have built in their home can become the basis for new churches to be started in their community.

It may be that this type of witnessing appeals to your own life and situation.

What are some ways you can use friendship evangelism in your own life? How might you open your home to others for the purpose of teaching them about Jesus?

∽

Blessed One, make me open to the possibilities that my own hospitality can provide for witnessing in Your name.

August 15: Not Giving Up

"Do not be weary in well-doing" (1 Thess. 3:13 RSV).

One of the most famous Roman Catholic missionaries in history, he died at the age of 46. It has been said that the industrious Jesuit missionary literally "burned himself out" in his work. Jesuits credit him with the phenomenal statistic of 700,000 conversions.

Born in the Basque region of Spain to aristocrats, Francis Xavier (1506-1552) studied law and theology at the University of Paris. He came under the influence of his roommate, Ignatius Loyola, the founder of the Society of Jesus (Jesuits), and was converted in 1533. On August 15, 1534, the two men took vows of poverty and charity. Ordained in 1537 in Venice, he spent two years there serving the poor.

In 1542 he arrived in the Portuguese settlement of Goa (India). There he preached, cared for the sick, learned the languages, composed a native catechism, and founded a college. From 1545 to 1549 he traveled more than 5,000 miles ministering in India and surrounding countries including present-day Sri Lanka and Indonesia.

He set out in 1549 to Japan, a largely Buddhist country. After 2 years, he had established a community of about 2,000 believers. Returning to Goa in 1552, he then left for China. While awaiting permission to get into the country, he died.

Do you ever feel like giving up?

∽

Lord, give me strength to stay with the work You have given me to do.

August 16: Tough Christians

"I press on toward the goal to win the prize for which God has called me" (Phil. 3:14 NIV).

Drugs, gangs, street violence, illiteracy.

The streets of El Paso, Texas, can be tough ones. Drugs and gangs are a way of life for many Hispanic teenagers. Only 1 to 2 percent of them go on to college.

At the Houchen Community Center, a United Methodist mission, leaders reach boys in a unique way—they challenge them physically.

Around 30 boys from fifth grade to post-high school work out two nights a week and do long-distance running every Saturday through the center's Los Duros program. Los Duros (The Tough Ones) encourages youth to channel their energies and frustrations into physical exercise. The program concludes each year in May with a competition that consists of a seven-mile run, four rounds of boxing bouts, and a strength competition.

Sherron Courneen, the executive secretary for community and institutional ministries for the United Methodist's Board of Global Ministries, says that Los Duros empowers troubled youth.

"It provides them with an alternative, a new way of being in the world, of living and thinking," she says. "It gives them some hopes and dreams that weren't there before."

Los Duros also emphasizes academic and spiritual pursuits. Tutoring, youth camps, and Bible study are also part of the program.

How can you reach out to teenagers in your community?

Dear God, help me be a witness to a teenager today.

August 17: Enduring Hardships

"Keep your head in all situations, endure hardship, do the work of an evangelist, discharge all the duties of your ministry" (2 Tim. 4:5 NIV).

He endured incredible hardships on his many journeys. Hostile natives, wild animals, poisonous snakes, disease, lack of food and water, and physical exhaustion didn't keep him from his dream of following in the steps of David Livingstone.

Early in his life, Frederick Stanley Arnot (1858–1914) felt God calling him to Africa.

The native of Glasgow, Scotland, went as a Plymouth Brethren missionary to South Africa in 1881 and journeyed up the Zambezi River, the first of nine journeys of exploration he would make. Preaching the gospel to Lewanika, the Barotse chief, he was received favorably. His relations with Lewanika would become legendary.

After beginning work in Benguela (now Angola), Frederick set up the Garenganze Mission of the Plymouth Brethren in the Belgian Congo in 1886. He established many mission stations in his exploration of central Africa.

In addition to his preaching, he and his wife, Harriet, founded schools and medical clinics. Because of poor health, he returned to Britain several times.

Frederick had a direct influence on the founding of two missionary societies—the South African General Mission (now the Africa Evangelical Fellowship) and the South African Baptist Missionary Society.

Are you prepared to endure hardships for the sake of Christ?

~

Today, dear Lord, help me to face the obstacles that confront me with serenity coupled with perseverance.

August 18: Friend to Immigrants

"You are no longer foreigners and aliens, but fellow citizens with God's people" (Eph. 2:19 NIV).

The Southern Baptist missionary was an angel on the waterfront for immigrants landing in the Port of Baltimore between 1893 and 1918.

Marie Buhlmaier (1859–1938) greeted immigrants with a big smile as they disembarked their ships. She brought them drinks and lovingly answered their questions about their trip to their new homes. Out of the pockets of her large kitchen apron she distributed tracts and answered any questions about Jesus. She gave them New Testaments written in their language.

Marie knew firsthand how an immigrant felt because at 9 years old she had arrived in New York City. Meeting their father there, the family discovered he had lost his job. Immediately Marie went to work earning 75 cents a week crocheting trims for dresses. She never went to school.

At 14 Marie met a doctor whose daughters invited her to Sunday School. By October 1873 she and her family were members of a German-speaking Baptist church. The doctor asked Marie to be a part-time home missionary for the church. Working as a missionary, housemaid, and seamstress, she became known as a soul winner. Baptist leader Annie Armstrong and other church officials recruited her as an immigrant missionary to Baltimore.

With many ethnic groups now in America, are you willing to reach out to them?

~

Lord, give me a heart today to witness to people who have a different ethnic origin than I.

August 19: A Special Call

"May he give you the desire of your heart and make all your plans succeed" (Psalm 20:4 NIV).

A series of events showed one missionary couple where they should serve and reinforced their belief that God always has a plan.

The first event happened in the 1980s when Sheila Everett and her pastor husband heard a presentation about the need for the gospel in Albania. Sheila began praying for the country.

Soon after, her church decided to sign up to pray for an unreached people group. Their assignment? The people of Albania.

Meanwhile, in Texas, David and Mary Carpenter's church also prayed for Albania. Soon they felt God calling them to missions work in the nation but were told that missionaries couldn't serve there.

The Carpenters moved to Fort Worth and began attending the Everetts' church—where the people were still praying for Albania. "We met Sheila, and she was in tears. When we stood there in front of her, she saw us as an answer to her prayers," Mary says. "God orchestrated to bring us together."

Two years later, Albania opened to missionaries, and the Carpenters joined other Southern Baptist missionaries there. They served for four years. Looking back, Mary says: "I believe God uses prayer to open up the hearts of people and to open up countries."

When have circumstances worked to advance God's plans in your life?

Keep me open, God, to the possibilities You put in front of me.

August 20: Rejoicing

"Rejoice in the Lord alway: and again I say, Rejoice" (Phil. 4:4 KJV).

"I . . . have been called upon to make sacrifices that have caused my heart to bleed. But, in spite of it all, I have found inexpressible joy and happiness in the Master's service," said the Presbyterian missionary.

Born in Russellville, Alabama, Althea Brown Edmiston (1874–1937) graduated in 1901 from Fisk University in Nashville with the highest honor. The only woman to make a commencement address, she spoke on "What Missions Have Done for the World."

Althea sailed for the Congo on August 20, 1902, and worked at Ibanche where she became head of the day school and supervisor of a girls' home. In 1905 she married Alonzo Edmiston. She went on two furloughs to America because of her two sons' illnesses. After 1918 the Edmistons worked at three different mission stations.

In addition to her work as a teacher and administrator, Althea translated the Bakuba language, a formidable task that took her 11 years to complete and which resulted in a 619-page grammar book and dictionary.

She and Alonzo developed sleeping sickness and had to take treatments in the States. Between 1927 and 1937 the couple translated and printed the entire Bible into the Baluba-Lulua languages. After 35 years of tireless work, she died on June 9, 1937, of malaria and sleeping sickness and was buried at Mutoto station.

Can you rejoice in the good—and bad—times?

Dear Lord, give me strength to rejoice in all circumstances.

August 21: Working Together

"If you have any encouragement from being united with Christ, if any comfort from his love, if any fellowship with the Spirit, if any tenderness and compassion, then make my joy complete by being like-minded, having the same love, being one in spirit and purpose" (Phil. 2:1–2 NIV).

One person can complete a task, though it may take much time and dedication. Two people can do it faster and more effectively. Three people can make the process even smoother. Four people . . .

Get the picture? When Christians work together with a spirit of unity, great things can be accomplished.

When mudslides ravaged Venezuela in December 1999, missionary and relief agencies from a variety of denominations came together to bring aid and support. World Relief worked with evangelical churches to distribute supplies. Trans World Radio worked with churches and other agencies to relay information. Adventist Development sent bread, blankets, and other supplies to survivors. Catholic Relief Services provided invaluable emergency supplies.

When a massive earthquake measuring 7.8 on the Richter scale hit Turkey in August of the same year, the same kind of cooperation brought relief to the thousands of injured and displaced victims. The International Mission Board, Texas Baptist Men, and Southern Baptist Disaster Relief were some of the first on the scene. They joined hundreds of other religious and missions organizations attempting to ease the human suffering.

∽

Remind me, Almighty God, that all Christians should be united in love. Help me get past any barriers I may feel between other believers and me.

August 22: Famine Relief

"When all Egypt began to feel the famine, the people cried to Pharoah for food. Then Pharoah told all the Egyptians, 'Go to Joseph and do what he tells you.' . . . Joseph opened the storehouses and sold grain to the Egyptians" (Gen. 41:55–56 NIV).

In times of famine Christians have an opportunity to reach out to the hurting. Sometimes far-reaching results may occur.

During the terrible famine of 1876–1878 in South India, Baptist missionary John Clough (1836–1910) organized relief work among the Telugus, a low-caste tribe. In order that the starving could have food, he contracted with the Indian government to dig 4 miles of the 100-mile extension of the Buckingham Canal. Organizing camps and relief stations, he and his staff provided food, shelter, and work as well as met the spiritual needs of the people.

John refused to baptize anyone desiring to join the church during this time because he wanted to avoid "rice Christians." In the weeks following the famine, 9,000 were baptized and joined the church. The Ongole Baptist Church, which he and his wife Emma had started in 1867 with 8 members, rose to 21,000 members before it was divided into smaller congregations.

Upon leaving India in 1910, he left behind nearly 60,000 church members in a missions field that had been almost abandoned in discouragement before his coming.

∼

Today, Lord, help me meet both the physical and spiritual needs of people.

August 23: "I Could Have Done More"

"The man who plants and the man who waters have one purpose, and each will be rewarded according to his own labor" (1 Cor. 3:8 NIV).

One of the most dramatic moments in Mitch and Vivian Lea Land's tenure as Southern Baptist missionaries in the Ivory Coast took place in a drought-ridden village.

As a last resort, the village chief and healer invited the Lands into the village to show the Christian film *Le Combat*. After viewing the video, at least 60 people said they wanted to become Christians. Then they burned their idols on a bonfire. As they did so, a miracle happened—it began to rain.

Mitch worked as a director of Christian publications in the African country. *Le Combat* and another movie he produced helped introduced the gospel story to thousands.

Despite such amazing stories, Mitch says he wished he'd been able to do much more. "As I reflect on our years there, I must say that I would like to do a lot of things over and do them better," he says. "I think I could have done much more to win people to Christ."

Mitch says that he knows how much people remember acts of kindness and that "I wish I had cared more about others than I did."

When have you felt as if you could have done more for God?

∼

I confess, O God, that I often don't do everything I can for You. I want to be bolder in my faith.

August 24: A Refuge for the Poor

"You have been a refuge for the poor, a refuge for the needy in his distress" (Isa. 25:4 NIV).

At the Trinity Methodist Church in Atlanta she pioneered the Trinity Home Mission, a church home and industrial school to serve the poor and needy. It became a model for city missions projects.

A native of Watkinsville, Georgia, Laura Askew Haygood (1845–1900) served as a home and foreign missionary. At the age of 7 she moved with her family to Atlanta. At the age of 16 she enrolled at the Wesleyan Female College in Macon, Georgia, and graduated after two years.

In 1866 she established a private school for girls. Six years later she became teacher, and later principal, at Girls' High School, the first Atlanta public school for girls. During this time she organized the Trinity Home Mission at her church. In 1883 she helped initiate the women's home missions work of the Methodist Episcopal Church, South. As a writer and speaker, she addressed issues of women's rights and the needs of the poor.

In 1884 Laura went to China. The McTyeire Home and School in Shanghai was dedicated in 1891. It remains today a visible symbol of her work. She died in Shanghai and is buried there. In 1916 the Laura Haygood Normal School, which honors her work, was built in Soochow.

Are you attuned to the needs of the poor and needy in your city?

∼

God of mercy, show me today how to reach out to those in distress.

August 25: Your Experiences

"In everything, do to others what you would have them do to you, for this sums up the Law and the Prophets" (Matt. 7:12 NIV).

What experiences from your life could help you be a witness?

In Delores Garza's case, it's her childhood experiences that now help in her work as a United Methodist community developer in San Antonio, Texas. Her experiences as a needy, often hungry child shape her witness to others in the same situation today.

"I come from a dysfunctional family where there was a lot of neglect," Delores says. "We were hungry a lot of times and no one ever looked in on us."

When Delores sought spiritual counseling as an adult from a local minister, she found out about the Community Developers Program, an organization that empowers local neighborhoods. She saw in the program an opportunity to give back to her neighborhood.

Delores often talks to local congregations and challenges members by asking, "How can you say you understand hunger when you've never been hungry? There's always someone out there who is hungrier than you."

She encourages Christians to go into their communities and knock on doors to learn about people's needs. "If you've found the Lord, I don't care how many times they slam the door in your face, you just keep knocking."

She knows that a great difference could have been made if someone had knocked on her family's door when she was a child.

∼

Empower me, dear God, to knock on people's doors and on the doors of people's hearts.

August 26: God's Protection

"You are my hiding place; you will protect me from trouble and surround me with songs of deliverance" (Psalm 32:7 NIV).

"What! You are going after Afrikaner with a Bible instead of a gun? You must be mad," the old Boer woman exclaimed when she heard that the missionary was setting out for the home of a notorious outlaw.

Robert Moffat (1795–1883), though, was not to be deterred. Traveling north from Cape Town among several cannibalistic tribes, he set out to find Afrikaner, a barbarous chief. Robert not only found him and brought him back to Cape Town, he also led the man to Christ!

The burly, bearded Scot who endured incredible hardships during his 53 years in Africa is known as the father of South African missions. He was the father-in-law of David Livingstone, Africa's most famous missionary. In fact, Robert's words about having seen "the smoke of a thousand villages" where no missionary had ever been inspired David to go to Africa.

Representing the London Missionary Society, Robert departed for South Africa in 1816. Two years later he married Mary Smith who became his faithful partner. God's protecting hand was upon him as he opened up vast areas beyond the Zambezi River establishing churches as he went. As an educator, he introduced skills such as agriculture and carpentry. He also translated the entire Bible, many hymns, *Pilgrim's Progress*, and textbooks into the Bechuana language.

Have you thanked God today for His protection?

∽

Thank You, Lord, that You are "my hiding place."

August 27: Share Christ—Even in Danger

"My mouth will speak words of wisdom; the utterance from my heart will give understanding"(Psalm 49:3 NIV).

Yeni was part of the most disliked people group in Southeast Asia where Lisa and Ross O'Brien volunteered as English teachers. In the country's class system, Yeni and Lisa lived a world apart. "We were at the top, and they were at the bottom," Lisa says. "So why did we care about them?"

But Lisa and her family did care and befriended Yeni's family. They yearned also to teach them of Christ's love.

When Yeni and her husband's baby became sick, Ross took the baby to the doctor. He then asked if he could pray for her in Jesus' name, and they agreed. Several days later, the couple reported the baby was better and thanked them for the prayer. "In that country, God often uses signs and wonders to bring people to Christ," Lisa explains. "Some barriers were torn down that day."

A year later, when Lisa returned to the country and visited Yeni, she brought a wrapped Bible with her. "I was deep in a neighborhood full of radical Muslims with a Bible in my hand," she remembers. "Never had I felt so scared, excited, protected, and empowered at the same time." God gave Lisa the words to say, and she and three other women had a wonderful visit.

∽

You are so mighty and miraculous, my Redeemer. You give me the words to say and the protection I need when I need them the most.

August 28: Joy Is Strength

"The Lord is my strength and my shield; my heart trusts in him, and I am helped. My heart leaps for joy and I will give thanks to him in song" (Psalm 28:7 NIV).

"The joy of the Lord is our strength for service and testimony," he said. "It makes all our work easy and delightful. . . . It goes with the foreign missionary and the one who works all night in the heart of the slums."

A. B. (Albert Benjamin) Simpson (1844–1919) was a prodigious worker in many areas of Christian service. A native of Prince Edward Island, Canada, he served as a Presbyterian minister in Canada as well as Kentucky and New York. He was known as an outstanding preacher. Evangelist D. L. Moody once said of him: "No man gets to my heart like A. B. Simpson."

Concentrating much of his energy to missions, in 1887 he established the Evangelical Missionary Alliance which later became the Christian and Missionary Alliance. More than 350 missionaries had sailed to foreign countries by 1897.

He was responsible for the continent's first illustrated missionary periodical called *The Gospel in All Lands*. He established Missionary Training College (now Nyack College), which is North America's earliest surviving Bible college.

An author of over 70 books, he edited his denomination's *Alliance Weekly* and wrote 300 songs.

Do you have the kind of joy in your work that A. B. Simpson had?

∼

Help me, Lord, with joy claim You as the strength for my service.

August 29: Set Apart

"There was at Joppa a disciple named Tabitha, which means Dorcas.... She was full of good works and acts of charity" (Acts 9:36 RSV).

Carmen Camacho and her sister, Mercedes, rushed to the hospital—it was almost time for Carmen to give birth. As they drove, Mercedes felt a voice tell her that her niece should be named Dorcas. She ignored the voice, though, until the baby arrived. Then Mercedes exclaimed, "She really does look like a Dorcas!"

Carmen kept the name she had already selected, but when she talked later to her husband, who was serving in the military in Panama, he said that the other name must be God's will. His younger sister had died at 12 years old; her name was Dorcas.

As Dorcas grew, her family members stressed repeatedly that God loved her and had a plan for her. They often told her: "Dorcas, you are unique. Nobody looks like you, acts like you, is you. God loves you. He has a special plan just for you. Polish the good qualities He has given you."

Dorcas grew up to dedicate herself to missions and today serves with husband, Emerson Byrd, an MK (missionaries' kid) from Guatemala. She is the director of Houston's Baptist Missions Center, where 15 avenues of ministry reach out to broken lives with the love of Christ.

Do you believe that God has a special purpose for your life? Are you living up to that purpose?

Thank You for loving and calling me, O God.

August 30: God of All Generations

"One generation will commend your works to another, they will tell of your mighty acts" (Psalm 145:4 NIV).

She was called the Mother of a Thousand Daughters.

Eliza Agnew (1807–1883), a New York native, was only eight years old when she resolved to become a missionary. She arrived in Ceylon in 1839 to become a principal of a Presbyterian girls' boarding school. Called Mother by the girls, she ran the school at Oodooville for 41 years. She had the children and grandchildren of her first students and became known as the Mother of a Thousand Daughters.

Eliza had great success with her students. Author R. Pierce Beaver wrote: "The cumulative effect of her influence was unequaled in the pioneer period. In contrast to the schools for boys in Ceylon and India at the time, which had few converts, more than six hundred of Miss Agnew's pupils became Christians." After her girls graduated, Eliza continued to minister to them by visiting and encouraging them in their faith. Many of these girls became teachers in village schools. Others became the influential wives of teachers, preachers, doctors, lawyers, merchants, and farmers.

In the 43 years Eliza labored in Ceylon she never returned home.

Are you telling the next generation about the "mighty acts" of God?

∼

Lord, help me to realize that my children, grandchildren, and great-grandchildren need to know of Your faithfulness. May I share lovingly and humbly what You have done in my life and encourage them in their walk.

August 31: A Good Helpmate

"She brings him good, not harm, all the days of her life" (Prov. 31:12 NIV).

She is known as the second wife of Adoniram Judson.

Sarah Hall Boardman Judson (1803–1845) was also a missionary in her own right, a poet, and a dedicated wife and mother.

Ironically, Sarah's early life was intertwined with that of the Judsons. At the age of 13 she wrote a poem on the death of Ann Judson's 8-month-old son, Roger. When Ann visited New England, Sarah read one of her poems for Ann.

After Sarah married George Dana Boardman in 1825, they left to pioneer in Burma alongside the Judsons. Their work took them to Calcutta, Moulmein, and then Tavoy among the wild mountain tribe called Karens. Sarah established a girls' school there.

Two of their three children died before George died in 1831. She worked alone for three years ministering among the Karens.

Sarah and Adoniram were married on April 10, 1834. A tireless partner, she translated religious tracts into Burmese and wrote 20 hymns in Burmese. At her death she was translating *Pilgrim's Progress.*

Exhausted by having eight children in ten years, she died of dysentery on August 31, 1845, on the way to America. Her last words to Adoniram were, "I ever love the Lord Jesus." She was buried at St. Helena, an island off the African coast where Napoleon died.

Are you a dedicated helpmate?

∽

Loving Lord, help me to daily be a force for good to those around me.

September 1: Do You Believe?

"'He who believes in me will live, even though he dies; and whoever lives and believes in me will never die. Do you believe this?'" (John 11:25–26 NIV).

One of the greatest joys of the Christian life is sharing Christ with others. Asking someone, "Do you believe this?" can be incredibly rewarding.

Ellamae Elder, a Southern Baptist missionary in Cape Town, South Africa, says that reaching men, women, and children for Christ is the ultimate goal for her and other missionaries. She reaches this goal in many ways.

Through literacy classes, Ellamae finds joy in teaching adults to read for the first time in their lives. They then can read the Bible and learn about God in their own language.

Ellamae and her husband also mentor others in Bible study and have showed the *Jesus* film in their home to tell others the story of Christ's life and mission.

At a recent Franklin Graham crusade, Ellamae saw life-changing conversions. Many people came to know Christ that night. Ellamae personally counseled nine children who decided to trust in God. She now follows up with these children through mentoring relationships.

"It was really great to see thousands come to the Lord!" she exclaims about that experience.

What are you doing to reach out to others? What are you doing to ask them, "Do you believe this?"

Lord, reveal to me how I can reach others for You.

September 2: A Mission of Literacy

"'One thing I do know. I was blind but now I see'" (John 9:25 NIV).

"I have longed to read the Bible. You have taken away my blindness," a Guatemalan woman tearfully said to the Apostle to the Illiterates. The grateful woman was one of more than 100 million lives that Frank Laubach (1884–1970) reached through his literacy program.

Even though literate people may not consider the inability to read a type of "blindness," it is a major handicap to those who cannot read.

Sent by the Congregationalists' American Board of Commissioners for Foreign Missions, Frank and Effa Laubach went to the Philippines in 1915. In 1929 Frank set up a program to teach the illiterate Muslim Moros of Mindanao to read by phonetic symbols and pictures. Effa promoted literacy among the Moro women. Frank's method, Each One Teach One, involved a nonreader who learned to read teaching another nonreader to read. Known as the Laubach Method, it was imitated internationally. At his death on June 11, 1970, Frank had taken his ministry to 103 countries and had developed literacy primers in 313 languages.

Motivated by his love of Christ and sustained by fervent prayer, Frank Laubach brought millions to knowledge of God through his visionary literacy work. This month is National Literacy Month. Millions still can't read the Bible. Is God calling you to contribute your time or money to literacy education?

∼

Reveal to me today, dear Lord, how I can help those blinded by their circumstances.

September 3: Learning About Jesus

"'Heaven and earth will pass away, but my words will never pass away'" (Mark 13:31 NIV).

The story of Jesus' birth. Jonah and the whale. Noah's ark. The feeding of the 5,000.

The words of the Bible live on in the lives of Cambodian children who learned of Jesus through a special literacy program. The Cambodian Adult Literacy Program teaches reading skills through a curriculum based on such familiar Bible stories.

The program—a cooperative effort of several internatinal agencies—has seen outstanding results. Of 4,000 Cambodian children involved in 176 rural classes, about half have accepted the truth of the Bible stories and made commitments to Christ.

Three reading primers teach how to speak the Khmer language, and volunteer teachers lead the classes.

Literacy programs are important in Cambodia, where 40 percent of rural Cambodians and 15 percent of city dwellers can't read.

We who can read often take the act of reading the Bible for granted. Yet millions of people around the world can't read. And how else can people learn the truth of the Bible for themselves if they can't read it? A program teaching children how to read Bible stories is a wonderful starting point.

Do you take your reading ability for granted? Can you work in a literacy program?

Thank You, Lord, for dedicated teachers who are giving young children the new skill of reading.

September 4: A Faithful Servant

"And what you have heard from me before many witnesses entrust to faithful men who will be able to teach others also" (2 Tim. 2:2 RSV).

It was said of him after his death: "His faith was the greatest thing about him."

Charles Kelsey Dozier (1879–1933), a native of LaGrange, Georgia, displayed faith early in life. When his father lost his hardware business, higher education seemed out of reach. "I did not know where the money would come from for my education," Charles later said, "but I did believe in God and was willing to commit my life into his hands." Through his working and help from an aunt and a brother, Charles graduated from Mercer University and Southern Baptist Theological Seminary.

On September 4, 1906, Charles and his new bride, Maude, left for Japan where they served for 27 years. Charles taught at the new Baptist seminary in Fukuoka and served as a principal at a night school there. It became the largest missionary-operated night school in Japan. On April 11, 1916, he opened a successful day school for boys, Seinan Gakuin, which he led for 13 years. Pastor of the Seinan Gakuin Baptist Church, he also was an evangelist for years.

On his tombstone is written the last message that Charles sent to his beloved school, "Seinan yo Kirisuro ni chujitsu nare" (Seinan, be true to Christ).

Would you like to be known for your faith?

∼

Lord, enable me to be Your faithful servant.

September 5: New School Year

"The only thing that counts is faith expressing itself through love" (Gal. 5:6 NIV).

How can you lovingly and practically demonstrate your Christian faith to others?

For a group of women in East St. Louis, Illinois, the answer was to reach out to needy schoolchildren in their community.

As the beginning of the school year approached in their city, a group of women representing the area's WMU organization realized that many school children wouldn't be able to buy their necessary back-to-school supplies. They decided to organize the WMU Back-to-School Event at the East St. Louis Christian Activity Center to do something about it.

Women collected notebooks, paper, pencils, and other school supplies in addition to underwear, socks, and other clothing from area churches. The items went into special back-to-school kits, which were then distributed to 520 children and youth. The involved women say that the parents were very appreciative and were surprised at the number of items their children received.

Michelle Cantrell, wife of center director Chet Cantrell, says that such outreach activities show how Christians can live their faith in practical ways. "The women talk of what a blessing it was to share time together," she says.

∼

Help me remember, Lord, that there are many children in my community who aren't blessed with material things. Give me eyes to see them as You see them.

September 6: A Gift of Leadership

"We have different gifts according to the grace given us.... If it is leadership, let him govern diligently" (Rom. 12:6,8 NIV).

"Judged by any standard, M. Theron Rankin was a great man—one of the greatest of his generation."

"Baker James Cauthen will go down in Baptist history as one of its truly great giants."

These were descriptions of two executive directors of the Southern Baptist Foreign Mission Board (now International Mission Board). Both were foreign missionaries in China before becoming visionary administrators.

Theron became a missionary teacher in China in 1921 and later president of Graves Theological Seminary in Canton. Married to missionary teacher Valleria Greene, he became the FMB's secretary for the Orient in 1935. During World War II the Japanese imprisoned him for nine months. During his tenure (1945–1953) as FMB executive director, missionaries increased from 500 to 913 in 32 countries.

Baker James and his wife, Eloise, became missionaries in 1939 in China. On the eve of the Japanese invasion, they were in language school in Peking when they were forced to leave. They continued their ministry at Kweilin in Free China until forced out again by the Japanese army. In 1954 Baker James became FMB's secretary for the Orient. In his tenure (1954–1979) as FMB executive director, 908 missionaries in 33 countries increased to more than 3,000 in 95 entities.

Is leadership one of your spiritual gifts?

~

Eternal God, give our leaders a vision for the future that will take the gospel into unreached areas.

September 7: Teaching in Faith

"Hold on to instruction; do not let it go; guard it well, for it is your life" (Prov. 4:13 NIV).

Teaching Christian concepts in Latvia and other countries of the former Soviet Union is challenging and sometimes frustrating. Prayer, though, has helped break through the challenges for one missionary.

Gail Smith, a missionary with Campus Crusade for Christ International's CoMission II project, recently met a teacher reaching out to her students with both instruction and prayer.

In the town of Riga, where the woman teaches at a public school, teachers stay with the same group of students throughout their elementary years. The teacher had earnestly prayed three years earlier for the class to be one she could reach for Christ.

She lost several students in the second grade when their parents became suspicious of the religious instruction. The parents moved the children to a different elective class.

The rest of the students? All 17 of them have become Christians and are learning to grow in their faith.

The teacher continues to pray daily for the students, knowing that none of their parents are believers and that they will face many obstacles at home.

Do you feel led to teach children in some capacity? How can you reach children in local schools for Christ?

∽

Dear Lord, empower Christian teachers as they reach out to children in Your name.

September 8: A Virtuous Example

"Many daughters have done virtuously, but thou excellest them all" (Prov. 31:29 KJV).

Did you know that the first American woman to reach China was a Baptist missionary?

Henrietta Hall Shuck (1817–1844) was born in Kilmarnock, Virginia. In 1831 while she was away at school at Fredericksburg, a camp meeting was held near her home. Her father, Rev. Addison Hall, sent for his daughter to return home and attend the revival meetings. As a result, she became a Christian and was baptized on September 2, 1831.

Four years later she met missionary J. Lewis Shuck. They were married on September 8, 1835, in Richmond. They sailed on September 22 for China.

Arriving in Macao, they worked there until 1842 and then moved to Hong Kong. Henrietta's health began to deteriorate, and when she died on November 27, 1844, she left five children. She was buried in Hong Kong's Happy Valley Cemetery.

During her nine years in China she assisted her husband in starting the first evangelical church there. In Hong Kong she organized the first Western-style education for females in China. Today the Baptist-supported Henrietta School of Hong Kong is a tribute to her work.

A minister friend who labored with the Shucks sheds more light on her character: "Her house was ever open to the stranger, and her heart ever sympathized with the needy and afflicted, and her hands were diligently employed in acts of kindness and charity."

Holy God, thank You for virtuous lives that serve as our examples today.

September 9: Fast for Children

"If one of you says to him, 'Go, I wish you well; keep warm and well fed,' but does nothing about his physical needs, what good is it?'" (James 2:16 NIV).

"It really helped me appreciate what I have and made me realize that a lot of children don't have food."

"I didn't think I could do it, but God was there for me and helped me."

These are a couple of the things teenagers had to say about being involved in the 24 Hour Fast, an outreach project sponsored by Just Jesus Ministries. The teenagers commit to go without food for 24 hours to raise awareness about hungry children in the United States. The youth ask for monetary donations if they complete the daylong fast. When they approach sponsors, they say something like: "There are thousands of children who go hungry each night in America, and I am so serious about wanting to help them that I am going to go without eating for 24 hours to raise money to do it."

Ninety percent of the money raised goes directly to hungry children, with just 10 percent remaining with Just Jesus Ministries.

According to Johnny Walker, the director of Just Jesus Ministries, the fast is just one of many ways the group challenges the teens to put their faith into action.

Are you serious enough about the hungry that you would fast?

∾

Give me a heart, loving God, to help the hungry children.

September 10: Reaching the Destitute

"Give justice to the weak and the fatherless; maintain the right of the afflicted and the destitute" (Psalm 82:3 RSV).

When he opened his children's home, he limited it to 25 boys because of lack of funds. One day he refused a boy called Carrots. A few days later the boy was found dead because of "frequent exposure and want of food."

Blaming himself for the tragedy, Thomas Barnardo (1845–1905) decided that he would never again refuse a destitute child. His motto became No Destitute Child Ever Refused Admission.

Born in Dublin, he became a Christian as a teenager and worked for four years among the poor. In 1866 he went to London to train to become a doctor for the China Inland Mission. He registered as a medical student at London Hospital and was soon drawn to helping the poor instead of going to China.

In 1867 he founded the East End Juvenile Mission which expanded into Dr. Barnardo's Homes. His wife and helpmate, Syrie, formed a nursing organization to help the needy. After receiving his degree as a surgeon, Thomas opened a hospital.

He also provided centers for working men, a boarding-out system, and an emigration plan where boys and girls were sent to Canada for settlement. Rescuing and training almost 60,000 children and aiding about 250,000, he died of sheer exhaustion.

What can you do to help the destitute?

Lord, show me how to help those who don't have food, clothing, and shelter.

September 11: House Raid

"Although the Lord gives you the bread of adversity and the water of affliction, your teachers will be hidden no more; with your own eyes you will see them" (Isa. 30:20 NIV).

"This is a raid!" Security officers tore through his home as Brother Q. (not his real name), his wife, his son, and his mother sat quietly on their living room sofa. In searching for Christian literature, the guards pulled down furniture, opened drawers, and looked under mattresses.

Brother Q. watched with a heavy heart. "Not far from me were two boxes filled with Christian books printed inside China. Christian literature that came from outside the country was one thing. But I knew authorities would treat us far more severely if they ever discovered Christian books printed inside China."

Moments later, the guards approached the box. They walked around it, but didn't look inside it. Brother Q. says it was as if they didn't even see the box!

Brother Q. became a Christian when elderly pastors who had been imprisoned under Communist rule were released. He was mentored by the pastors and found inspiration in the above words from Isaiah. Today, he leads more than 2,000 house churches with 125,000 Christian believers in 11 Chinese provinces. Partners International, an organization that works with indigenous missionaries and leaders in 50 different countries, aids him in his work.

Former Partners International president Chuck Bennett says that he has never met a Christian with a "keener mind or greater vision."

What is your vision for reaching others for Christ?

Give me a vision, Lord, of how I can reach others for You.

September 12: Hungry No More

"Then Jesus declared, 'I am the bread of life. He who comes to me will never go hungry, and he who believes in me will never be thirsty'" (John 6:35 NIV).

When you think of missions groups, what type of work comes to your mind first? You may think of groups of people building houses or teaching Vacation Bible School to children, but the first image many people have is of Christians helping hungry people. Hunger has always been, and continues to be, a mainstay of Christian missions work.

Drive through your community and you will probably see evidences of this. Churches have food banks where hungry people can come and get free food. Churches and organizations operate soup kitchens where people come and eat free meals. Meals on Wheels programs take food to the elderly and disabled.

National and international missions-oriented organizations also reach out to the hungry. World Vision, an international Christian group, educates people to the needs of the poor and hungry all around the world. Through its child sponsorship program, individuals can help children with basic needs like shelter, education, and food. Bread for the World members lobby their senators and representatives to meet the needs of the hungry and address the root causes of hunger and poverty.

September is Hunger Awareness Month. How can you make a difference in the lives of the hungry?

Gracious God, give me empathy for the hungry men, women, and children of my community and the larger world today.

September 13: A Top Ten List for Poor Children

"Faith ... if ... not accompanied by action, is dead" (James 2:17 NIV).

The world's poor children will have a future in this century—if Christians act on their faith and do something about it.

Richard Stearns, the president of World Vision in the US, says that poor children have many problems, but many of those problems can be solved.

World Vision, an international Christian relief organization working to beat hunger and poverty, says ten things can change the lives of impoverished children around the world: (1) a livable income (more than half of the world's population live on less than $2 per day); (2) food for everyone (malnutrition affects four of every ten children); (3) primary education for children (more than 130 million children have no schooling); (4) clean water (contaminated water claims the lives of 5 million children each year); (5) debt relief (debt repayment takes the place of children's immunizations, schooling, and proper nutrition); (6) peace building (4 million people were killed in the 1990s in more than 100 wars and conflicts); (7) girls as equals (girls are more likely to be aborted, abandoned, and neglected); (8) a sustainable future (environmental destruction happens more in poor areas); (9) end to child exploitation (more than 250 million children work so their families can eat); and (10) freedom to believe (intolerance has fueled many wars).

Which of these ten things can you work to achieve?

∽

Bless the world's poor children, Lord, and let me work to help them.

September 14: Good Work

"Comfort your hearts and establish them in every good work and word" (2 Thess. 2:17 RSV).

"Will not someone come and help in this good work?" she wrote from her mission station in the Congo.

Lillian May Thomas DeYampert (1872–1930) was a missionary educator in Africa for 21 years. She helped start the Luebo day school which educated thousands. In 1903, when Lillian asked for someone to join her in the "good work," only three instructors were teaching almost 250 students.

Lillian was born on September 14, 1872, in Mobile, Alabama. While attending Talladega College, she responded to a call for missionaries to the Congo. She sailed to Africa with four other missionaries on May 26, 1894. She and two of the other women were the first female black missionaries the Southern Presbyterian Church sent to the Congo.

Lillian wrote many articles focusing on educational needs in the *Kassai Herald*, the journal of the American Presbyterian Congo Mission. Referring to her first year in Luebo, she said, "We had no books, charts, black-boards or anything to teach with."

In 1915 she and missionary husband, Lucius A. DeYampert, whom she had married in 1908, went home on furlough. Because of poor health, she was not able to return to Africa. She and her husband retired to Selma, Alabama.

Are you attentive to those who ask for help in doing God's work?

~

God, open my heart to respond to genuine needs around the world.

September 15: Starving Christians

"Each of you should look not only to your own interests, but also to the interests of others" (Phil. 2:4 NIV).

The ABC late-night show *Nightline* explained the sad situation in the Sudan this way: "The less we have in common with the victims of tragedy, the more distant that tragedy is, the further down our own list of priorities it falls. By all of those standards, famine in Sudan is a long way off."

Fifteen years of civil wars and years of drought had left Sudan in a state of disaster by 1999, when that broadcast was aired. More than 2.5 million people were at risk of starvation. Thousands died each day.

In any other situation, the words from the television show would ring true. The irony of this situation, though, is that we have much in common with the starving Sudanese. The Christian church is rapidly growing in Sudan. The men, women, and children there are our brothers and sisters.

World Relief, an ecumenical Christian relief agency, puts it like this: "These are not simply suffering people in a far-off land; these are our brothers and sisters in Christ—part of one of the fastest growing churches in the world, alive with the Spirit, rejoicing in their salvation. Yet, they cannot survive in isolation."

Do you identify only with the Christians in your own church, community, or nation? We must remember that we have brothers and sisters in Christ in all corners of the world.

∽

Unite us together, O God, in our common beliefs.

September 16: A Sacred Holiday?

"I hate, I despise your religious feasts; I cannot stand your assemblies" (Amos 5:21 NIV).

In September Ethiopians celebrate one of their most sacred holidays. The Meskel holiday is based on the legend that the Queen of Ethiopia found Christ's cross and brought it back to her homeland. Ethiopians, and in particular the 250,000 members of the Ethiopian Orthodox Church, gather together and celebrate the legendary return of the Cross.

Karen Simons and ten other team members from Houston, Texas, witnessed the holiday firsthand in the capital of Addis Ababa. They went to Ethiopia to develop a possible partnership between the city and their 500-church Baptist association. While there, they also participated in evangelistic efforts.

Karen says there was real irony in the Meskel celebration. The people celebrate the holiday with religious fervor; yet, there is no connection to what the Cross truly means. "The celebration focuses solely on the Cross as an icon, not Christ," she explains.

David Emmert, another member of the team, agrees: "It was like watching a 600-foot foul ball. It's very impressive, but it doesn't really count."

As Karen watched the two-and-a-half-hour celebration conclude with the final act of setting a two-story high tower of sticks and flowers ablaze, she prayed: "May the light of the gospel spread as quickly across this land."

Do you sometimes participate in superficial rituals of faith?

∼

Remind me today, Lord, that You don't desire my rituals. I want to worship You in a true, loving, faithful manner.

September 17: Abounding in God's Work

"And God is able to make all grace abound to you, so that in all things at all times, having all that you need, you will abound in every good work" (2 Cor. 9:8 NIV).

"Miss Bertha was a woman who truly loved the Lord, and sought to become all that God intended her to be in this life. She spent hours in daily Bible study and prayer. She practiced meeting with God before meeting with men," said a minister friend.

One of her favorite verses was 2 Corinthians 9:8. Certainly, she did "abound" in her work for God.

Bertha Smith (1888–1988), known all over the world as Miss Bertha, led countless people to Christ. A Southern Baptist missionary for 41 years in China and Taiwan, she returned home to an active ministry for almost 30 years.

The native of Cowpens, South Carolina, arrived in China on September 17, 1917. She labored in Shantung Province primarily as a Bible teacher and conference leader. She was actively involved in the Shantung Revival where many conversions took place.

Expelled by the Communists in 1948, she relocated on Formosa (now known as Taiwan) as the first Southern Baptist missionary. She led Bible classes, held conferences, and taught at the Taiwan Baptist Theological Seminary.

Returning in 1959 to Cowpens, she established the Penial Prayer Center. She led prayer retreats and Christian life conferences around the world.

Are you seeking to know God better?

∼

Faithful God, give me a passion for Bible study and a deeper prayer life.

September 18: Breaking the Cycle

"For God is not a God of disorder but of peace" (1 Cor. 14:33 NIV).

An act of domestic violence occurs, on average, every 15 seconds in the United States. More than 2.5 million individuals are victims of domestic violence every year in America. Domestic violence is believed to be the leading cause of injury of women between the ages of 15 and 44.

For Margaret Allen, a Southern Baptist missionary and director of the South Richmond Baptist Center in Richmond, Virginia, these sobering statistics are a sad reality. Margaret deals almost daily with women, teenagers, and children who are the victims of violence, from women whose boyfriends beat them, disfiguring their faces; to teenaged girls whose boyfriends mentally abuse them; to preschoolers whose mothers are in jail for violent acts.

The needs in such cases often seem overwhelming. Violence is bred in many of the young people's lives and if it is not dealt with, the cycle of violence will repeat.

"Many of their [preschoolers] family members are involved in violence," Margaret says. "They see police arresting uncle and brothers and they have to deal with it."

Margaret yearns for prayers for all of the people caught in such desperate circumstances (victims and offenders) and for herself, as she tries to bring peace and healing.

This month is Domestic Violence Month and draws attention to the plight of those who are abused.

How can you bring peace to disorderly, violent situations?

∼

Loving God, thank You for the peace and restoration You bring to lives.

September 19: Counted Worthy

"They will walk with me, dressed in white, for they are worthy" (Rev. 3:4 NIV).

One day a missionary came to the Mount Holyoke seminary to find a teacher for a girls school. Fidelia Fiske (1816–1864) answered the call by saying, "If counted worthy, I shall be willing to go."

When Fidelia went to Persia (now Iran) in 1843 to become the director of a female boarding seminary, she found the government intolerant and parents unwilling to educate their daughters. Writing home to a friend, Eliza said that the first foreign word she learned was *daughter,* and the next was *give.* She went to the people saying, "Give me your daughters."

Since it was a disgrace in that culture for women to know how to read, Fidelia at first found it difficult to get students, but they gradually began to come. Fidelia and her teachers taught the Bible three hours a day and required students to memorize a lot of Scriptures. Through their prayer and hard work, their students began to make progress.

Beginning in 1846, the first of many revivals broke out in the school. Many of the students became Christians. District women's assemblies were organized that took the work far beyond the school.

Fidelia had certainly been found worthy. Worn out after 15 years, she returned to her childhood home in Shelburne, Massachusetts, where she died. She was only 48 years old.

Will you be found a worthy servant?

Today, Lord, send me where I am needed.

September 20: Tough Questions

"'What I tell you in the dark, speak in the daylight; what is whispered in your ear, proclaim from the roofs'" (Matt. 10:27 NIV).

Answering questions about our faith is sometimes difficult.

What if, though, your work, future, or life depended on the way you answered?

A missionary who works in the Russian Federation as an English teacher, Maureen (not her real name) must be careful about how she talks about her work and faith. She cannot openly say she is a missionary.

One day at school a fellow teacher began asking Maureen questions about her life. Do you have another job? What you do when you're not in school? Do you meet with groups in your home? What do you study?

Maureen wanted to tell her that she taught Bible studies and would love for the woman to join her, but she couldn't. "I naturally sidestepped those questions, thinking some authority had put her up to asking them," she says. "Then about five minutes later, she finally tells me that the reason for the questions is that she's met an old friend who studies in our group and she simply wants to come and study the Bible with us also."

Maureen's suspicions kept her from being open. She says she's glad a friend of hers is right in saying, "God is much bigger than my attempts at being cautious."

~

Dear God, when I am in situations where it is difficult to share my faith, give me courage and creativity to find ways to do so.

September 21: Strength Through Christ

"I can do everything through him who gives me strength" (Phil. 4:13 NIV).

She formed her own women's missionary society based on the words of Philippians 4:13.

Frances Xavier Cabrini (1850–1917) was the first American citizen canonized by the Roman Catholic Church.

Born in Lombardy, Italy, she trained as a teacher. She wanted to become a missionary in China but was denied the opportunity because she had not completely recovered from contracting smallpox. In 1880, three years after taking her vows, she and seven orphan girls founded the Missionary Sisters of the Sacred Heart.

Because of her success, Pope Leo XIII sent her and six sisters to New York City in 1889 to work among the many Italian immigrants there. She soon founded orphanages, schools, training centers, and hospitals in cities across the United States and in other countries. Traveling widely, she established 67 houses—1 representing each year of her life.

In 1909 she became a citizen of the United States. Canonized in 1950, Pope Pius XII later named her patron saint of immigrants.

She frequently inspired her nuns to accomplish the impossible. "Nothing is ever to daunt you. . . . None of us will fail if we leave everything in the hands of God," she said. "Under Him the question of possible and impossible ceases to have any meaning."

Have you incorporated Philippians 4:13 into your life?

~

God, thank You that I can rely on Your strength—because without You, I am weak.

September 22: Commitment of Self

"Commit your work to the Lord" (Prov. 16:3 RSV).

When the Triennial Convention of Baptists met in 1835, a seminary student was in the audience. After a stirring missionary speech, the offering plate was passed. He placed a piece of paper in the plate on which he had written, "I give myself."

J. Lewis Shuck "gave" himself to both home and foreign missions.

Ordained on August 30, 1835, he married Henrietta Hall on September 8. On September 22 they sailed for China, becoming the first Baptist missionaries to China. Working in Macao, Lewis baptized his first convert in 1837. They moved to Hong Kong in 1842 and the next year formed the first Baptist church in China.

After Henrietta's death, Lewis returned to America with his five children and a young Chinese convert, Yong Seen Srang, who attracted crowds of admirers everywhere. When they visited Judson College in Marion, Alabama, the students contributed more than $500 to the China fund.

Returning to China representing the newly formed Southern Baptist Convention, Lewis and Yong established the first Baptist church in Shanghai in 1847 with Lewis serving as its pastor. When his second wife died in 1851, he went back to America.

Appointed by the SBC's Home Mission Board (now North American Mission Board) in 1854, he founded the first Chinese Baptist church in America in Sacramento and a black Baptist church. He later returned to China with his third wife.

Have you found your place of service?

Dear God, empower me daily to give myself to Your work.

SEPTEMBER 23: RELIGIOUS FREEDOM?

"Now the Lord is the spirit, and where the Spirit of the Lord is, there is freedom" (2 Cor. 3:17 NIV).

What is life like for Christians in post-Communist Russia?

You might be surprised to discover that many Christians face persecution in the former Soviet Union. While the trappings of democracy have slowly begun to appear in the country, religious freedom has not.

That denial of freedom—primarily in the form of the On Freedom of Conscience and Religious Associations (FCRA) law—now threatens to force many missionaries from their work. It also makes it harder for the private citizen to openly worship Christ.

The FCRA law prohibits any religious group from practicing its religion unless it is registered with the Russian government. To register, the church must prove that it has been organized for 15 years or more. Since most churches kept their existence a secret for years, that is a hard thing to prove. The law encourages worship at the Russian Orthodox Church. It works against most Protestant and Catholic congregations. It even keeps groups like the Salvation Army from working effectively in the country.

In 1999, Dan Pollard, an American independent Baptist missionary, was expelled from Russia because of problems stemming from this law.

Sergei Nikolaev, the president of the St. Petersburg Theological Seminary, says: "We did not have this type of discrimination even in the confines of Communism."

∼

Blessed Lord, I pray today for the health and growth of Christian churches in Russia. Give Christians there strength and courage.

September 24: Prayers and Persecution

"'Bless those who curse you, pray for those who mistreat you'" (Luke 6:28 NIV).

Paula Eddins, a Southern Baptist missionary in Sri Lanka, is a pray-er. She knows firsthand that prayer truly makes a difference!

In a small Sri Lankan village at a viewing of the *Jesus* film—a movie used as an evangelization tool throughout the world—a group of angry spectators began throwing rocks and sticks. A fight ensued, and one woman, seriously injured, was rushed to the hospital. After the incident, Paula and other Christians were told they could never return to the village.

Paula felt her heart collapse. They had to have more opportunities to reach these villagers for Christ.

Her response? She and other missionaries asked Christians in America to pray.

She is pleased now to report that "God has protected us and others, and we are now back in the village doing a weekly children's Bible study."

This response to the Christian film shows the resistance to the gospel in Sri Lanka, an island nation near India. Paula says that the people there are slow to respond to Christianity, and she often feels impatient because of that. Her love for the people, though, outweighs any impatience she may feel.

"God has given me a love for the people of Sri Lanka and a passion to tell them the good news," she says.

Have you ever battled persecution with prayer?

Prince of Peace, thank You for listening to our prayers and for answering them.

September 25: Laboring Out of Love

"I have known hunger and thirst and have often gone without food; I have been cold and naked. . . . I face daily the pressure of my concern for all the churches. . . . If I must boast, I will boast of the things that show my weakness" (2 Cor. 11:27,28,30 NIV).

He started a Baptist college, a publication society, and the first Baptist weekly newspaper. Luther Rice (1783–1836) helped to create a denomination out of scattered churches, one that would become the world's largest missionary denomination.

Hailed as a man of great virtues, Luther Rice's critics complained of his great faults. His visions were vast, and he was criticized for attempting things too fast. Immensely popular, his detractors said that his wit in preaching was unbecoming. Hostesses expressed amazement at the number of cups of tea and coffee he could drink at one sitting. He once drank 16 cups of tea.

Luther had a dream of a great Baptist university. In 1821 Columbian College opened in Washington, D.C. It was a financial failure, and he spent the rest of his life trying to save it. Eventually Congress bailed out the school. Its name was changed to George Washington University.

Exhausted, he died in September 25, 1836. To the last he labored for his dear college. On his deathbed he instructed that his beloved horse Columbus and his carriage be sold and proceeds be given to the college.

Do you work wholeheartedly for God?

~

Dear Lord, give me a longing to sacrifice for Your church.

September 26: The Persecuted Church

"Remember the words I spoke to you: "No servant is greater than his master." If they persecuted me, they will persecute you also" (John 15:20 NIV).

Persecution is a common experience for Christians in many parts of the world.

In 1999 Christians and American lawmakers focused on Sudan, one of the most repressive regimes in the world to people of many different religious beliefs. November 14 served as the official day of prayer.

The Khartoum regime and the Sudanese Peoples Liberation Army have warred since the late 1980s. Their civil war has caused famine, death, and destruction for millions of Sudanese.

Actions by the regime against the church include regular raids of Christian villages. Soldiers also are known to kidnap women and children to sell them into slavery; burn crops and kill livestock; and conduct bombing campaigns, sometimes with hospitals as the targets.

War-related causes were responsible for 1.9 million deaths in the 1990s, and 100,000 died of starvation in 1998 because of the regime's refusal to deliver food to its own people.

Christians and missionaries in this environment face an uncertain future and the reality of persecution and death every day.

Can you even imagine the kind of persecution Sudanese Christians undergo?

∼

Our Lord, You tell us that we will be persecuted if we are Christians. Give me the kind of faith that could survive harsh persecution.

September 27: Giving Testimony

"And this is the testimony: God has given us eternal life, and this life is in his Son" (1 John 5:11 NIV).

"I bore my testimony for the Lord before the King unto whom I was sent, and he was very noble unto me."

Mary Fisher (1623–1698), a Quaker missionary, walked alone from the southern coast of Greece almost 600 dangerous miles to Turkey for an audience with the sultan. Warmly received by him, she gave her testimony about Christ. Although no visible results resulted from her 1657 trip, her witness inspired Christians everywhere.

Before her pilgrimage to Turkey, Mary had braved many hardships. She had been imprisoned twice in her native York, England, for speaking to her village priest about the Quaker doctrine. She and another woman took their message to students at Sidney Sussex College. After complaints about their teaching, they were unmercifully stripped to the waist and savagely flogged.

In 1656 she and a woman companion traveled to Boston. In order to prevent the Quaker doctrine from being introduced, authorities burned their books and imprisoned them. Mary was finally able to get back to England.

After 12 years of teaching and persecution, she married a Quaker minister and was happily married 40 years, raising three children. She worked until her death in Charleston, South Carolina, in women's work among Quakers.

Are you willing to go anywhere to give your testimony?

Faithful God, give me courage to daily testify of Your salvation and love.

September 28: War and Fear

"If we live, we live to the Lord; and if we die, we die to the Lord. So, whether we live or die, we belong to the Lord" (Rom. 14:8 NIV).

Shirley and Maurice Randall gathered with their pastor and his wife to pray and wait. Their good friend, Archie Dunaway, a fellow Southern Baptist missionary, was missing. They feared the worst.

The next morning, news came that Archie had been stabbed and beaten to death. Shirley remembers that morning well: "There was a feeling of fear so strong you could almost touch it." Then, however, she remembered the above verse from Romans that she and Archie had shared just days before. She suddenly understood how close they all stood to heaven, and she felt, amidst the fear, a sense of peace.

Shirley and her husband had ample reason for fear: 21 missionaries and their children were killed in Rhodesia in June 1978, the same month Archie died. Rhodesia's war for independence brought government soldiers and rebel forces into their village almost daily.

After Archie's death, they wondered if they should stay. Prayer and the support of their children told them they should. They continued working in the hospital treating gunshot wounds and other injuries.

Today, Rhodesia is called Zimbabwe, and the war is over. Shirley says, though, that different battles wage. The hospital, for example, is flooded with AIDS patients.

Could you survive in such a fearful situation? Would your faith grow or falter?

~

Dear God, give me strength always, even in fearful circumstances.

September 29: In Their Own Language

"And we all hear these men telling in our own languages about the mighty miracles of God!" (Acts 2:11 TLB).

A Cakchiquel Indian challenged him: "If your God is so great, why doesn't He speak in my language?"

William Cameron Townsend (1896–1982) was serving as a missionary to the Cakchiquels in Guatemala when he caught the vision for Bible translation.

He and his wife, Elvira, worked among the tribe for ten years. They learned their language, reduced it to writing, and translated the New Testament in 1931.

Taking the name of John Wycliffe, who was the first to translate the Bible into English, Cameron founded Camp Wycliffe in 1934 as a linguistics training school for missionaries. Two students came the first year to a farm in Sulphur Springs, Arkansas, and five people the second year.

By 1942 "Camp Wycliffe" had grown into Wycliffe Bible Translators—the largest independent Protestant missions agency in the world—and the Summer Institute of Linguistics.

The first translation by Wycliffe personnel was completed in 1951 in the San Miguel Mixtec language of Mexico. Today over 400 translations exist, and hundreds more are in process.

The inscription on Cameron's burial stone in North Carolina is a fitting one to a great innovator: "Dear Ones: By love serve one another. Finish the task. Translate the Scriptures into every language. Uncle Cam."

This month calls attention to Bible translation. Did you know that 2,000 people groups still do not have the Bible in their languages?

~

Our Lord, today help Bible translators in their tedious task.

September 30: Trusting in God's Strength

"He gives strength to the weary and increases the power of the weak" (Isa. 40:29 NIV).

After a paralyzing illness, he still managed to translate the Bible.

Born into an orthodox Jewish family in Lithuania, Samuel Schereschewsky (1831–1906) studied at the University of Breslau. He was converted to Christianity through reading a New Testament that had been translated into Hebrew by the Black Jews of India. He sailed to America and studied at the General Theological Seminary in New York. While at the seminary, he decided to become a missionary and translate the Bible into Chinese.

After his ordination, he left for China. He spent 16 years translating the Bible and the Anglican Book of Common Prayer into the Mandarin language. He was named bishop of the Episcopal Church in Shanghai. In 1881 he was smitten with a paralyzing disease. He resigned the episcopate and spent his last years translating the Old and New Testament into the colloquial speech of China. Unable to use a pen and able to use only one finger of each hand, he typed the entire Bible, experiencing pain with each stroke of the keys. He completed the arduous task in 1902. Countless numbers of Chinese have been introduced to Christ through his translation.

Are you attempting to do the impossible trusting in your strength instead of God's strength?

Today, Lord, help me to rely on Your strength alone. Give me a task that You can accomplish through me.

October 1: A Vision for Missions

"'Therefore go and make disciples of all nations, baptizing them in the name of the Father and of the Son and of the Holy Spirit, and teaching them to obey everything I have commanded you'" (Matt. 28:19 NIV).

Fourteen people met at the home of one of his church members, widow Mrs. Beeby Wallis, on October 2, 1792. After prayer and discussion, the group founded a Baptist society for spreading the gospel.

Andrew Fuller (1754–1815), known as the founding father of the Baptist Missionary Society, was its secretary for 22 years and led in fund-raising and planning for the society.

With no formal training in theology, Fuller is considered by many to be the greatest theologian English Baptists ever produced.

A native of Wicken, Cambridgeshire, he joined the Soham Baptist church at the age of 16 and became its minister 5 years later. In 1783 he became the pastor of Kettering Baptist Church which he led until his death. In 1785 he published *The Gospel Worthy of All Acceptance,* an influential book which made possible the missionary movement embodied in William Carey, the first missionary sent out by the Baptist Missionary Society.

A broad-shouldered man over six feet tall, Andrew was a wrestler in his youth. Self-taught, he was a thinker of great depth and power who wisely used his incredible energy.

Are you using your energy and intellect to help carry out the Great Commission?

Heavenly God, today give me a vision to share the gospel.

October 2: Reaching Christian Athletes

"For physical training is of some value, but godliness has value for all things, holding promise for both the present life and the life to come" (1 Tim. 4:8 NIV).

Sharon, a record-setting sprinter and hurdler who dreamed of the Olympics, faced an injury that left her despondent and threatened to end her athletic career. Contemplating suicide, she realized she needed Christ.

John, a college football player, looked at his line of injuries (he'd just had his fifth surgery) and realized he needed God in his life.

Today, these two athletes—the now-married Sharon and John Williamson—serve as Assemblies of God home missionaries with Chi Alpha Athletic Ministries. Their experiences as athletes at the University of Arkansas help them identify with the athletes they try to reach for Christ.

"God has given us a passionate burden for the college athletes of the world," John says. "They have been given talent by God and a platform by man."

Each fall, they travel to different Chi Alpha campus ministries around the nation. Each spring, they help plan the annual Athletes International Ministries conference. Speakers in the past have included such high-profile athletes and coaches as David Robinson, Deion Sanders, and the late Tom Landry.

"Our hearts' desire," they say, "is to see our athletes give Christ the glory."

Can you encourage any Christian athletes?

∽

I praise You, Lord, for bestowing physical ability upon us. Help us use it for Your glory.

October 3: Obeying the Teachings of Christ

"Jesus replied, 'If anyone loves me, he will obey my teaching'" (John 14: 23 NIV).

"I have done my duty; may Christ now teach you yours."

These were the last words of Francis of Assisi (1181–1226) before his death in October 1226.

The son of a wealthy cloth merchant in Assisi, Italy, he worked with his father until he was 20. When Assisi went to war with a neighboring city, Francis enlisted and was captured. He was imprisoned for a year and then became very ill. These experiences and two others led to his disenchantment with materialism.

On a pilgrimage to Rome, after seeing a leper who had the face of Christ, he kissed the beggar and gave him alms. Later Francis received a revelation at a ruined church. He heard a voice from a crucifix ordering him to restore the church. After renouncing his father's wealth, his father disowned him.

Dedicating himself to a life of poverty, he became a beggar. A diverse group of men and women joined him. In 1208 the Friars Minor (Franciscans) began their mission of preaching repentance, singing, aiding peasants, and caring for lepers—while renouncing wealth and begging alms.

Much to the dismay of Francis, the order entered the political and intellectual life of the universities. Francis retired and received the stigmata (wounds of Christ) on his body. Two years after his death he was canonized.

Do you sometimes get caught up in worldly pursuits and forget your "duty" to God?

Lord, enable me to focus on the teachings of Christ.

October 4: Glitter and Despair

"You say, 'I am rich; I have acquired wealth and do not need a thing.' But you do not realize that you are wretched, pitiful, poor, blind and naked" (Rev. 3:17 NIV).

Today Liverpool, England, represents success and beauty. It played an important part in World War II, and, of course, the Beatles hailed from the city. Lying on the River Mersey, the city has beautiful views of the mountains of North Wales. It is just an hour drive from the English Lake District and numerous castles. A two-hour drive will take you to Scotland.

The beauty, however, hides an underlying discontent and sense of despair. Bob and Debby Bogart, Global Outreach missionaries who serve at the Liverpool City Mission, say that things in the famous city "aren't always as they appear to be on the surface."

"Behind the glitter of lights we discover the gloom and despair of suffering humanity," says Bob. "We are part of a vital team seeking to ease some of the human pain and, at the same time, share the love of Christ."

The Liverpool City Mission feeds, clothes, and cares for more than 100 homeless men and women every two days. One of its most important times of the year is in October, when area churches hold Harvest Celebrations to gather food for the mission.

When have beautiful things often appeared to you on the outside before you discovered hidden despair or ugliness?

Eternal God, help me look below the surface and see things as they really are.

October 5: A Diary's Influence

"Let this be written for a future generation, that a people not yet created may praise the Lord" (Psalm 102:18 NIV).

"My soul was so captivated and delighted with the excellency, loveliness, greatness, and other perfections of God. . . . I continued in this state of inward joy, peace, and astonishment, till near dark."

In his diary David Brainerd (1718–1747) poured out his desire to sacrifice himself for God. He lived only 29 years, but through his diary he influenced generations of Christians and achieved more fame in death than in life.

Beginning in 1742, Brainerd labored among Native American Indian tribes in Massachusetts, New York, Pennsylvania, and New Jersey. In April 1747 tuberculosis forced him to abandon his work. He traveled to theologian Jonathan Edwards's home—he was engaged to Edwards's daughter—and died there in October.

Edwards was so impressed with Brainerd's pious journal that he published *An Account of the Life of the Late Reverend Mr. David Brainerd* in 1749. He hoped it might "afford instruction to missionaries in particular." Edwards was not disappointed. The diary became a best-seller with more than 30 editions appearing before the end of the nineteenth century. The journal inspired some of the greatest names in missions such as Baptist William Carey, Methodist Thomas Coke, and Anglican Henry Martyn.

Do you keep a journal of your inward spiritual thoughts? Consider the benefits it would afford you and others.

~

Thank You, God, for the writings of great Christians who continue to influence us today.

October 6: Simple Acts

"'If anyone gives a cup of cold water to one of these little ones because he is my disciple, I tell you the truth, he will certainly not lose his reward'" (Matt. 10:42 NIV).

A kind word, an encouraging hug, a cup of cold water.

Sometimes it's the simple things that make a difference in the lives of those who are suffering.

In October 1998, Hurricane Mitch roared through Honduras. It was the most destructive hurricane to hit Central America in 200 years. Tegucigalpa, the capital city of Honduras, felt the brunt of the storm. Thousands dead, millions more left homeless, homes and businesses destroyed, churches gone—the destruction was devastating.

Southern Baptist missionary Marvina Hooper wondered what to do. Her answer came in the form of college students from nearby Centro Universitario Bautista. They immediately began distributing cups of water and warm baby clothes. They shoveled mud and helped residents look for belongings. They distributed food and supplies. They played with the children and gave hugs of support.

In reaching out to those in need, the students did what they could, even though many of the acts of service were small and simple.

Marvina says that the experience changed her life.

"The memory of the university students will always remind me of the blessing and joy in serving in Christ's name," she says.

What simple acts can you do today to help someone in need?

∼

Lord Jesus, empower me also to do simple acts for others in Your name.

October 7: She Gave Everything

"As he looked up, Jesus saw the rich putting their gifts into the temple treasury. He also saw a poor widow put in two very small copper coins. 'I tell you the truth,' he said, 'this poor widow has put in more than all the others. All these people gave their gifts out of their wealth; but she out of her poverty put in all she had to live on'" (Luke 21:1–4 NIV).

She never received more than $.50 a week, but she managed to save the remarkable sum of $345.83 which she gave to missions. Her gift was the first one offered to the American Board of Commissioners for Foreign Missions.

Like the widow in the Bible, Sally Thomas (1769–1813), a servant girl in Cornish, New Hampshire, gave all she had. A member of the Congregational Church in Cornish, Sally worked for 23 years for the Daniel Chase family.

She died on October 1, 1813, at the age of 44. Little is known of Sally, but her gravestone inscription speaks volumes: "By the labor of her hands she had acquired property amounting to about $500; which by her last will; excepting a few small legacies, she gave for the spread and support of the Gospel."

Do you generously give of your resources to further the Lord's work?

∼

Thank You, God, for the example of sacrificial giving that Sally Thomas has left us. May her legacy inspire us to give beyond our means.

October 8: In His Time

"Now, Lord, consider their threats and enable your servants to speak your word with great boldness" (Acts 4:29 NIV).

Faced with persecution, they have learned to be patient and wait upon the Lord.

When missionaries Susan and Mark Sutton began their work in Lyon, France, they were surprised to find themselves persecuted by the large population of Muslims in the area. Those persecuting them slashed tires, broke windshields, attacked their new church, shot at members, and set fire to members' cars.

The couple has learned, however, to remain faithful to God and wait upon Him patiently. They believe that God can do great things, even amidst trying and threatening times.

As time has gone by, the Suttons have seen change come to the area and their church grow. They have even seen their persecutors come to know Christ.

Serge, a man who practiced witchcraft, is one of the many who has accepted Christ and changed his ways. He now witnesses to his friends about his new life in Christ.

"At the proper time, one by one, the people are giving their lives to Christ," Susan says. "We discovered that God works in His own time and in His own way."

Do you wait upon the Lord, even amidst persecution? Or do you second-guess God and attack the problem by yourself?

~

Dear Lord, help me turn my eyes upon You, even when I am threatened. Enable me to rely on Your power, and not my own.

October 9: Strength Out of Weakness

"But as for you, be strong and do not give up, for your work will be rewarded" (2 Chron. 15:7 NIV).

God sometimes uses the most unlikely of people to be trailblazers.

Mary Webb (1779–1861) was such a person. A crippling disease at the age of five kept her confined to a wheelchair for the rest of her life.

After reading a missionary sermon based on 2 Chronicles 15:7, Mary found strength to take a leadership step that was not common—and to some, controversial—for a woman of her day. In October 1800, Mary with 13 other women—7 Baptists and 6 Congregationalists—formed the Boston Female Society for Missionary Purposes.

She was the first woman to publicly organize women in support of missions. Her society was the second known women's organization in America. (Isabella Graham had organized the Society for the Relief of Poor Widows with Small Children in 1797.)

Mary served as secretary and treasurer of the society for over 40 years and remained treasurer and correspondent until her death.

Her enthusiasm for missions spawned numerous other missionary groups such as the Female Cent Society, the Children's Friend Society, and the Penitent Females' Refuge. Other organizations ministered to immigrants, African Americans, and Jews.

Are you allowing a physical or emotional handicap to keep you from being obedient to God?

Lord, empower me to serve You when I feel inadequate. Teach me daily that I am weak but You are strong.

October 10: "Broken" for Others

"As he approached Jerusalem and saw the city, he wept over it" (Luke 19:41 NIV).

It is said that she died of a broken heart following the atomic bombings of Hiroshima and Nagasaki at the close of World War II.

Susan M. Bauernfeind (1870–1945) arrived in Japan on October 10, 1900, and faithfully labored there for 43 years. She was one of the first two women missionaries sent to Japan by the Woman's Missionary Society of the Evangelical Association. Born in a log house in Goodhue County, Minnesota, Susan was a multitalented and versatile woman, accomplished as a teacher, linguist, social worker, administrator, and evangelistic missionary.

Two years after arriving in Japan she began a social center in the country's largest spinning factory. In 1904 she established the Tokyo Bible School and then founded the Aisenryo Orphanage for homeless girls. She organized the Japan branch of the Woman's Missionary Society in 1918. Because of her work, a church in Japan was named for her.

The emperor of Japan recognized her twice for her achievements for the people of Japan. Posthumously, she was cited as one of 700 major contributors to Japanese culture from outside Japan.

Is your heart broken for the hurting people of the world? Do you pray daily for them?

Lord, give me a burden today for those around the world who are living in war zones. I pray for all who have physical and emotional wounds.

October 11: Amidst the Headlines

"O Lord my God, I take refuge in you; save and deliver me from all who pursue me" (Psalm 7:1 NIV).

"Riots Raise New Tensions in Indonesia." "Eyewitnesses Provide Evidence of Mass Murders." "Religious Attack in Indonesia Sets Back Peace Bid."

Headlines such as these, gleaned from newspapers around the world at the beginning of 2000, showed the uncertainty of life in Indonesia. Political upheaval and tumultuous election days had left people fearful. Murders of Christians created fear among religious communities. The barbarism against East Timorese citizens demanding freedom shocked the world.

Missionaries working in the midst of such crisis have incredible challenges. Yet, they continue to reach many for Christ. Eugene (not his real name) is one such missionary.

Eugene says that the year of those headlines was one of the most difficult. Christian friends feared the worst and echoed the words of Psalm 7 in their worship services. Election day, however, turned out to be free of violence and church members rejoiced in the fact that "our Lord was working overtime that week."

Amidst such turmoil, life does go on. Eugene trains medical students, leads Bible studies, and helps in worship services. He celebrated when his church baptized 17 new believers around this time.

When difficult circumstances engulf you, do you stay focused on Christ? Or do you get overcome with worry?

Thank You, God, for Your protection and unending care. I know that You are my refuge always.

October 12: Heart for Missions

"The people walking in darkness have seen a great light . . . they rejoice before you as people rejoice at the harvest" (Isa. 9:2,3 NIV).

Did you grow up with a heart for missions?

Lucille Reagan (1897–1937) did. She learned about missions as a child in her Sunbeam Band missions group in Big Spring, Texas. During high school she read pleas from Dr. B. L. Lockett, the first Texas missionary to Nigeria: "Pray for this field and send us help. . . . There is a great joy of harvest in Africa."

At age 17 Lucille dedicated her life to missionary service in Africa. After receiving her degree from Baylor University and completing Woman's Missionary Union Training School, she received her appointment to Nigeria.

On October 12, 1921, she arrived in Africa. She soon learned the Yoruba language, often practicing with three African boys she was sending to school. The boys all became Baptist preachers in Nigeria.

In 1924 she became vice-principal of the Baptist Academy in Lagos and became its principal in 1928. She organized other schools at Ebute Metta and Apapa. Serving on the textbook committee of the Nigerian Education Department, she helped write textbooks used by Nigerian schools. In addition to her educational work, she was active in evangelism. Her career was cut short by disease. She died on July 12, 1937, of yellow fever and was buried in Ogbomosho alongside another missionary who also died of the disease.

∽

Today, precious Lord, prepare the hearts of youth to respond to the call of missions.

October 13: Who Are the Hungry?

"'Simon son of John, do you love me?' Peter was hurt because Jesus asked him the third time, 'Do you love me?' He said, 'Lord, you know all things; you know that I love you.' Jesus said, "Feed my sheep"' (John 21:17 NIV).

Hunger is not something unique to people in Third World countries. Thirty million Americans go without food at some time each month. Hungry people are everywhere—just down the road from you.

Christians in Mammoth Springs, Arkansas, realized hunger was in their community and started a food shelter. Mary Doss, the director of the shelter, says that the ministry has taught church members that there is a face behind hunger.

One family the shelter assisted began attending church regularly. One of their sons became a Christian at a church camp. Another family with six children began sending their children to church activities and children's choir.

For a hunger ministry to be effective, it must do what this shelter does—feed the hungry and also reach out to individuals spiritually.

"We do the hungry no favors if we give them bread for the body while neglecting the soul," says Steven Nelson, director of hunger concerns for the Ethics and Religious Liberty Commission.

World Hunger Day, a day Southern Baptists observe every October, reminds us to consider what we can do to help alleviate hunger around the world.

Does your church have a food pantry? Are you giving money to alleviate hunger?

∽

Lord, bless those who are hungry today.

October 14: Neighborhoods, Then the Nation

"'You will be my witnesses in Jerusalem, and in all Judea and Samaria, and to the ends of the earth'" (Acts 1:8 NIV).

In Indiana, a knock on the door can bring more than just a visit from a friend or a special delivery. It can bring hope to the hungry and a witness for Christ.

Canning Hunger, an evangelism project organized by Southern Baptist missionaries Bob and Susan Bailey, reaches out to neighborhoods in the southeastern area of Indiana. Church members from different congregations go door-to-door to collect canned goods that are then donated to six centers in the area. As members knock on doors on their streets, they meet neighbors they never knew before.

As they collect the food, visitors also ask if they can come back later to collect more (realizing that the need for canned goods is a continual process). This allows the neighbors to visit with each other on a regular basis. Then, hopefully, comes the opportunity for Christians to share their faith with their neighbors.

Bob says that the project is wonderful because it is twofold—it helps the hungry, and it fosters witnessing relationships.

"The bottom line is that we will not reach our nation until we reach our own neighborhoods," Bob says. "Jesus gives us a strategy in Acts 1:8."

How well do you know your neighbors? Is there some way you can foster better relationships with them?

Lord, be with my neighbors today. Enable me to be a witness to them for You.

October 15: A Strong Mind

"Thou wilt keep him in perfect peace, whose mind is stayed on thee, because he trusteth in thee. Trust ye in the Lord forever; for in the Lord God is everlasting strength" (Isa. 26:3–4 KJV).

"A woman of feeling, piety, and good sense, of strong mind...fitted in every respect to be an associate in the great undertaking to which the life of her husband was devoted."

John Clark Marshman paid this tribute to his extraordinary mother. The first woman to leave England for missionary work in India, Hannah Marshman (1767–1847) was a great influence behind the early Serampore missionaries who were sent by the Baptist Missionary Society.

Already a mother of three, Hannah willingly set out on the perilous voyage in 1799 with her husband, Joshua. Her unfaltering trust in God was a source of strength to those on the voyage and later in India.

She and Joshua established the first schools for children in North India. For many years she managed a large school which helped support the Serampore Mission. William Carey valued her practical wisdom, calling her "a prodigy of prudence."

Mother to nine more children born in India, Hannah worked closely with her husband until his death in 1837. When she died, she was the last survivor of those who had labored with her husband, William Ward, and William Carey 47 years before.

Have you trusted in God for strength to face life's challenges?

Today, God, help me to rely on You for perfect peace.

October 16: Troubled Nations

"Then the nations will know that I am the Lord . . . when I show myself holy through you before their eyes" (Ezek. 36:23 NIV).

Bloody violence. Intense hatred. Political mayhem.

For years, these characterized life in Zaire. The military government ruled with an iron fist.

Now, however, the situation has changed, and the country is known as the Democratic Republic of the Congo and is heading in a different direction. The changes have not been easy, and the road to a truly peaceful nation is still a long one.

Liz and Tom Ryder serve as United Methodist missionaries in this area and live with cautious optimism because the Congolese government wants churches to stay involved in health care, agriculture, and education.

"It is a rare privilege to be part of this new country despite its growing pains," Liz says. "Doing what God wants us to do at this time in our lives is peace in itself."

Living in the midst of such a violent upheaval and unsure times have given the Ryders a special perspective. "We have experienced war up close and mourned with our friends who have lost loved ones," Liz explains. "We accept gratefully the plan of God to oversee the running of this universe."

Do you appreciate the peace in your life? Do you accept God's plan for your life and this world?

∼

Dear Lord, thank You for Your hand in the work of people and governments throughout the world. Guide them today as they seek change.

October 17: Restoring Sight

"Then he touched their eyes and said, 'According to your faith will it be done to you'; and their sight was restored" (Matt. 9:29 NIV).

The first Protestant medical missionary to China was an eye doctor. Peter Parker (1804–1888) is considered the most influential person in introducing Western scientific medicine into China.

A Massachusetts native, Peter graduated from Yale College in 1831. Three years later he received both divinity and medical degrees there.

He was only 30 years old when he arrived in Canton in 1834. The American Board of Commissioners for Foreign Missions sent the energetic physician before China was officially opened to the West in 1842.

He opened a Christian ophthalmic hospital that was immediately successful. His fame in enabling the visually impaired to see spread far and wide. In 1837 he founded the China Medical Missionary Society and headed its hospital. He had a genius in being able to train Chinese medical students to be as skillful as he was.

An excellent linguist, Peter served as an interpreter for the American diplomatic mission that negotiated a treaty after the Opium War. Later he was engaged in the United States foreign service giving his income to his hospital. Because the American Board objected to his diplomatic work, it terminated his service in 1947. He continued to support his ministry through part-time diplomatic work.

Do you take for granted your physical sight? Your spiritual sight?

∼

Today, Lord, thank You for both physical and spiritual sight.

October 18: Break Through Prejudice

"But if you show favoritism, you sin and are convicted by the law as lawbreakers" (James 2:9 NIV).

In their own country, they are scorned and ridiculed. The majority of the population views them with prejudice.

The Mapuche Indians, the only South American tribe never conquered by the Spaniards, live in isolation in remote Chile. Their lives are ones of poverty and rampant social problems.

Southern Baptist missionaries Carol and Hawk Hawkins have seen the prejudice leveled against these people. Carol says that the Chilean's prejudice, as well as the prejudice of most people, comes from a fear of the unknown. "As Christians, we are instructed to love our neighbor as ourselves, but how can we love someone we do not know, cannot understand, and who is different from us?" she asks.

To reach out to the Mapuches, Carol and Hawk seek to understand the group and to respect their cultural identity. That has led them to use the *Jesus* film, translated and dubbed into the Mapudungan language, and to utilize the Mapudungan Bible translated by Wycliffe Bible Translator missionaries.

Carol says, "Truth and knowledge have a way of setting one free to become an open vessel through which God's love can flow."

Examine your feelings. Do you have any prejudice?

O God, help me realize that we are all created in Your image. Empower me to overcome any prejudice I may have in my life.

October 19: A Growing Church

"Then the church throughout Judea, Galilee and Samaria enjoyed a time of peace. It was strengthened; and encouraged by the Holy Spirit, it grew in numbers, living in the fear of the Lord" (Acts 9:31 NIV).

In his first year of ministry in India, he had only one convert. Near the end of his second year, his church had only six members. When he transferred to Calcutta in 1874, though, he found himself preaching to 1,600 worshipers who thronged to hear his sermons.

Missionary statesman John R. Mott called him "possibly the greatest ecclesiastic of the nineteenth century."

James Mills Thoburn (1836–1922) was an American Methodist Episcopal missionary bishop who served in Asia for over 50 years. A native of Ohio, he graduated from Allegheny College (Pennsylvania) in 1857. His sister was Isabella Thoburn, missionary educator in India, who established the first Christian college for women in Asia.

Ordained in 1858, James left for India as a missionary in 1859. He learned the language quickly and began preaching his first sermons after only a short time.

A man of strong faith and determination, he was the founder of Methodism in Burma (1879), in Malaysia (1885), and in the Philippines (1899). Preaching throughout India, he was appointed bishop of India and Malaysia in 1888, the first resident Methodist bishop in Asia.

Are you gaining strength daily in your walk with God?

∽

Dear Lord, thank You that Your church has grown because of the Holy Spirit working through Your servants.

October 20: Unexpected Answers

"Whatever you ask for in prayer, believe that you have received it, and it will be yours" (Mark 11:24 NIV).

Answers to prayers often come in unexpected places. For one missionary, it came at a corner hamburger and chicken stand.

Southern Baptist missionary Jim Hogg and members of an established church in Esmereldas, Mexico, felt led to start a church in the nearby town of Quinind. Months of failed Bible studies and other outreach attempts, however, had left Jim discouraged.

One night Jim prayed to God, through tears, that an opportunity for outreach might soon appear. Moments later, he and church members dropped by Jenaro's hamburger and chicken stand, a favorite eating establishment owned by the friendly Jenaro.

Then came the unexpected answer to the prayer Jim had voiced just minutes before. "I was talking to Jenaro, and God's answer hit me like a lightning bolt," says Jim.

Jenaro wanted to host a Bible study in his home. Two months later, Jenaro asked Christ into his heart. The study grew from 8 to 40 members, with 3 people becoming Christians. Jim's next step is to teach members about baptism and form the group into a church. He prays that Jenaro will serve as their leader.

"This is something only God can do," Jim says.

Has God ever answered one of your prayers in an unexpected way?

~

God, thank You for listening to all of my prayers. Help me have faith that You will answer my prayers in Your time and in Your way.

October 21: A Tract Leads to a Legacy

"'I will also make you a light for the Gentiles, that you may bring my salvation to the ends of the earth'" (Isa. 49:6 NIV).

One day a sick woman in New York City sent for her physician. The doctor arrived, and while waiting to see her, he picked up a tract called "The Conversion of the World." The message of the tract made such an impression on him that he could not forget it.

John Scudder was so moved by the tract that he gave his life to missions work.

In 1819 he sailed for Ceylon representing the American Board of Foreign Missions. He was the first medical missionary from America and in 1820 the only medical missionary in the world.

After working in Ceylon, John went to Madras, India, where he spent most of his 36 years as a missionary. He began an extraordinary family legacy in missions, including seven sons and two daughters who worked in India. John Scudder Jr. was also a missionary doctor. His daughter, Ida Scudder, who founded the Vellore Medical College and hospital in Madras State, became a world-famous physician.

A missionary tract was the impetus that eventually led 43 members of the Scudder family to give over 1,100 years to missionary service.

Is God leading you to distribute Bibles or tracts that can change a person's life and affect generations to come?

~

Lord, show me how I can be a light to lead others to You.

October 22: A Home for Sinners

"The Lord lifts up the downtrodden" (Psalm 147:6 RSV).

A hungry would-be thief. A man eating his dinner from a trash can. A teenager looking for a friend.

At the Baltimore Hispanic Ministry, United Methodist pastor and missionary Fidel Compres reaches out to a wide variety of searching, struggling individuals. On the front door of the downtown ministry's building we find the words *Bienvenidos* and *Welcome*—Fidel's invitation to the Hispanic community in the area.

The day after the ministry opened, Fidel answered a knock at his door and found a young man asking him, "May I have a drink? Do you have some food?" Fidel shared food and drinks left over from the opening celebration the day before and invited the man inside. He then told him of God's love for him. When the man started to leave, he handed Fidel a key. Fidel realized it was the key to the ministry's building—the man had intended to break in and steal from the ministry. Fidel's message changed his mind.

The ministry's message is truly that God loves us all, whether we are a potential thief or homeless person or struggling teenager.

"The church is a hospital for sinners," Fidel says. "My hope is to give everyone an opportunity to become a disciple of Jesus."

How can you reach out to those struggling around you with a message of hope and love?

∼

Dear God, make me a witness to the downtrodden in my life and community.

October 23: Changed, But in Chains

"Since, then, you have been raised with Christ, set your hearts on things above, where Christ is seated at the right hand of God" (Col. 3:1 NIV).

New inmates entering MacDougall Correctional Institute in Ridgeville, South Carolina, are signed up for the Starter-Kit Ministry. The program, organized by nearby Summerville Baptist Church, reaches out to prisoners with both physical and spiritual help.

Phil and Vicki Dougherty work with the ministry because they believe God's Word clearly commands Christians to minister to prisoners. "God had implanted the desire in my heart to reach out to this particular segment of society," says Vicki. "As Phil had to pass the facility en route to work, God began to speak to him about it."

They and two men lead Sunday evening worship services twice a month. At the end of the program, each participant receives a starter kit with hygiene items, a Bible, and tract.

Phil and Vicki believe that prison ministries can result in many transformed lives. "Some inmates," says Phil, "turn loose of their sin and accept the gospel." Others grasp some of the truth, but don't hold onto it. Still others reject the message.

"Hearing someone who is convicted to life in prison testify that his life is better in prison because of knowing Jesus than it was on the outside not knowing Jesus" is a wonderful testimony, the two say.

You are my freedom from sin, Lord. I praise You for the deliverance You have brought to my life.

October 24: A Career Change for God

"But I am like an olive tree flourishing in the house of God; I trust in God's unfailing love for ever and ever" (Psalm 52:8 NIV).

He didn't start his missionary career until he was past 50.

Johannes Theodorus Vanderkemp (1747–1811) was an eminent Dutch scholar, soldier, and physician before he became the only medical missionary in Africa in the early nineteenth century.

Born in Rotterdam, he was the son of a Lutheran professor of theology. After studying at the University of Leyden, he spent 15 years in the army. He studied medicine at the Edinburgh University and then served as a physician until 1795.

After the death of his wife and child, he became a Christian in 1791. The newly formed London Missionary Society accepted him for service in 1796, and he was ordained the next year as a minister in the Church of Scotland.

Arriving in Cape Town, South Africa, in 1799, he worked for two African people groups—the Kaffirs and the Hottentots. Identifying closely with the native population, he married an African woman. He labored hard to defeat the slave trade—in 3 years he paid $5,000 to redeem slaves.

Johannes was only able to serve 12 years before his death. It is said that for 100 years the Kaffir Christian converts were called by his name.

Lord, am I where You want me to be today? Reveal to me where I can best be of service to You.

October 25: God's Blessings

"'Bring the whole tithe into the storehouse.... Test me in this,' says the Lord, 'and see if I will not throw open the floodgates of heaven and pour out so much blessing that you will not have room enough for it'" (Mal. 3:10 NIV).

Samuel, a devout Muslim in the African country of Niger, questioned Southern Baptist missionaries David and Tami Wood about their faith. What, he wondered, made them come to his country? Becoming friends with the couple, and then viewing a video about Jesus, made him believe that Christianity was true. When he told his father, though, Samuel was told he would be shunned and lose his inheritance.

"We prayed with and for Samuel that God would reveal Himself in a way that he would know he needed God," Tami says. After returning from furlough, Tami and David found Samuel waiting at their home. His wife, who had almost died two days before, had been completely healed. Samuel believed it was a sign from God and asked to be publicly baptized.

His father, seeing the miraculous healing, said he wouldn't take Samuel's land from him. "That was the worst year for rainfall, but Samuel's field produced 110 storage huts of grain," says Tami. "And Samuel set aside 11 huts of grain to be used for the work of God."

Do you give God credit for the miracles and blessings in your life?

∽

Today fill my heart, Lord, with gratitude for the miracles You perform in my life. I want to return gifts to You.

October 26: A Daily Renewal

"Therefore we do not lose heart. Though outwardly we are wasting away, yet inwardly we are being renewed day by day" (2 Cor. 4:16 NIV).

She was unable to raise her head from her pillow. She could only move her hands and forearms. Yet, she raised over $120,000 for missions.

Lizzie Johnson (1869–1909), a member of the Woman's Foreign Missionary Society of the Methodist Episcopal Church, didn't let infirmity stop her from contributing to missions. A back injury at age 13 had resulted in the Casey, Illinois, woman being bedridden at the age of 27.

Amid much pain, Lizzie stitched a quilt for six months in order to sell it to raise money for missions. Disappointed when the quilt didn't sell and physically exhausted from the undertaking, she waited four years, until with the help of her sister and brother, she made and sold bookmarks to every state and 16 foreign countries. She contributed the $20,000 profit to home and foreign missions. When Francis Wesley Warne, missionary bishop to India, heard of the quilt, he borrowed it and circled the world three times telling Lizzie's story. Donations came in totaling $100,000. Following Lizzie's death, her family raised $5,000 more to build a church in Cawnpore, India. The Casey United Methodist Church continues to support it.

Have you ever lost heart because physical or emotional difficulties became stumbling blocks to your dreams?

∽

Almighty God, today renew in me a sense of purpose even amid any struggles I encounter.

October 27: Hope in Suffering

"We rejoice in our sufferings, knowing that suffering produces endurance" (Rom. 5:3 RSV).

In her work as a church planter in Taiwan, Southern Baptist missionary Siu Miu became friends with a 17-year-old who suffered from nose cancer. Several operations had left her face disfigured and, despite the medical work, the cancer kept recurring. "Without any hope and financial support, she wanted to kill herself," says Siu.

Siu visited the young woman many times and shared Christ's love with her. She yearned to show her that, even in the midst of her suffering and pain, God loved her.

The day came when the teenager believed what Siu told her. She believed in the message of Christ. "Her attitude changed, she wasn't depressed as before, and she became a witness to her Buddhist family," she remembers. When the young woman died six months later, her family had become Christians.

The message in this experience, Siu says, is that God knows about our troubles and cares for us in the hard times. "I trust that in the midst of our suffering everything will come out positive because God cares and He loves us," she says.

Sui served in Taiwan for two years and now works in Chile. Her missions work, she says, is filled with struggles—learning new languages, learning to work effectively with others. In all struggles, though, God is beside her.

When have suffering or struggles overwhelmed you?

Thank You, Lord, for Your help in difficult times.

October 28: A Life of Sacrificial Giving

"'But a Samaritan, as he traveled, came where the man was; and when he saw him, he took pity on him. He went to him and bandaged his wounds, pouring on oil and wine'" (Luke 10:33–34 NIV).

She performed all surgeries in her bathroom. Once when she amputated the leg of an unskilled laborer, he needed skin grafts. Asked about the scars on her own leg, she brushed away the question. A nurse later complained that a skin graft for the "good-for-nothing coolie" had come from the doctor's own leg.

Eleanor Chestnut, a Presbyterian medical missionary to China, epitomized agape love.

Eleanor displayed sacrifice early in life. She wore castoff clothing to get through Park College in Missouri. While at Chicago's Woman's Medical College, she lived in an attic and had very little to eat.

While building a women's hospital in Lien-chou, she lived on $1.50 a month so the remainder of her salary could go for bricks. When her missionary board insisted on repaying her, she refused saying, "It will spoil all my fun."

On October 29, 1905, she and other missionaries were working at the hospital when a mob attacked. After alerting authorities, she could have escaped, but she returned to aid others. Her last heroic act was to tear strips from her dress to use as a bandage for a wounded child in the crowd.

Are you sacrificially giving of yourself to help others?

Help me, God, today to exhibit agape love for those around me.

October 29: The Fearless Missionary

"For I am already on the point of being sacrificed; the time of my departure has come" (2 Tim. 4:6 RSV).

Have you ever heard of the missionary with one thumb?

"Tell your king that I have purchased the road to Uganda with my death!" the missionary said before he was speared to death.

Although Bishop James Hannington (1847–1885) represented the Anglican Church Missionary Society a brief time in Uganda, his legacy of courage lives on. James grew up in Sussex, England, the son of a wealthy businessman. Known for his childhood mischief and fearlessness, he once used dynamite to destroy a wasp nest and lost his thumb in the process.

The boy prankster became a parish priest with a heart for evangelism. After hearing about the murder of two CMS missionaries in Africa, James was challenged to lead an expedition to Uganda in 1882. Attacked by wild animals and warriors, he trekked on until fever and dysentery stopped him. Twice left for dead, he revived but had to return to England where doctors forbade him to return to Africa.

Consecrated as bishop of East Equatorial Africa on June 24, 1884, he arrived in Kenya in January 1885. On an expedition to Uganda to encourage missionaries and believers he was murdered on orders from the evil King Mwanga on October 29. Fifty men soon volunteered for CMS service.

Today, O God, empower the Christians of Uganda.

October 30: Operation Teddy Bear

"Praise be to . . . the God of all comfort, who comforts us in all our troubles, so that we can comfort those in any trouble with the comfort we ourselves have received from God" (2 Cor. 1:3,4 NIV).

A soft, cuddly teddy bear often lies in a place of honor on a child's bed. It serves as a dedicated friend for years, its crumpled and worn fur a sign of its devotion.

Now teddy bears serve another purpose, thanks to Alabama's WMU. The organization's teddy bear ministry provides the plush toys to children in crisis situations: after auto accidents and fires, during hospital stays, and after the loss of a loved one.

Marsha Johnson, a WMU member in Clanton, helps in the collection of 600 to 800 teddy bears every year and says she "sometimes sees teddy bears in my sleep."

Marsha says one young girl fell in love with a bear she bought for the project and wanted to keep for herself. She and her mother decided she needed to give it away, though, and said a special prayer over the bear. "A while later, the girl and her mother were involved in an accident," says Marsha. "The paramedic grabbed a bear when he found out a young girl was at the scene. The girl received the bear and said, 'Mommy, don't be afraid.' The girl showed the bear to her mother. It was the same bear the girl had picked out for someone in need."

Dear Lord, help me reach out to children in need today.

October 31: A Protective Shelter

"In the shelter of your presence you hide them from the intrigues of men" (Psalm 31:20 NIV).

"The father of a bright little thirteen-year-old girl sold her to Mr. Froman the storekeeper, for twenty blankets," she wrote to the superintendent for the Presbyterian Board. "I had a hard time to rescue her, but I succeeded. Now Mr. Froman is angry at me."

Amanda McFarland (c. 1837–1898), the first woman missionary to Alaska, is known for her work rescuing Indian girls who were fleeing from white traders to whom they had been sold by their parents.

Amanda had served with her husband among the Indians of New Mexico and Idaho until his death in 1875. Two years later the Presbyterian Board sent her to Alaska.

At Fort Wrangell she rented a house as a shelter for the girls. She instructed them in the Bible as well as in domestic skills such as sewing. Soon she was caring for more than 100 girls.

After three years of work and often using her own money for supplies, she moved into a larger house with 21 girls. Three years later after the home and everyone's possessions were destroyed in a fire she relocated to a house at the fort. From there she settled in Sitka where her school became the Sitka Training School, now known as Sheldon Jackson Junior College.

Are you sensitive to the needs of children often trapped by circumstances?

I pray today, Almighty God, for children who need Your loving shelter.

November 1: Saving the Oppressed

"He will save them from oppression and from violence, for their lives are precious to him" (Psalm 72:14 TLB)

"The girls were led down the hill to the icy cold river, in which they sat all morning until they were numb. They were then rushed back to the hut where screaming women carried on a frenzied ritual to build up the girls' courage."

In her book, *Road to Kilimanjaro: An American Family in Maasailand*, missionary Ruth Shaffer wrote about the female circumcision ceremonies she witnessed in East Africa.

According to Ruth, the puberty initiation rites were done to show that the girls "have been able to withstand extreme pain honorably, and have earned the status of women." Citing the damaging effects of the rituals, she wrote that it "causes so much scar tissue that few Maasai babies can survive birth alive, and mothers often die in childbirth as well."

After graduating from Moody Bible Institute, Roy and Ruth Shaffer began work with the Africa Inland Mission in 1923. Over a 35-year ministry they developed a powerful bond with the Maasai tribe.

Through their efforts and those of other missionaries, they helped to reduce the practice of female circumcision. The tradition still persists in parts of the world today despite active campaigns by many religious, health, and women's organizations to ban it.

How can you reach out to the oppressed?

∼

Holy Lord, empower those battling centuries-old destructive traditions. Thank You that all lives are precious to You.

November 2: Ambushed!

"When the three hundred trumpets sounded, the Lord caused the men throughout the camp to turn on each other with their swords" (Judg. 7:22 NIV).

Tim and Ann Tidenberg, Southern Baptist missionaries in Tanzania, saw this Old Testament story of Gideon reenacted when members of a Maasai tribe came to destroy Christians in their village.

The native Maasai tribe has had many converts to Christianity. Conflict has erupted between Maasai, recent Christian converts, missionaries, and other Christians in the area. In late 1999, it turned violent as warriors attacked Baptist and Pentecostal churches.

On one occasion, 70 warriors stormed a church and attacked members with clubs and spears. They chanted that "black blood or white blood" would be shed.

Tim and other Christians inside the church tried to fight back but soon realized that prayer was the only match for the physical assault. As they prayed, the Maasai began to battle among themselves. Unexpectedly, then, the warriors retreated.

Tim remembers: "The battle continued around us as a story from the Old Testament began to unfold—confusion of the enemy. The army Gideon fought against was confused and fought themselves while Gideon's army stood and watched. That is exactly what happened."

A while later, Christians met with village elders and Maasai. Elders shared how God had helped their villages, and Maasai asked for forgiveness. The Christians shared openly with them.

When have you been attacked for your faith?

Be with me, Lord, when I am attacked. Remind me to turn to You in such situations.

November 3: A Home of Her Own

"Now we know that if the earthly tent we live in is destroyed, we have a building from God, an eternal house in heaven, not built by human hands" (2 Cor. 5:1 NIV).

Daughter of missionaries Robert and Mary Moffat, Mary Livingstone (1820–1862) grew up in Kuruman, South Africa. Mary Moffat had made a stable home that was called "an oasis in the desert." Her daughter would never know such a home.

In their 17-year marriage, David and Mary Livingstone were together only 4 years. The remaining years David spent exploring deeper into the interior of Africa. Mary and the children were left behind waiting to join him.

After their marriage on January 2, 1845, the Livingstones left for Mabotsa 220 miles away. Mary worked hard to create a home there, but within 2 years David moved 40 miles north to a new station. Over and over in the years ahead, they pulled up roots and moved. Mary gave birth to five children, losing one to disease, and battled jungle fevers. With deteriorating health, she and four children finally went home to Scotland. David joined them 4 years later. Returning to Africa, Mary died in the Zambezi Delta. Writing in his journal, the famous missionary/explorer grieved, "Oh, my Mary, my Mary! How often we have longed for a quiet home."

When did you last thank God for your home?

∼

Thank You, Everlasting God, for the eternal home You have prepared for those who trust in You.

November 4: When It's Hard to Forgive

"In him we have redemption through his blood, the forgiveness of sins, in accordance with the riches of God's grace that he lavished on us with all wisdom and understanding" (Eph. 1:7 NIV).

What is the greatest wrong anyone has ever done to you? Did you forgive the person who did it?

Imagine that your husband and two children have been killed. Could you ever forgive their murderers? Missionary Gladys Staines did.

Graham, Philip, and Timothy Staines died in January 1999 in Manoharpur, India, when mobs set fire to the car in which they slept.

The Staineses spent 16 years together on mission in India, where their primary work centered at the Mayurbhanj Leprosy Home. The home serves more than 60 patients at one time, all who receive medical treatment and can then stay at the facility for vocational training. The patients' children can also stay and attend a free local school.

After the death of her husband and sons, Gladys and teenaged daughter, Esther, decided to stay in India. "I thought about leaving but then I think, What do I gain by going back? I believe that God brought me here. He will give me strength to continue," she says.

Gladys has also forgiven the murderers, saying: "All of us deserve forgiveness. Christ forgave us. Did any of us deserve forgiveness? He expects us to forgive others."

Whom do you need to forgive?

Your forgiveness is sometimes hard to fathom, Lord. Thank You for it.

November 5: Physical and Spiritual Healing

"If there is a natural body, there is also a spiritual body" (1 Cor. 15:44 NIV).

Ruth Bell Graham grew up as the daughter of a great missionary doctor. A surgeon at the largest Presbyterian hospital in the world in the mid-1930s, her father was concerned with both the physical and spiritual needs of his patients.

Nelson Bell (1894–1973) felt called to be a missionary doctor while studying at Washington and Lee University. He married Virginia Leftwich after graduating from the Medical College of Virginia.

Representing the Presbyterian Church, the couple arrived in China in 1916. Nelson joined the staff of a Presbyterian mission hospital in North Kiangsu Province. Because of his innovative surgical and medical techniques, he became a fellow of the American College of Surgeons in 1934.

For most of his career in China, civil disorder existed, and the mission carried on its work under extreme difficulties. Concerned about his patients, he would give his own blood at times to save a patient. More importantly, he cared about the condition of their souls.

When the Japanese invaded, he and his family returned to America in May 1941 and settled in Montreat, North Carolina, where he established a surgical practice in nearby Asheville.

Nelson, son-in-law Billy Graham, and Carl F. H. Henry, established *Christianity Today* magazine in 1956. In 1972 Nelson was elected the moderator of the Presbyterian Church in the United States.

Are you attentive to both your physical and spiritual needs?

Lord, help me daily to nurture my spiritual side.

November 6: Genuine Love

"And he has given us this command: Whoever loves God must also love his brother" (1 John 4: 21 NIV).

She once said, "One who works with the Indians must love them and not just think he does."

Mary Posser Jayne (1867–1937), pioneer missionary in Oklahoma, demonstrated her love for Native American Indians by her service to them.

An Iowa native, Mary determined at an early age to become a missionary to the Native American Indians. After graduating from the Western Normal School at Shenandoah, Iowa, she attended the Baptist Missionary Training School in Chicago for 2 years. On November 6, 1896, she joined two other missionaries in Kingfisher, Oklahoma. Working with the Cheyenne and Arapahos, she became a wandering evangelist, going from one camp to another holding church services and women's meetings.

After 17 years among the Cheyenne and Arapahos, she joined the Southern Baptist Home Mission Board (now North American Mission Board) as a missionary to the Pawnees. She pioneered women's missionary groups. She also began work among the Otoes, a tribe kin to the Pawnees. In 1925 she became a counselor to Native American Indian boys at Bacone College. She died there on January 4, 1937.

On her death the Bacone president said of her: "To the third and fourth generations they will remember that a good woman came among them. . . . They learned a way of life from her and they will never forget it."

Can others tell you genuinely love them?

~

Today, blessed Lord, help me to love others with a deep agape love.

November 7: God's Aloha

"The cords of the grave coiled around me; the snares of death confronted me. In my distress I called to the Lord; I cried to my God for help" (Psalm 18:5–6 NIV).

Suicide, he thought, was the only option left.

Jeff, an Australian businessmen visiting Hawaii, looked down from the 31st floor of the hotel. If he jumped from the balcony, he reasoned, his problems would be over. "I decided that suicide was a real option and definitely in the best interest of my family," he says now.

Jeff, however, soon felt his heart change and knew that God had better plans for him. He stepped back into the room and found a Bible called *The Greatest Is Aloha*. In its pages he found hope and salvation.

The Bible placement was the work of the Wakiki Beach Chaplaincy, a group founded by former Lutheran minister of youth Bob Turnbull. The interdenominational ministry reaches out to tourists, businessmen, military personnel, and residents of Hawaii. It uses hula, music, and other avenues to present the gospel on the beach, in hotels, and on the streets.

The chaplaincy also places 5,000 Bibles in area hotels every year. The Scriptures tell of God's invitation to all (or God's aloha) and bring hope to readers like Jeff.

Have you ever felt desperate or alone? Did God reach down to you in your despair?

Lord, thank You for Your Word and the message of healing and hope it brings to everyone.

November 8: The Greatness of God

"Great is the Lord and most worthy of praise; his greatness no one can fathom" (Psalm 145: 3 NIV).

A British missionary in Eastern Europe wrote one of the twentieth century's most beloved hymns. He got his inspiration from a Russian song that had its origin in a Swedish poem, "O Store Gud" ("O Great God"), written by lay preacher Carl Boberg.

In 1927 Stuart Hine (1899–1989), inspired by the folk tune and the opening line, wrote "How Great Thou Art." He got the idea for the first verse after hearing thunder rolling across the Carpathian Mountains. The second verse came to him as he tromped through the woods with a group of young people. After a number of people were converted, he conceived the third verse. When Stuart returned to Britain during World War II, he added a fourth verse. The hymn then was published in a missionary magazine and also in leaflets. It soon found a worldwide audience.

In 1954 a book publisher gave one of the leaflets to George Beverly Shea saying it was something he might want to sing. Shea sang it in a Toronto Billy Graham Crusade in 1955. It became one of his trademarks and helped to popularize the song.

How often do you take the time to consider the greatness of God? It can be a life-changing experience.

∼

Almighty God, open my eyes to Your great majesty. May I be reminded afresh each new day how truly awesome You are.

November 9: A Call to Christ

"I urge you to live a life worthy of the calling you have received" (Eph. 4:1 NIV).

When did Christ call out to you? Have you followed that call during your life?

Jim and Jo Goodwin's work as Methodist missionaries in Brazil really began more than 50 years ago when Jim first felt called to Christ.

During World War II, Jim visited a small country church where the minister, Rev. Charles Hamby, shared some sad news with his parishioners. He had just received news in a telegram that his son, whose naval ship had been missing, had died. Overcome with grief, he faced his congregation.

Jim says he'll always remember the prayer the pastor prayed that day. He asked God to help him forgive those responsible for his son's death and to keep them safe from harm so their parents wouldn't have to suffer the sorrow he now faced. Amazed by the man's sense of peace and willingness to forgive, Jim made a decision. He committed his life to Christ at that moment.

Later in life, Jim and his wife felt another call—to serve as missionaries. They were appointed to Brazil and served there for decades. They reached out to others with the same sense of peace and forgiveness that led Jim to Christ years before.

∽

Give me peace today, Lord, and help me reach out in forgiveness to others.

November 10: A Heart to Hear

"When you received the word of God, which you heard from us, you accepted it not as the word of men, but . . . the word of God" (1 Thess. 2:13 NIV).

Sharon and Harvey McCone pored over the bilingual tract, "Have You Heard of the Four Spiritual Laws?" They hoped the tract, produced by Campus Crusade for Christ, would help them learn some basic Spanish before they left for the Caribbean Basin as International Service Corps missionaries.

Later that day, on the way to a prayer meeting at church, they saw a young Hispanic woman outside. She had just come from the children's hospital across the street from their church where her son had recently had heart surgery. They invited her to the prayer meeting and dinner.

Elizabeth spoke in broken English, and Sharon immediately realized that this woman could help her and Harvey with their Spanish. They asked her to teach them how to read the gospel tract properly. Her aid with pronunciation, voice inflection, and grammar helped immensely.

The next day brought wonderful news. Elizabeth came to the church and asked for guidance in becoming a Christian. She, her husband, and child came to church the next Sunday.

Sharon says the bilingual tracts help them today in their missions work, making it easier for them to share the gospel in a language they are still learning.

How could learning another language help you reach out to others?

∽

God, help me remember today the many people who don't speak my language.

November 11: Reaching Everyone Everywhere

"'You are to go into all the world and preach the Good News to everyone, everywhere'" (Mark 16:15 TLB).

In a small cottage in Moulton, England, in the 1780s he covered his walls with hand-drawn maps of the world. On the different countries he wrote their population, climate, vegetation, animals, and religion. It is has been said that "he had a fuller account on his wall maps of the state of the whole world than anyone else living of whom we have record."

William Carey (1761–1834) was "mapping" out a biblical perspective on taking the gospel to the entire world—a revolutionary thought for his day.

In 1792 he published *An Enquiry into the Obligations of Christians to Use Means for the Conversion of the Heathen* which stated that it was the *duty* of Christians to evangelize. That same year he preached at a Baptist associational meeting his now famous sermon on Isaiah 54:2. His two main points were (1) Expect great things (from God), and (2) Attempt great things (for God). Before the meeting ended, the participants had voted to establish a foreign missions organization, the Particular Baptist Society for the Propagation of the Gospel.

William reached India on November 11, 1793, where he would labor tirelessly for more than 40 years. By 1834, 14 missionary societies in England, as well as others in America and Europe, owed their existence to him.

How can you carry out the Great Commission?

O Lord, give me a vision of how to reach others.

November 12: Clothe Yourself with Patience

"As God's chosen people . . . clothe yourself with compassion, kindness, humility, gentleness and patience" (Col. 3:12 NIV).

Lucy McGuire did not feel kind or patient. She, instead, felt tense and stressed.

She and her husband had driven for two days from Novi, Michigan, to Monterrey, Mexico, to check out the location for a missions trip for their Presbyterian church. Because both of them were perfectionists, the trip—with its exhausting pace and unexpected delays—had left them ill-tempered.

Arriving in Monterrey, they were intent on meeting their contact, an evangelist named Enrique. But he wasn't at the hotel restaurant, their designated meeting place. Their fatigue and impatience mounted.

Enrique finally arrived, his face beaming with excitement and gratitude. He couldn't wait for the opportunity to work with their church.

Over the next week, Lucy and her husband learned much about the pace of the Mexican lifestyle. "Enrique's family didn't rush to get from one event to the next," Lucy remembers. "His church members did not disappear as fast as they could after the Sunday morning service."

Daily, their tension disappeared, and by the week's end, they looked forward to their church members' experiencing the same thing. "We knew they would come back blessed and richer for seeing this kind of love in action," Lucy says.

Do you often feel tension and impatience in your daily life? How would God rather you act?

Precious God, thank You for others who can teach us from their different lifestyles.

November 13: A Man of Honor

"Too much pride brings disgrace; humility leads to honor" (Prov. 29:23 CEV).

After his death, one obituary said that "earth had lost and heaven gained a soul whose life had been an inspiration, and whose memory will be honored while honor remains among men."

Given an honorary doctor of divinity degree by Cambridge University, pioneer missionary John Gibson Paton (1824–1907) was honored in his lifetime as well as after his death.

His Scottish parents dedicated him at birth to missionary work. He served with the Glasgow City Mission from 1847 to 1856 while studying theology and medicine at the University of Glasgow.

Ordained by the Reformed Presbyterian Church in 1858, he sailed for the cannibal island of Tanna in the New Hebrides, a group of islands in the southwest Pacific (now Vanuatu). Facing many hardships including the loss of his wife and son and attempts on his life, he escaped on a passing ship to Australia with his Bible and some translations. There he sought support for missions work in the islands.

Back in Scotland he was elected moderator of his church in 1864. After his remarriage, he returned to the New Hebrides in 1866 where he had success on the island of Aniwa for 15 years.

An inspiring speaker, he is said to have raised more than $400,000 for South Pacific missions.

Do you want to be known as a person of honor?

∽

May I, Lord, in humility, bring honor to Your name.

November 14: All Are Missionaries

"We, however, will not boast beyond proper limits, but will confine our boasting to the field God has assigned to us, a field that reaches even to you" (2 Cor. 10:13 NIV).

"I personally never liked the term *missionary.*"

These words come from a Christian who has served as a missionary in Alaska since 1949. Despite his missions experience, though, Richard Miller says, "Each one of us has a place to fill, and filling that place is what is important."

An experience back in 1949 first clarified this belief in him.

Richard stepped forward following a call at a missions meeting for people who would commit to career missions. Standing at the front, he says, "It looked like the sheep and the goats. The good ones were doing what the Lord wanted them to do, and a small number would not surrender."

Then, suddenly, a young man came down the aisle sobbing uncontrollably. He lived in a rural area and felt God wanted him to take up his father's medical practice. He asked, "Would it be all right for me to stand here with the others?"

Richard says that moment still rings clear and new to him today.

"I've heard preachers 'brag' about how the greatest call in the world is to preach the gospel," he says. "I have always believed the greatest thing one can do is to do what God wants one to do."

What does God want you to do with your life? He wants you to know that this calling is as valid as any career missionary's.

∽

Help me, Lord, to surrender to Your call on my life.

November 15: Standing Firm

"Stand firm then, with the belt of truth buckled around your waist, with the breastplate of righteousness in place" (Eph. 6:14 NIV).

She not only obtained a missionary appointment—a hurdle for an African American woman in the early twentieth century—but also founded a mission society.

Eliza Davis George (1878–1978) graduated from Central Texas College where she dedicated herself to missions work in Africa. She faced opposition, though, from her denomination, the Southern Baptist Convention. Never before had an African American woman from Texas become a foreign missionary. Presenting her case at a special missions meeting, she gripped the hearts of the men. One said, "Your eloquence and sincerity have moved us deeply. I for one can no longer stand in the way of your fulfilling your life's ambition."

Arriving in Liberia in 1914, she helped establish the Bible Industrial Academy. Within two years 50 boys were enrolled. When the National Baptist Convention took over work in Liberia, a married couple replaced her.

She married Thompson George, and they started a new mission. Following her husband's death in 1939, she persisted in fulfilling her call.

In 1943 the National Baptist Convention retired her at age 65. Supported mainly by Eliza Davis George Clubs in America, her work became known as the Elizabeth Native Interior Mission. By the 1960s there were 27 churches in the Eliza George Baptist Association. She labored past the age of 90.

Do you stand firm when your convictions are challenged?

Faithful Lord, give me courage when I face opposition.

November 16: Overcoming with Fortitude

"Be strong and courageous. Do not be afraid or discouraged" (1 Chron. 22:13 NIV).

"Yesterday I swam my horses across Maumee River. . . . Preached by candle light to about a dozen hearers," he said in his diary. "I have traveled all day along a dreary wilderness, have seen no one since I left Defiance except four Indians."

The best known Baptist missionary to the Native American Indians, Isaac McCoy was a man of restless energy and great fortitude. He traveled by horseback to Washington, D.C., 13 times to plead Indian causes before three Presidents and many cabinet members.

Born in western Pennsylvania, Isaac grew up in Kentucky. He settled in the Indiana Territory in 1804 with his bride, Christiana, to do pioneer work.

One of the first Baptist home missionaries, Isaac was appointed in 1817 to start a mission station among the Indians near Fort Wayne. A passionate advocate for Indians, he established a school where the children were housed and fed.

He organized the American Indian Mission Association in 1842 in Louisville, Kentucky. It became a part of the Southern Baptist Home Mission Board (now North American Mission Board) in 1855.

Christiana was an ideal helpmate. According to Isaac, she was a woman of "uncommon fortitude and mild disposition." Once she traveled down the Wabash several hundred miles in a canoe with her small children to reach a settlement before giving birth to another child.

How do you overcome fear and discouragement?

∼

Lord, endow me with Your strength to conquer my fears and overcome hardships.

November 17: To Scottish Children

"Then Philip ran up to the chariot and heard the man reading Isaiah the prophet. 'Do you understand what you are reading?' Philip asked. 'How can I,' he said, 'unless someone explains it to me?' So he invited Philip to come up and sit with him" (Acts 8:30–31 NIV).

When you think of Scotland, what picture comes to your mind? You probably conjure up an image of green hills and historic castles. You might also be surprised, though, to find that Scotland is a land open to evangelization.

Peggy DuCharme, a Southern Baptist missionary in Scotland, describes the area this way: "I live and work in Stirling, which is in the central part of Scotland and is a very historical place," she says. "In fact, it's where the events in the movie *Braveheart* took place."

And of the missions opportunities, Peggy says, "One advantage we have in Scotland is that Christian leaders have the opportunity to go into local public schools and share about God."

Peggy was asked to participate in Millennium Day at a local public primary school and learned how Scottish schools are open to Christian influences. "I was invited to talk to the children about the spiritual significance of a new millennium," she remembers. "It was a true joy and privilege to introduce the Lord to the boys and girls, and even the teachers who were listening in."

∼

Empower me, O Lord, to share Your love and hope with the children around me.

November 18: Bringing Comfort

"Praise be to ... the God of all comfort, who comforts us in all our troubles, so that we can comfort those in any trouble with the comfort we ourselves have received from God" (2 Cor. 1:3–4 NIV).

"If ever there was a Christlike work in this world, it was to go among these poor sufferers and bring to them the consolation of the gospel," he said after visiting his first leper asylum.

Irish missionary Wellesley Bailey (1846–1937) first visited a leper asylum while a teacher with the American Presbyterian Mission in India. He saw the spiritual poverty of the lepers and also their need for proper housing, food, clothing, and medical care.

After his marriage, he and his wife, Alice, continued these visits. In 1873 while in Ireland they spoke of their work, and a fund, Lepers in India, was established to raise money.

They joined the Church of Scotland Missionary Society in 1875 and opened up a small leprosy asylum in Chamba in the foothills of the Himalayas. As their ministry grew, the organization became known as the Mission to Lepers in India. Wellesley became the secretary of the Mission, running it from Edinburgh and making extended tours to India. The work then spread around the world.

Now called the Leprosy Mission, the organization continues to comfort millions suffering from this horrible disease.

Are you bringing the "consolation of the gospel" to others?

~

God of comfort, today enable me to minister to the suffering around me.

November 19: Missions on the Best-seller List

"Repentance and forgiveness of sins will be preached in his name to all nations, beginning at Jerusalem" (Luke 24:47 NIV).

The story of today's missions work has even made it onto the best-seller list at the local bookstore—penned by no other than popular author John Grisham.

The Testament, a 1999 release by the author of *The Firm* and other legal thrillers, told the story of the fictional Rachel Lane, a missionary in the interior regions of Brazil. The book's main character, attorney Nate O'Riley, searches for Rachel to tell her that she has inherited millions of dollars. She turns down the money, telling Nate that her work for Christ is the most important thing in her life.

At a time when a Christian message is usually completely absent from popular fiction, *The Testament* was a welcome change. It provided an up close and accurate view of South American missions work and presented the plan of salvation in a natural way.

The accuracy of the story was created from firsthand experiences with missions work. Grisham traveled and researched with good friend and Southern Baptist missionary to Brazil, Carl King.

Grisham found himself talking about his Christan faith and missions work when the book was released. How can you talk about your Christian faith through your work?

∼

O Lord, I want to tell nonbelievers of your love. Give me an opportunity to do so.

November 20: Risk Takers for Christ

"Who have risked their lives for the name of the Lord Jesus Christ" (Acts 15:26 NIV).

Would you have risked your life to witness to cannibals?

The words of Acts 15:26 are written on a monument at Martyr's Church on Erromanga, known as the Martyr Isle. This small island in the New Hebrides was the site of a number of missionary deaths.

Probably the most famous island martyr was John Williams (1796–1839). He was an ironmonger's apprentice when the London Missionary Society sent him and his young wife in 1816 to the Society Islands.

He evangelized, built churches and schools, trained converted cannibals as Christian teachers, and translated the Gospels into island languages. Educating the natives in trade and economics, he built machines for crushing sugar cane. Amazingly, he built a ship with the help of only three tools and no iron but a rusty anchor chain. In it he sailed thousands of miles over the Pacific.

He discovered the island of Rarotonga. It was there that he completed his translation of the New Testament. Returning to England in 1834, he found himself famous.

He returned to the South Seas in 1837 with 16 missionaries, a new ship, and funds. On a pioneering venture to Erromanga he and colleague James Harris were killed on November 20, 1839, by cannibals who had suffered cruelties at the hands of sailors years earlier. The missionaries' remains were buried on the island of Upolu, Samoa.

Lord, thank You for risk takers for Christ.

November 21: Potatoes for Pennies

"Blessed is he who is kind to the needy" (Prov. 14:21 NIV).

What can you buy for 2 cents?

Not much today. Even so-called "penny candy" costs a whole lot more than 2 cents these days.

Through the Potato Project of the Society of St. Andrew ministries, though, 2 cents can actually buy a serving of food for a hungry person in America.

The Society of St. Andrew is an ecumenical Christian ministry that attempts to fulfill Jesus' command to feed the hungry. Its ministries include Harvest of Hope, a hunger education program; the Gleaning Network, a project that has volunteers gathering leftover crops after harvest; and the Potato Project, which salvages the produce and distributes it.

Methodist Carolyn Vines serves as a district coordinator of the Potato Project and says that the results are incredible. One event gathered 47,640 pounds of sweet potatoes, which had a market value of almost $38,000. The only cost was $700, which paid for transportation. Carolyn says that another event resulted in food that cost just 2 cents a serving.

Methodist churches started a Your Change Can Change the World thrust to spotlight the project. "I am absolutely convinced that church members contributing their pocket change weekly can raise the money that we need," Carolyn says.

How do you spend your pocket change? Could you use it for more worthwhile causes?

∼

Dear God, I want to be more grateful for the material wealth I have.

November 22: The First Bible in America

"Because our gospel came to you not simply with words, but also with power, with the Holy Spirit and with deep conviction.... You became imitators of us and of the Lord" (1 Thess. 1:5–6 NIV).

He translated and published the first Bible in North America.

Born in Widford, England, John Eliot (1604–1690) graduated from Cambridge University in 1622. Leaving England in 1631, he served as chaplain to a group of Puritans sailing to America. The next year he started his almost 60-year ministry with the congregation who settled in Roxbury, Massachusetts.

John's ministry to the Indians began when an Algonquin captured in the Pequot War of 1637 was given to him as a bond servant. John painstakingly learned the Indian language. He started work among the tribe in 1646, preaching to them in their language and beginning work on a translation of the Bible in the then unwritten Algonquin dialect. He published the New Testament in 1661 and the Old Testament in 1663.

By 1674 John had established 14 self-governing "praying Indian" villages with nearly 24,000 Christian Indians. Because he believed the Indians were best suited to evangelize their own people, he trained 24 as preachers.

Known as the Apostle to the Indians, he died in Roxbury on May 21, 1690. A monument to him stands at Natick, Massachusetts, the site of his first "praying Indian" village.

Do you share the gospel with conviction and power?

∽

Lord, today enable me to reach others through Your Word.

November 23: God Speaks Their Language

"'With your blood you purchased men for God from every tribe and language and people and nation'" (Rev. 5:9 NIV).

It can be found in millions of homes across America. Every bookstore has a copy of it. It is a totally accessible book. We never doubt that the Bible is available to us in our language.

There are millions of people around the world, however, who cannot read the Bible because it has not been translated into their language.

Larry and Sonya Marhenke, missionaries with Lutheran Bible Translators, recently made passages from the Bible available for the first time to a people group in Central America.

Stories from the Gospel of Mark have been translated and published for the first time into Cunenteco, a Mayan language spoken in a remote part of Guatemala. The translation is called *The Power Book*.

"This publication focuses on God's power in and through the life of Jesus," Larry explains. "It will show the Cunenteco people that Jesus is more than simply someone to be respected, but He has unlimited power to change lives."

Lutheran Bible Translators has brought the Bible to about 5 million people through the translation of 11 New Testaments. More than 100 missionaries work with the organization.

Its executive director, Bob Roegner, says that the ministry's power is this: "There is a certain pride when people realize that God speaks their language."

This month National Bible Week focuses on the Word of God. Do you ever take the Bible for granted?

∼

Holy God, thank You for giving me Your Word.

November 24: An Active Mind

"Therefore, prepare your minds for action" (1 Peter 1:13 NIV).

The pioneer missionary earned the accolade "the superior man." Small, quiet, and scholarly, Presbyterian James Hepburn (1815-1911) appealed to the Japanese mind.

A native of Pennsylvania, he became a Christian while at Princeton Seminary. After practicing medicine in New York and China, he arrived in Japan in 1859, the year Japan was opened to the West. The first Presbyterian missionary to Japan began language study and medical practice in an abandoned Buddhist temple near Yokohama. He opened Japan's first dispensary, held the nation's first classes for medical students, and pioneered ophthalmology.

His wife, Clara, taught English to sons of nobility and pioneered education for women for 25 years.

Known equally for his linguistic and medical skills, James invented the system for writing Japanese in Roman letters and published the first Japanese-English dictionary and Japanese grammar. With co-workers he translated the entire Bible which was published in 1888 and a dictionary of the Bible published in 1891. He also translated the Westminster Shorter Catechism and Confession of Faith. He helped found and was first president of a Presbyterian college. Several of the first great leaders of the Protestant church in Japan resulted from his ministry.

James opened the heart of the nation to the gospel. His years of tireless work resulted in the emperor conferring on him an imperial decoration.

Is your mind prepared to do God's work?

Lead me daily to use my mind for Your service, Lord.

November 25: Standing Tall

"He set my feet on a rock and gave me a firm place to stand" (Psalm 40:2 NIV).

Have you ever felt defeated by the circumstances of life? Have you felt as if a huge weight pulled you down?

Jan Kerns, a missionary at Christian Encounter Ministries in California, says she literally saw the weight of despondency lifted off of a young man's shoulders.

In the late 1980s, a man came to the camp for troubled youth. Very skinny, his long, stringy hair fell across his face. "His posture was bent and, in general, he looked very defeated by life," Jan recalls.

Several months later Jan went to the chapel to participate in the Sunday morning worship service. On the stage stood a tall man playing his guitar and exuding confidence.

"Who's that?" Jan asked her husband, assuming he was a new intern. She learned that it was the man she had encountered just months before.

"He had dedicated his life to the Lord and testified that he literally felt a physical burden lifted from his shoulders," Jan says. "That's why he could now stand tall."

Jan, formerly a children's director in a church, and her husband, a former short-term missionary in Africa, began work at Christian Encounter Ministries in 1980. The ministry houses troubled youth, aged 16–26, who also attend high school on the 80-acre property.

Jan says that the greatest reward in the work is seeing lives transformed.

Savior, give me strength today when I feel defeated.

November 26: Instructing Others

"Keep hold of instruction, do not let go; guard her, for she is your life" (Prov. 4:13 RSV).

In seven years he completed degrees in the arts, medicine, and theology.

After reading David Livingstone's *Travels*, Robert Laws (1851–1934) desired to follow in the great missionary's footsteps. Coming from a poor family, Robert struggled to get an education by working as a cabinetmaker by day and attending evening classes to gain entrance to the University of Aberdeen.

After obtaining his three degrees, he joined a United Free Church of Scotland expedition in 1875 that established a mission named Livingstonia (in honor of Livingstone) near remote Lake Nyasa. Robert became mission leader and in 1880 moved his base to Bandawe near Lake Malawi. This location led to productive work among the Tonga and Ngoni peoples.

His prodigious labor in Africa included not only medical work but also establishment of hundreds of schools, publication of a missionary magazine, and translation of the Scriptures in tribal languages.

In 1894 he founded an institution for training teachers, pastors, health workers, and craftsmen. Many of the trained leaders became a part of the Church of Central Africa Presbyterian that Robert established. When the pioneer missionary left Africa in 1927, a Christian community of 60,000 with 13 ordained African pastors carried on what he had begun 52 years before.

Are you using your education, expertise, and experience as a tool for equipping others?

O Lord, show me today how to use my unique abilities for Your service.

November 27: A Good Samaritan

"But a Samaritan, as he journeyed, came to where he was; and when he saw him, he had compassion, and went to him and bound up his wounds, pouring on oil and wine; then he set him on his own beast and brought him to an inn, and took care of him" (Luke 10:33–34 RSV).

The most important word in the story of the good Samaritan is *compassion*. At the Good Samaritan Clinic in Tuscaloosa, Alabama, volunteers try to make compassion their mission, as they give free medical care to those in need.

The vision for the clinic came from Jerry Wilkins, the director of the Tuscaloosa Baptist Association. When he shared his idea with Linda Boyd, she initially told him it was a bad idea. "I told him we couldn't do this without the support of the medical community," she remembers.

As she worked with substance abusers who were mostly uninsured women, though, Linda opened up to the idea.

Today, the clinic offers high-quality medical, dental, and pharmaceutical care to the uninsured and the underinsured.

True reward comes from the lives touched through the clinic's services, Linda says. One man who had come in for a blood pressure check now volunteers as an interpreter for Hispanic patients.

Another woman who had been addicted to drugs and alcohol told Linda that she wanted to be a better woman and grandmother. They prayed together, and Linda is confident that the woman will turn her life around.

Do you operate daily by the principles set forth in the story of the good Samaritan?

~

Gracious God, I want to be a Christian who practices compassion.

November 28: A Reward Earned

"Give her the reward she has earned" (Prov. 31:31 NIV).

In 1928 she was the first person to be inducted into the Oklahoma Hall of Fame.

Elizabeth Fulton Hester (1839–1929), a member of the Methodist Episcopal Church, led a full life as an educator, nurse, civic worker, and church leader. She traveled west at the age of 17 to become a teacher at the mission school at Tishomingo, Indian Territory (now Oklahoma). It is said that five of her students became chiefs of their respective Indian nations.

In 1859 she married George B. Hester, a prominent merchant. During the Civil War she served as a nurse. After attending the Methodist General Conference with her delegate husband in Atlanta in 1878, she returned home to organize the first unit in her area of the newly established Woman's Foreign Missionary Society. She helped to establish auxiliaries throughout the Indian Territory.

In 1928 she was honored at the 50th celebration of the East Oklahoma Conference Woman's Foreign Missionary Society. She had been its president for 15 years. She also served as conference treasurer of the Woman's Home Missionary Society for 18 years and as a member of the Woman's Missionary Council. Also a spokesperson for woman suffrage during this time, she was active in many other civic organizations.

Are you actively involved in a missions organization? If you are, is God calling you to take on a leadership role?

Lord, reveal to me today how I can serve You more effectively.

November 29: Labor Not in Vain

"Be steadfast, immovable, always abounding in the work of the Lord, knowing that in the Lord your labor is not in vain" (1 Cor. 15:58 RSV).

"Tell my sister that I died at my post."

These were the last words of pioneer missionary Narcissa Whitman (1808–1847) who was killed in an Indian attack along with her physician husband, Marcus, on November 29, 1847, at their Presbyterian mission.

The Whitmans established the mission in 1836 seven miles from present Walla Walla, Washington. The site is now home to Whitman College, founded in their memory in 1859.

Working with her husband to minister to the physical and spiritual needs of the Indians, she often rode beside him on horseback carrying medicines and surgical instruments.

After her daughter drowned, she became mother to numerous other children. Some were half-Indian children. Others were children of parents who had died on the Oregon Trail. Their home often overflowed with travelers. Once in 1846, 69 men, women, and children crowded inside their mission walls. Nineteen were members of her family.

The president of Whitman College said of the couple in 1950, "So greatly did they live, so magnificently did they labor and serve, that forces they set in motion will forever enrich the civilization they helped to plant on the western slopes of the Continental Divide."

Are you involved in work that has eternal benefits?

∽

Enable me, God, to labor daily for You.

November 30: The Blessings of God's Work

"Now to him who by the power at work within us is able to do far more abundantly than all that we ask or think, to him be glory in the church and in Christ Jesus to all generations, for ever and ever! Amen" (Eph. 3:20–21 RSV).

At one time the woman wouldn't leave her house, spending her days watching television. Her low self-esteem kept her from pursuing any dreams. After enrolling in a Christian Women's Job Corps® program, though, she began working as a part-time employee at Wal-Mart. Since then she has received two promotions, bought her own house, and become involved in her church. A piece of paper inside a container attached to her key ring displays the Scripture passage above. She gives God glory for the work He's done in her life.

This woman is just one blessed through the ministries of the San Antonio Baptist Association. Coordinator of ministry missions Camille Simmons says that the association's work includes literacy missions, hunger ministries, family ministries, inner-city ministries, CWJC[SM], and coordination of missions groups and summer missionaries visiting the city.

"What happens when we give ourselves to our awesome, almighty Father is nothing short of miraculous," she says. "That He should allow us to be a part of what He is doing is a blessing beyond measure."

Can you join in God's work today?

~

Empower me to work for You, Lord. All glory from any of my work is Yours.

December 1: Victory over AIDS

"Jesus reached out his hand and touched the man. . . . And immediately the leprosy left him" (Luke 5:13 NIV).

Almost everyone today knows that HIV stands for human immunodeficiency virus.

To pastor Bruce Sonnenberg, though, the letters stand for something entirely different—He Intends Victory.

Bruce came face-to-face with HIV and AIDS in 1990, when he learned that two men in his Irvine, California, church had AIDS. Bruce felt it was time for his church to make a stand. The result was the He Intends Victory ministry.

The ministry encourages individual churches to set up ministries to people with HIV and AIDS. He urges churches to use Jesus as their model, for He cared for diseased people with love.

"We believe that the Christian church has on many occasions failed to reflect the heart of Jesus Christ toward those affected by HIV and AIDS because of fear, ignorance, or critical judgment. This must change," says the ministry's statement of purpose.

The power of the ministry is seen in such women as Renee Austin, a young woman who developed HIV after years of drug use. After discovering He Intends Victory, she became an active Christian spokesperson for people with the disease. Of the people she has met through the group, Renee says, "We are called to bear one another's burdens, and do we ever!"

How do you feel about people with HIV and AIDS? How would Jesus want you to feel?

∽

Give me a heart today, blessed Lord, for those suffering from HIV and AIDS.

December 2: Living for God

"'For in him we live and move and have our being'" (Acts 17:28 NIV).

In 1771 when John Wesley asked for volunteers to go to America as missionaries, the blacksmith-preacher enthusiastically responded. On the ship he recorded his desires: "I am going to live to God, and to bring others so to do."

Francis Asbury (1745–1816) began the practice of the Methodist itinerant preacher. Believing wholeheartedly in evangelism, he wrote: "Go into every kitchen and shop; address all, aged and young, on the salvation of their souls."

Spending much of his time on horseback, he traveled 270,000 miles during his lifetime. Crossing the Allegheny Mountains more than 60 times, he may have been the best-known man in North America. Braving blizzards, swollen rivers, and treacherous mountain paths, Francis experienced poor health for many years. He played down his difficulties writing, "This is a very small thing when compared to what the dear Redeemer suffered for the salvation of precious souls."

In 1784 John Wesley appointed Francis general superintendent of the Methodists in America. In December 1784 the Methodist Episcopal Church in the United States was organized in Baltimore with Francis as its leader.

When he arrived in America, there were four Methodist ministers. During his lifetime he ordained 4,000 preachers. The 300 members of the movement in 1771 grew to 214,000 in 1816.

Are you being an example to others?

Lord, empower me to live daily for You and tell others about You.

December 3: Mudslide!

"He heals the brokenhearted. . . . His understanding has no limit" (Psalm 147:3,5 NIV).

Devastating mudslides that hit Venezuela in December 1999 destroyed entire towns. Not one person was left to report the dead.

World Relief, the international assistance and refugee resettlement arm of the National Association of Evangelicals, went to Venezuela as soon as word of the disaster was reported. The destruction from the mudslides was beyond description for many in the organization. The numbers told part of the story—more than 30,000 dead, 400,000 homes destroyed, 200,000 jobs lost, entire villages wiped out.

The organization quickly began by giving aid to churches in distributing relief supplies. The churches then began the difficult task of getting water, food, medical supplies, and volunteers out to the people who needed these the most.

World Relief's Dave Larson said he heard people say things like, "What will we do? I have no home and no job." Confusion and despair reigned. He says that their work can only start to answer such questions for the people.

World Relief began in 1944 and represents more than 75 denominations and their missions counterparts. Its mission statement says that it will "work with the church in alleviating human suffering worldwide in the name of Christ."

When you see disasters like the Venezuelan mudslides on the news, do you feel like you are worlds away, or that you can help somehow?

∽

I ask You, Almighty God, to be with those affected by natural disasters. Give them comfort and peace.

December 4: Blankets of Love

"Lacking clothes, they spend the night naked; they have nothing to cover themselves in the cold" (Job 24:7 NIV).

A cold, harsh winter awaited ethnic Albanians as they returned to their homes in the Kosovo province of Yugoslavia.

More than 850,000 Albanians became refugees in the summer of 1999 after their expulsion from their homelands. The cold winter greeted them as they returned in October of the year.

Christians from around the United States provided one form of help: warm, comforting blankets.

The International Mission Board, a Southern Baptist missions agency, sponsored the Blanket Kosovo with Love project and encouraged Baptists to send in their contributions. And the call worked, says IMB's transportation freight specialist Jean McDaniel.

Jean says that more than 36,000 blankets came into her warehouse from across the country.

"In my wildest imagination, I couldn't have imagined the response this big in such a short time," she says. "It was unreal."

Blankets came in all shapes and sizes. All were new and made of wool or other warm materials. Some were store-bought, and others were homemade.

"There were baby blankets and children's blankets," Jean recalls. "People had crocheted blankets. There were handmade quilts."

This project reminds us that even a simple gesture can reach across the oceans to a war-torn people. All Christians can make a difference.

How might I make a difference to people in other nations?

∼

Lord Jesus, give hope today to the people in Yugoslavia and all nations wracked by war.

December 5: A Firm Hope

"For God alone my soul waits in silence, for my hope is from him" (Psalm 62:5 NIV).

After he was converted on one of his voyages, he resigned from the British Royal Navy and dedicated himself to missions.

Captain Allen Gardiner (1794–1851) had witnessed firsthand the plight of Indians in South America. He had made several missions journeys there before his final one in 1850.

On December 5, 1850, Allen and six men representing the Patagonian Missionary Society went ashore on the remote island of Tierra del Fuego off the southern tip of South America. The Indians whom they had come to evangelize drove them back to their ship. Taking refuge in Spanish Harbor, they awaited a supply ship. The vessel arrived in January 1852—three months too late. All the crew had died of starvation.

Allen's last diary entry read: "Great and marvelous are the loving-kindnesses of my gracious God unto me. I neither hunger nor thirst, though five days without food." On a rock near where he lay down to die he had inscribed Psalm 62:5.

When news of Allen's heroism reached England, other missionaries volunteered to continue his work among the Indians. The schooner, *Allen Gardiner*, sailed from Bristol in 1854 with members of the (Anglican) South American Missionary Society. Today churches in southern Chile and Argentina have connections to Allen Gardiner's visionary work.

Do you continue to praise God in the most difficult of times?

~

Gracious God, help me to be faithful today when I encounter the unexpected.

December 6: Home Away from Home

"Prepare a guest room for me, because I hope to be restored to you in answer to your prayers" (Philemon 22 NIV).

Have you ever wondered where missionaries live when they come to the United States for a visit or an extended stateside assignment? Their own home is oceans away, and they may be unable to stay with relatives or friends. The solution to the problem often comes from the Missionary Housing ministry. WMU regularly helps missionaries hook up with homes provided by the ministry.

When Rodney Coleman's missionary work in Colombia began to be threatened by guerrilla warfare, he knew he'd be coming back to the States soon. He called upon individuals at WMU to help. They helped him find a temporary home at Fairview Baptist Church's missionary house in Grand Prairie, Texas.

Rodney says that such help answers missionaries' prayers. "You do not know how much your help, your service, your ministry means to those of us far away or to those of us under fire," he says. "Our lives have been in danger this year and just to find a place like this to go to catch our breath and come back is fantastic."

Rodney's family is just one touched by the housing ministry. More than 470 homes are available across the country; they are offered by churches, associations, and individuals. Arrangements are usually made for free rent, with missionaries paying utilities.

～

Thank You, Lord, for those willing to open their homes to strangers.

December 7: Exploring for God

"Let us send men before us, that they may explore the land for us" (Deut. 1:22 RSV).

Missionary explorers played a significant role in the history of missions. They not only set up mission sites but also many made important geographical discoveries.

Jacques Marquette (1637–1675), French Jesuit missionary, ministered to the Algonquin, Ottawa, and Huron Indians. Jacques, together with Louis Joliet, made a 2,500-mile, four-month canoe trip down the Mississippi River in 1673. They determined that the Mississippi led to the Gulf of Mexico.

Most famous missionary explorers have been associated with Africa.

Scottish missionary Robert Moffat (1795–1883) opened up the African continent from Cape Colony in South Africa to beyond the Zambezi River. He inspired his son-in-law David Livingstone to explore new lands.

Probably the most famous missionary explorer was David Livingstone (1813–1873). A member of the London Missionary Society, he traveled north of the Zambezi River through unexplored territory, covering 6,000 miles in four years. Constantly ill and beset with malaria, he persevered. After returning to England a hero, he went on his next expedition mapping out much of central Africa and discovering Victoria Falls. He also identified the natural resources of the area and showed that malaria could be diminished by the use of quinine. In 1866 he began his final expedition and died in search of the source of the Nile.

Thank You, God, for the great contributions of missionary explorers.

December 8: No Greater Love

"'The greatest way to show love for friends is to die for them'" (John 15:13 CEV).

John knelt—obeying the commands of the ruthless Chinese Communists that fatal morning of December 8, 1934. Betty, quivering and thinking of the fate of her three-month-old daughter, fell to her knees. The sword flashed twice: John (1907–1934) and Betty Stam (1906–1934) were with Christ.

The martyrdom of the young missionaries influenced hundreds to volunteer for missionary service.

Meeting at Moody Bible Institute, John and Betty joined the China Inland Mission (CIM) and married in 1933. They had been at Miao-shou only a few weeks.

Although their ministry had been brief, their devotion to Christ had made an impression. A Chinese Christian doctor, who begged for their lives that morning, was also killed.

A Chinese evangelist named Lo recovered the couple's bodies and buried them. Conducting their funeral, he said, "They came to China and to Miao-shou, not for themselves but for you, to tell you about the great love of God, that you might believe in the Lord Jesus and be eternally saved."

After finding baby Helen Priscilla in a deserted house, Lo and his wife carried her in a rice basket 100 miles by foot to a missionary family. She became known as the Miracle Baby.

Would you be willing to lay down your life for the cause of Christ?

∽

Loving God, give me daily a sacrificial, obedient spirit.

December 9: New Friends and New Opportunities

"We proclaim to you what we have seen and heard, so that you also may have fellowship with us" (1 John 1:3 NIV).

In delivering relief to earthquake-ravaged Turkey, Don Presley learned important lessons about miracles and friendship.

Don, who was part of a disaster relief team sponsored by Alabama Baptist Men, set up semipermanent kitchens in three different areas.

"The first thing that was miraculous about our trip was how we got there," Don says. Turkey—which has just a few Protestant churches, and missionaries work in secret—would never seek help from Christians. Some of the Protestant church leaders, however, had government contacts and signed an agreement for the Baptist Men group to provide relief. "The missionaries there just couldn't believe it," he says.

The other thing that surprised Don and the seven other members of his team was the people's friendliness and curiosity. Despite the fact that most of them are Muslim, the people expressed interest in their faith.

"Many of the people we dealt with were young Turkish soldiers," Don says. "They were so nice, courteous, and friendly. The interaction we had with them was great."

Don says that individuals would often ask, "Are you American?" The next question would be, "Are you Christian?" In a country where Christians often worship in hiding, this surprised them. "We hope that, even though we couldn't openly witness, we used our actions and words to plant some seeds."

How will you share your faith today?

∼

Open the hearts of men and women everywhere to You, Lord.

December 10: Nobel Prize Honors

"He who pursues righteousness and love finds life, prosperity and honor" (Prov. 21:21 NIV).

Did you know that three missionaries received the Nobel Peace Prize for their work?

Methodist layman John Mott (1865–1950) was the world's leading missionary statesman of the first half of the twentieth century. In 1888 he organized the Student Volunteer Movement. He founded the World Student Christian Federation in 1895 and in 1915 became general secretary for the American YMCA. He was cofounder of the International Missionary Council in 1921 and was active in the World Council of Churches. He shared the Nobel Prize in 1946 with Emily Balch.

Albert Schweitzer (1875-1965) had three passions in life: theology, music, and medicine. He authored several theological works including *The Quest of the Historical Jesus*. A musical historian, he was organist of Bach concerts. After receiving his medical degree in 1913, he went to the Congo where he established a hospital at Lambarene and served there the rest of his life. Also known for his quest for world peace, he received the Nobel Peace Prize in 1952.

Mother Teresa (1910–1997), one of the most respected religious leaders of the twentieth century, founded the Missionaries of Charity in Calcutta in 1950. In 1952 the Roman Catholic nun opened the Nirmal Hriday (Pure Heart) Home for Dying Destitutes in Calcutta. Her work spread to five continents. She was awarded the Nobel Peace Prize in 1979.

Thank You, God, for the honors that missionaries have received for their significant work to humanity.

December 11: Radios for Christ

"Incline your ear, and hear the words of the wise" (Prov. 22:17 RSV).

How many telephones do you have? What would you do if no telephone at all was available to you?

In many Mayan communities of Guatemala, the nearest telephone is a half-day's walk through a rain forest that at times is completely impassable. In such a situation, how can people and villages communicate with one another?

One missions group is solving this problem by installing ham radio equipment and, in doing so, also sharing the message of God's love.

DARF (Disciples Amateur Radio Fellowship) is a joint missions endeavor of the Disciples of Christ and United Church of Christ churches. They work through the Common Global Ministries Board and the country's Guatemala Christian Action Group to organize efforts to install ham radios in remote areas.

John Grigg serves as the group's president and has been on work trips to Africa and Central America. The project in Guatemala was especially important because of the Mayan communities' efforts to rebuild after the exploitation and destruction caused by years of civil war.

"They have many needs, but one need that now stands out is the need for communications," John says. "They need the advice, counsel, and support they could give each other if the isolated communities could share ideas, resources, and information."

Volunteers combine their love of ham radios with God's power to bring practical help and spiritual guidance to the people.

∼

Show me, Lord, how to use my interests to provide Your love to others.

December 12: The Greatest Is Love

"So faith, hope, love abide, these three; but the greatest of these is love" (1 Cor. 13:13 RSV).

The Chinese first called her Devil Woman. As she won herself into their hearts, she was called the Foreign Lady with the Big Love Heart.

Charlotte Digges "Lottie" Moon (1840–1912) was born on December 12, 1840, near Scottsville, Virginia. One of the first southern women to receive a master's degree, she was considered "the best educated and most cultured woman in the South" when she sailed to China in 1873.

She spent most of her 40 years in women's work at Tengchow. There in her living room she organized the North China Woman's Missionary Union. For 9 years she lived at Pingtu evangelizing where no woman missionary had ever gone.

Lottie had a great love for the Chinese, and they for her.

Her words speak volumes: "I would I had a thousand lives that I might give them to the women of China."

A fellow missionary said of her, "We all love her. And how the Chinese love her is beautiful to see."

After Lottie's death from starvation, the Chinese Christians at Tengchow spent 3 years gathering the love gifts that went into a marble stone monument for her. The three lines on it read: "1915; A Monument to bequeath the love of Miss Lottie Moon, an American missionary; The Tengchow church remembers forever."

Are you going to be remembered for your love?

∽

God, give me a sacrificial love for others.

December 13: Treasures at Christmastime

"Don't store up for yourselves treasures on earth, where moth and rust destroy, and where thieves break in and steal. But store up for yourselves treasures in heaven. . . . For where your treasure is, there your heart will be also" (Matt. 6:19–21 NIV).

Do you store up earthly treasures during the Christmas season, or do you stop and consider the less fortunate around you?

This time of year is perhaps the busiest for missions-minded Christians, as they extend the message of Christ's birth, life, and teachings to the needy in their communities. Churches everywhere have special Christmas programs and ministries.

At First United Methodist Church in Hueytown, Alabama, members work for months to get ready for their annual Community Children's Christmas Party. They obtain the names of poor children from local schools and social service agencies and invite these children to the party. Each child receives three wrapped presents; girls also receive a beanbag toy and boys a football. The children's families also receive help.

"Each family receives two bags of groceries from our food pantry and clothes from our clothes closet," says organizer Betty Rheuby. Volunteers also helped install a basketball goal for two brothers whose father is blind.

The joy in seeing children receive Christmas presents they might otherwise not receive is a true blessing, says Betty. And it wouldn't be possible, she says, without the generosity of church members. "We are truly a loving and giving church family," she says.

~

I want to store up heavenly treasures, Lord, instead of material things.

December 14: Peace Through Work

"Let the peace of heart which comes from Christ be always present in your hearts and lives" (Col. 3:15 TLB).

We all know that missions work is beneficial—both to the recipient of the ministry and to the worker. Karen Jones, a professor at Indiana's Huntington College, wanted quantitative proof of it and did her doctoral thesis on the topic.

Karen worked with five groups of World Changers youth volunteers and, before they began their work, asked them questions that tested their faith level and self-esteem. At week's end, she asked them follow-up questions. The results provided substantial evidence that the missions work vastly boosted both parts of their lives.

A former minister of youth who already had a heart for missions, Karen says her study reinforced her beliefs. She says that missions work "gives you a deep sense of peace and satisfaction that you are putting your faith into action. When you are serving in Christ's name, it is very profound."

Today, Karen works as a project coordinator for World Changers and has seen the effects on the lives of youth close-up. At one work project in Youngstown, Ohio, her group of teenagers prayed deeply for the homeowner they were serving, who was a known drug dealer. After leaving a gospel tract for him one day, they prayed that he would be unable to sleep without reading it. The next morning he announced that he had read it and believed in Jesus.

'That was miraculous," she says. "It gave the youth a great learning experience."

Have you experienced missions work firsthand?

~

Serving in Your name, Christ Jesus, is so powerful.

December 15: He Stills the Storm

"A squall came down on the lake, so that the boat was being swamped, and they were in great danger. The disciples went and woke him, saying, 'Master, Master, we're going to drown!'" (Luke 8:23–24 NIV).

With gunfire exploding in all directions, the only thing the missionary family could do was pray.

Lowell and Claudia Wertz's family knew this might be the end. Soldiers waged war outside their door and, though they prayed for deliverance, they were unsure and frightened. A knock on the door raised them from their prayers; Lowell opened the door to see the army's commanding officer.

The officer recalled an expression of friendship the family had given before and decided to return the favor. He escorted them to their nearby airplanes. Within hours, the place where they huddled in safety had been destroyed. "As I made the evacuation flight, I could only say one thing, 'God has been so good!'" Lowell remembers.

Lowell and Claudia served in Zaire for 12 years as United Methodist missionaries and today work in Tanzania with Joy in the Harvest, a ministry they helped establish.

In their years on the field, they have been robbed, looted, and abandoned by friends. Other friends have been martyred and their own children have stood at death's door.

In all circumstances, Lowell says that the message of Luke 8 speaks profoundly to him. He has often shouted at the Lord for help. And He has delivered him.

Have you had similar experiences?

∽

I pray to You today, Lord, for help in all circumstances.

December 16: An Obedient Devoted Follower

"Now that you have purified yourselves by obeying the truth so that you have sincere love for your brothers, love one another deeply, from the heart" (1 Peter 1:22 NIV).

Prenna was the first Hindu temple girl to find her way into the sanctuary of her bungalow.

Missionary Amy Carmichael (1867–1951) and her companions kept Prenna in 1901. Soon other temple runaways and abandoned children joined her.

Amy's life was characterized by spiritual passion, obedience to God, and devotion to others. "Oh, to care, and oh for power to make others care," she once said, "not less, but far, far, more!"

The oldest of seven children, Amy was born into a strong Presbyterian home in Northern Ireland. After serving 15 months in Japan, she arrived in 1895 in South India with the Church of England Zenana Missionary Society.

Amy focused her efforts on the children who were to be dedicated as Hindu temple prostitutes. She founded the Dohnavur Fellowship with more than 800 children in three homes, a hospital, and evangelistic work. She served faithfully 56 years without a furlough.

A prolific author, she wrote 35 books including *Things as They Are* (1903) which shocked many readers with its harsh truths about ministering in a foreign culture. Badly injured in a fall in 1931, she became an invalid but continued to write.

Do you "care" the way that Amy Carmichael did?

∼

Holy God, may I be obedient to Your message and then in love devoted to others.

December 17: A Memorable Millennium

"I thank my God every time I remember you" (Phil. 1:3 NIV).

The change of the millennium meant different things to different people—trepidation, excitement, and many celebrations.

Tom Berlin, pastor of Floris United Methodist Church, Herndon, Virginia, challenged his congregation to mark the millennium in a bolder way. "Why not use this opportunity to bless some of the poorest and most vulnerable people on Earth?" he asked his members at the first Sunday of 1999 Advent. "Why not build an orphanage in Sierra Leone?"

Three years earlier, Ray Buchanan of Stop Hunger Now spoke at the church and told them of an upcoming trip to Sierra Leone. Tom felt God call him to go on the trip. In the African country, Tom came face to face with poverty, war, hunger, and despair. He felt especially moved by the children, many of whom had been recruited as soldiers in the country's civil war. He also met Rev. John Yambasu, a national who not much later came to the States and visited Tom's church. In his sermon, John encouraged the congregation, "We need you to remember the people over there."

Tom then instituted his millennium challenge, asking members to give $20,000 for a new school. By the end of Advent, the church had given $125,000. Plans are now underway for a street ministry for hungry children, an orphanage, school, and church.

How can your generosity reach out to the world's poorest people?

~

Bless the poor children, Loving God.

December 18: A Fervent Believer

"Apollos... was a learned man, with a thorough knowledge of the Scriptures.... He spoke with great fervor" (Acts 18: 24,25 NIV).

Are you an enthusiastic, impassioned believer?

Thomas Coke (1747–1814), the Foreign Minister of Methodism, was.

He was dismissed from his Anglican parish in 1776 for being too "fervent" a preacher.

A native of Wales, Thomas graduated from Oxford in 1768 and became an Anglican curate. Influenced by one of John Wesley's evangelists, Thomas was converted and joined the Methodist cause.

In 1784 he arrived in America with instructions for Francis Asbury, the only one of Wesley's appointees who had stayed in America during the Revolution. Thomas chaired the Christmas Conference (1784) which led to the establishment of the Methodist Episcopal Church in America. Both he and Francis had strong antislavery feelings, and together they presented an antislavery petition to George Washington.

In his nine visits to America, Thomas paid his own expenses. A man of wealth, he generously gave it to Methodist missions. He donated more money to religion than any other Methodist and probably more than any Protestant of his day.

After his last voyage in 1803, he directed his efforts toward the West Indies, Gibraltar, and Africa. He became the president of the first Methodist missionary organization formed in England. While traveling to Ceylon (now Sri Lanka) with a group of missionaries, he died at sea.

~

Precious Lord, give me a fervent longing to reach others.

December 19: A Revolutionary Change

"Jesus answered, 'It is written, "Man does not live on bread alone, but on every word that comes from the mouth of God"'" (Matt. 4:4 NIV).

Rosario Rivera grew up poor in the Andes Mountains of Peru. Incensed by the injustice around her, she became a revolutionary. At 18 she went to Cuba and became the assistant of the notorious guerilla leader Che Guevara. After his death, she returned to Peru more bitter than ever.

In December 1971 after hearing that evangelist Luis Palau was speaking in the bull arena in Lima she became enraged. Deciding to kill him, she took a gun to the arena. At the end of the service, trying to maneuver into position to fire her gun, she went forward with 300 people. When an elderly counselor asked her if she wanted to receive Christ, she hit the woman in the face and ran away. That night she couldn't sleep. She got up and, searching her Bible, came across Matthew 4:4. Weeping, she received Christ.

Transformed by the power of Christ, she turned her leftist ideology into Christian social action. She tackled poverty, corruption, and injustice. The ex-Communist took evangelistic missionary trips throughout Peru. She started the I Am Jesus Christian elementary school in her home and initiated a breakfast program for children that fed 2,500 children in 1986.

Have you experienced a revolutionary change in your life?

∽

Help me to see needs around me, Lord, with the compassion of Christ.

December 20: Help Wanted

"During the night Paul had a vision of a man of Macedonia standing and begging him, 'Come over to Macedonia and help us'" (Acts 16:9 NIV).

An American soldier in Fort Wrangell, Alaska, wrote him, "Come and help them." The soldier was imploring the missionary to come assist eight Indian woodcutters from British Columbia who were evangelizing the Indians.

Providing help to Alaskans for three decades is what Sheldon Jackson (1834–1909) did in response to the letter. In 1877 when Sheldon left for Alaska, he had been a missionary for 18 years and was headquartered in Denver as superintendent of Presbyterian missions for most of the western frontier.

From 1884 to 1907 he supervised Alaskan missions for the Presbyterian Church. Through his government-appointed position as General Agent for Education, he established numerous schools for Eskimos and Indians.

The most dramatic way Sheldon helped Alaska was by introducing the reindeer—probably saving a whole people from extinction. Indignant that the Eskimos were faced with a famine because of unrestrained whale and seal hunting, he asked Congress to bring over reindeer from Siberia and teach Eskimo youth how to raise them. After delays from Congress, he collected over $2,000 and traveled thousands of miles in Siberia to bring over the first herd of domesticated reindeer in 1891. Congress then voted money for more reindeer.

Are you sensitive to the needs of people in other states and countries?

Lord, help me to be receptive when I receive a call for help.

December 21: God Wants Me!

"May the God of peace, . . . that great Shepherd of the sheep, equip you with everything good for doing His will, and may he work in us what is pleasing to him" (Heb. 13:20–21 NIV).

"God wants me!"

John and Rebecca Fulks say that this knowledge continues to be a marvel to them. They have learned, amidst the hectic pace of everyday life, that all God wants is their willingness to serve Him.

Of their work as Global Outreach missionaries in the African country of Uganda, Rebecca says: "We have found that the demands of the missions field and the ministry could take 24 hours a day if we let it. We find ourselves involved in 'work' from morning to night, go to bed, get up, and work from morning to night."

The solution to such a life filled with busy activity is to realize that God doesn't necessarily need our activity. He wants it—if it is glorifying Him!

"We soon realized that the work was not getting done the way God wanted it," she says. "God wants me! He does not need me, but He wants me!" She now prays that what they desire for the ministry will be in line with what God wants for it.

Do you realize that God wants you to serve Him? Isn't that an awesome thought?

~

God, I am humbled to know that You desire a relationship with me and want my service.

December 22: Rooted in Christ

"So then, just as you received Christ Jesus as Lord, continue to live in him, rooted and built up in him, strengthened in the faith as you were taught" (Col. 2: 6–7 NIV).

Can you imagine being on a missions field for 61 years?

Pioneer missionaries William Buck Bagby (1855–1939) and Anne Luther Bagby (1859–1942) are legendary in Southern Baptist history. The couple, married at Baylor University in October 1880, received missionary appointment during Christmas week of that year. Anne died (3 years after William's death) during Christmas week of 1942, making hers the longest tenure of any Southern Baptist missionary.

Landing in Brazil in March 1881, they organized the first Baptist church made up of Brazilians on October 15 in Salvador. Moving to Rio, they established the second Baptist church on August 24, 1884. Working there until 1900, William evangelized in the city and pioneered churches in other Brazilian states.

From 1900 to 1927 they settled in Sao Paulo where in 1902 Anne was founder/principal of the first Baptist school for women. William's training of Brazilian pastors and church leaders led to the formation in 1907 of the National Brazilian Baptist Convention.

Their last mission station was Porto Alegre. Following their deaths they were praised for "the ideals they planted taking root and permeating the hearts of men like a leaven in the nation." Their five surviving children continued their legacy, all becoming missionaries in South America.

Thank you, Almighty God, for those who have strengthened me in my faith.

December 23: Witnessing in "High" Places

"He sent for Paul and listened to him as he spoke about faith in Christ Jesus. As Paul discoursed on righteousness, self-control and the judgment to come, Felix was afraid and said, 'That's enough for now!... When I find it convenient, I will send for you'" (Acts 24: 24–25 NIV).

If the occasion arose, would you present the gospel to a high-ranking official?

Sometimes missionaries have been in positions to witness to people in high places. Such was the case of Lillias Underwood, the official medical attendant of the Korean queen.

Apprehensive at first about attending to the needs of the queen, the Presbyterian missionary nurse eventually became a familiar figure at court and was even able to dispense with an interpreter. Because of Korean etiquette, she was reluctant to present the gospel to the queen. She asked her fellow missionaries to pray that she would be given the opportunity. Her prayer was answered one Christmas Eve when the queen sent for her to inquire about the meaning of the Christian holiday. Lillias then explained the plan of salvation. Unfortunately, her hopes of reaching the queen disappeared in 1895 when Japanese assassins murdered the queen.

Though the death of her friend was a painful experience, Lillias continued her work with her missionary husband, Horace Grant Underwood, who organized the first Presbyterian church in Korea.

∽

Lord, help me to take advantage of every opportunity to present the gospel to those who do not know Christ. Tomorrow may be too late.

December 24: A Life of Sacrifice

"Therefore, I urge you, . . . in view of God's mercy, to offer your bodies as living sacrifices, holy and pleasing to God—this is your spiritual act of worship" (Rom. 12:1 NIV).

It was Christmas Eve 1912. Because she gave all her money and food to others during a famine in China, Southern Baptist missionary Lottie Moon (1840–1912) died of starvation.

Lottie Moon's life, as well as her death, was characterized by sacrifice.

The gifted, well-educated woman from an old Virginia family could have lived a comfortable life in America. Instead, she dedicated her life to sacrificial service among the women of North China. For 40 years she served as a counselor, comforter, teacher, and minister to them.

Lottie's words reflect her attitude about sacrifice:

"I have lived right down among the people, and I know they can be won by loving self-sacrifice on the part of the missionaries."

"Let them [missionaries] come rejoicing to sacrifice for that Lord and Master who so freely gave himself for them."

Another missionary wrote of Lottie's sacrifice:

"She makes very little ado about her sacrifices. I think I might safely say that no missionary is making greater sacrifices than she is making."

Initiated by Lottie in December 1887 (and named for her after her death), the Lottie Moon Christmas Offering® for International Missions is a fitting legacy of her sacrifice.

Where can you sacrificially serve?

O Lord, reveal to me this Christmas Eve where I need to give more to Your work.

December 25: A Thirst for Souls

"And the Lord added to their number daily those who were being saved" (Acts 2:47 NIV).

Jane (not her real name), a new Chinese Christian, knew she had to share the good news she had found. She started a church in a building that could hold 300. In seven years, attendance had grown from 14 to 1,000.

When city officials attended a drama about the birth of Jesus, Jane feared the worst. Instead, the two found her teaching positive and encouraged her to disciple others. She continued to reach out and invite others to church.

Soon after, a representative from the International Mission Board came to the area and met Jane. He was immediately impressed by her enthusiasm, feeling that she was an answer to the group's prayers for direction in that area. Together they developed a ministry to train and disciple new Christians. The training attracted 103 people. All attended 10- to 14-hour seminars and slept on floors and benches for 30 days.

In the three months after the event, those 103 participants had a profound impact on their communities. They led 1,300 to Christ, baptizing 1,200 of them. Three new churches, each with nearly 50 new believers, had been started.

The IMB representative wept upon hearing of these results. From one new believer had come thousands of new souls to Christ. Jane's thirst to reach others had truly worked.

This Christmas do you have a thirst to tell others the good news?

~

My Redeemer, give me a powerful need to reach others with the gospel.

December 26: Christ's Strength

"I can do all things through Christ which strengtheneth me" (Phil. 4:13 KJV).

Cheryl Derbyshire says she often feels as if she's stuck in the Israel of the Old Testament. She is reminded daily of religious practices that are in complete opposition to her Christian faith.

"Every day I see idol worship, corruption, and people far from God," says Cheryl, a Southern Baptist missionary to Thailand.

She remembers one night in particular, when neighbors' religious ceremonies became too much to bear. All Thai homes have a "spirit house" in their front yard used for prayer and rituals. The neighborhoods are built in an open style, so Cheryl can easily hear the ceremonies.

"As the monks began to chant I felt so oppressed by it all that I took my children and left the house," she says.

In such times, Cheryl relies on Philippians 4:13, the verse she has claimed as her own since beginning work with her doctor husband, Doug, and their four children. The verse gives her strength to endure various struggles.

To minister to new Thai friends and neighbors, Cheryl and Doug reach out through their home. Each December, she has a Christmas program in her front yard. Once a month they lead a Buddhist discussion group. Opposition to Christianity is hard to break through, however, since 95 percent of the population is Buddhist.

How do you confront situations where, as a Christian, you are in the minority?

∼

Dear God, give me strength today to rely on You totally.

December 27: Feliz Navidad

"And the angel said unto them, Fear not; for, behold, I bring you good tidings of great joy. . . . For unto you is born this day in the city of David a Saviour" (Luke 2:10 KJV).

"Feliz Navidad."

For hundreds of Honduran children injured and displaced by 1998's Hurricane Mitch, the Spanish version of "Merry Christmas" held little meaning.

Samaritan's Purse, an ecumenical ministry headed by Franklin Graham, reached out to these children through its Operation Christmas Child.

More than 800 children gathered at Estadio Olympico in San Pedro Sula, Honduras, to receive gift-filled shoeboxes. The children opened the boxes to find dolls, trucks, candy, crayons, socks, stuffed animals, and a variety of other gifts.

They also found colorful books and other Christian literature that told them of the birth of Jesus.

In addition to the gift distribution at the athletic stadium, distribution took place in the children's unit of a nearby hospital. Children wounded by the hurricane, as well as those suffering from illnesses, received shoeboxes.

Honduran children received 119,000 Christmas boxes!

Operation Christmas Child reaches out to children around the world—from Central America, to Europe, to the United States, to Africa—who often have never received a Christmas present. Boxes come from volunteers around the globe.

Do you know of children who will not receive the full benefit of a merry Christmas? How can you help them?

Everlasting God, I praise You today for the wonderful, ultimate gift of Christ. Give me a heart for others during this holiday season.

December 28: Giver of Strength

"In your hands are strength and power to exalt and give strength to all" (1 Chron. 29:12 NIV).

Before her death in December 1974 she said, "God has taken hold of me, and he gives me the strength I need each day. He uses me just because I know that I have no strength of my own."

When she died at the age of 95, Evelyn "Granny" Brand was a legend. In southern India decades after she had retired, she traveled on horseback from village to village preaching and teaching. She set up mission stations on six mountain ranges treating dysentery and malaria, instructing in hygiene, and telling the story of Jesus.

Evelyn had sensed a missionary calling to India after hearing Jesse Brand speak during his furlough in England. She went to India in 1911; they fell in love and married in 1913. They spent their honeymoon among the impoverished people of the disease-ridden Kollimalais Mountains of Death. By 1927 they had given medical aid to over 25,000 people. During one year Jesse preached over 4,000 times in 90 villages. After he died of malaria on June 15, 1928, Evelyn continued the work among the hill people they loved.

The missionary legacy of the Brands continued in their children. Daughter Connie married a missionary; son Paul became a pioneer in performing rehabilitative surgery on the hands and feet of lepers.

Are you looking to God or yourself for strength?

∼

Today, Almighty God, give me the strength I need.

December 29: False Gods

"You, dear children, are from God and have overcome them, because the one who is in you is greater than the one who is in the world" (1 John 4:4 NIV).

The people stand on the beach, their white outfits blowing in the breeze and reflecting the moonlight. They lift candles and clay pots, offering them as gifts to the goddess of the sea.

At midnight, they throw their offerings in the water, believing that the sacrifice will give them good fortune all year long.

This is the scene at beaches outside Rio de Janeiro, Brazil, every December 31. It shows the power of spiritism over Brazilians, and the struggle that Southern Baptist missionary Margaret Johnson faces.

Brazil is actually an open area for missionaries, since the government encourages religious freedom. Most Brazilians, however, practice a mix of religion and superstition that manifests itself into spiritism. It teaches that there are seven main nature gods that can be appeased with offerings.

As a teacher at a theological school, Margaret encounters students both from Christian and spiritist backgrounds. She also meets people through her church who have struggled with spiritism. She brings the news that Christ's message and love can overcome the spiritism of this world.

You may not practice spiritism, but do you ever rely on belief systems that counter Christ's power?

∼

Remind me, Lord, that only through You can I overcome the forces of this world. I want to rest in that assurance.

December 30: You Are Called!

"Therefore . . . be all the more eager to make your calling and election sure" (2 Peter 1:10 NIV).

Many Christians seem to know that God has called them to do something for Him. The problem is that few of us are able to figure out what that something is.

Is God calling you to teach children's Sunday School classes? Does He want you to sing for Him? Do homeless people have needs you can meet?

Missionaries have varied stories of how they learned that they were to serve God. They teach us that a call can come in many forms.

United Methodist missionaries Wayne and Mary Daniel had already been called to missions when God revealed a specific calling. Wayne, on a visit to Meru, Kenya, had the vision for a ministry to the country's street children.

Once someone asked volunteer Barbara Joiner where she got her heart for missions. Barbara, who has been on more than a dozen missions trips, answered him: "I learned to sing 'Jesus Loves the Little Children' before I learned 'Jesus Loves Me.'"

What is God calling you to do?

~

I'm not sure how You want me to serve You, God, but I am open to Your call.

December 31: Important Questions

"The Lord will fulfill his purpose for me" (Psalm 138:8 NIV).

Do You want me? How can You use me?

If you have never asked God these questions, perhaps now is the time to do so. Discovering God's purpose for your life is one of the most important steps you can take as a Christian.

Scott Chafee, who served as a Southern Baptist missionary in Zambia, says that this kind of introspection and an openness to God's will are the only reasons he now serves where he does.

"God never would have used me overseas if I had not taken that beginning step of asking Him, 'Do You want me?' Then the rest was easy. I simply walked through the doors that God opened for me and my family, and the last door He opened was the 747 hatch on the runway of Lusaka's International Airport!"

The door has led to a variety of ministries. Scott taught at a theological seminary, helped start new churches, and delivered Bibles to Zambians. He once gave a Bible to a tribal chief who, upon receiving it, said, "This is the first time in my life that I have ever held God's Word in my own hands." Today Scott helps enlist recruits for the International Mission Board's Journeyman and International Service Corps programs. He works at the IMB in Richmond, Virginia.

He could never have had such experiences if he had not opened himself to God's will in the first place. He challenges other Christians "to allow God to get them out of their comfort zones" and see where God wants to take them.

∽

Do You want me, O Lord? How can You use me in the coming year?

Index

Agnew, Eliza, 249
Allen, Margaret, 268
Allshorn, Florence, 38
Anderson, Kathryn, 82
Armacost, Ben and Judy, 214
Armstrong, Annie, 199, 237
Arnot, Frederick Stanley, 18, 67, 236
Asbury, Francis, 343, 359
Assisi, Francis of, 283
Aylward, Gladys, 81, 189
Bagby, Anne Luther, 62, 139, 363
Bagby, William and Anne, 139, 363
Bailey, Bob and Susan, 294
Bailey, Wellesley and Alice, 329
Barnardo, Thomas, 260
Barstow, Lori, 181
Bateman, Robert, 111
Bauernfeind, Susan M., 288
Behrens, Herbert, 176
Bell, Nelson. 316
Bennett, Chipley and Anne, 80
Berlin, Tom, 358
Bernsten, Annie Skau, 127
Bethune, Mary McLeod, 40
Bingham, Hiram, 129
Bingham, Rowland, 149
Bogart, Bob and Debby, 284
Boniface, 178
Booth, William and Catherine, 107
Borden, Lance and Carrie, 121, 170
Borden, William, 100
Boyd, Linda, 338
Brainerd, David, 67, 120, 285
Brand, Evelyn "Granny," 62, 369
Brand, Jesse and Evelyn, 369
Branstetter, David and Barbara, 161
Bretherick, George and Sharon, 50
Brown, Ken and Kathy, 41
Brunt, Deborah, 52
Buchanan, Ray, 358
Buhlmaier, Marie, 237
Butler, Cathy, 86
Butts, Tina, 68

Byrd, Emerson and Dorcas, 248
Cable, Mildred, 2, 149
Cabrini, Frances Xavier, 271
Calhoun, Darla, 39
Calvert, James and Mary, 222
Cantrell, Chet and Michelle, 255
Carey, Dorothy, 139
Carey, William, 1, 2, 67, 81, 122, 131, 139, 167, 281, 285, 295, 322
Carmichael, Amy, 62, 131, 232, 357
Carpenter, David and Mary, 238
Carver, William Owen, 232
Cary, Lott, 9
Cary, Maude, 165
Cauthen, Baker James and Eloise, 256
Chafee, Scott, 372
Chalmers, James, 104
Chappelear, Glenn and Donna, 204
Chestnut, Eleanor, 308
Choy, Leona, 47, 192
Clough, John and Emma, 241
Coggin, Lisa, 26
Coke, Thomas, 67, 285, 359
Cole, Sandy and Jerry, 219
Coleman, Rodney, 347
Columba, 168
Compres, Fidel, 302
Cox, Alan, 130
Cox, Melville, 93
Crawford, Daniel, 18, 67
Crawford, Martha, 177
Crawford, T. P.,177
Crosby, Fanny, 90
Crowder, Nona, 173
Crowther, Samuel Adjai, 144
Daniel, Wayne and Mary, 17, 371
Day, Fred and Janice, 105
de Arbañil, Nelly, 152
Derbyshire, Doug and Cheryl, 367
de Souza, Aias and Gecina, 148
Dickerson, Lori, 99
Dickson, Jim and Lillian, 162
Doremus, Sarah, 28
Doss, Mary, 293
Dougherty, Phil and Vicki, 303
Dozier, Charles Kelsey, 254

DuCharme, Peggy, 328
Duff, Alexander, 156
Dunaway, Archie, 278
Dye, Lisa, 136
Eddins, Paula, 274
Edmiston, Alonzo and Althea Brown, 239
Edworthy, Susie, 32
Elder, Ellamae, 251
Eliot, John, 333
Elliott, Elizabeth, 232
Elliott, Philip James "Jim", 14
Emmert, David, 266
Erwin, Monte and Janet, 211
Everett, Sheila, 238
Farley, Sandy, 34, 70
Father Damien, 118
Fearing, Maria, 153
Finley, Faithe, 146
Fisher, Mary, 2, 277
Fiske, Fidelia, 269
Francis, Mabel, 62, 220
Franson, Fredrik, 213
Freeman, John and Elizabeth, 171
French, Evangeline, 149
French, Francesca, 149
Fretheim, Peter and Miriam, 46
Fulks, John and Rebecca, 362
Fuller, Andrew, 281
Gardiner, Allen, 346
Garner, Amy, 84
Garza, Delores, 244
Gebhart, Eric and Cathie, 172
Geddie, John, 230
George, Eliza Davis, 2, 326
Glide, Lizzie Helen Snyder, 87
Goforth, Jonathan, 74, 139, 203
Goforth, Rosalind, 139
Golson, Martha, 64
Goodman, Ryan, 218
Goodwin, Jim and Jo, 320
Graham, Agnes, 21
Graham, Ruth Bell, 316
Graves, R.H., 62
Gray, Bill and Cheryl, 41
Grenfell, George, 18

Grenfell, Wilfred Thomason and Anne, 226
Grigg, John, 352
Grisham, John, 330
Gunter, Ron and Cynthia, 103
Gwathmey, Linda, 206
Hammer, Lilian, 135
Hannington, James, 309
Hardison, Alison, 130
Harvey, Bonnie, 44, 138
Hawkins, Bev, 34
Hawkins, Hawk and Carol, 298
Hawkins, Tom and Bev, 53
Hayes, Lucy Webb, 142
Haygood, Laura Askew, 243
Haynes, Helen and Gerald, 140
Haynes, Winford and Martha, 223
Heck, Fannie E.S., 174
Hepburn, James, 335
Hester, Elizabeth Fulton, 339
Higginbotham, Tom and Patti, 221
Hill, David, 60
Hills, Ken and Donna, 164, 170
Hine, Stuart, 319
Hogg, Jeff, 300
Hooper, Marvina, 286
Hucks, Claudia, 215
Hyde, John, 54
Jackson, Sheldon, 361
Jaffray, Robert, 74, 216
Jayne, Mary Posser, 317
Jessup, Henry, 62
Johnson, Lizzie, 306
Johnson, Margaret, 370
Johnson, Marsha, 310
Joiner, Barbara, 182, 371
Jones, Karen, 355
Jotcham, W.G.R., 212
Judd, Gerrit Parmele, 129
Judson, Adoniram, 56, 113, 122, 160, 185, 250
Judson, Ann, 42, 122, 232, 250
Judson, Emily Chubbock, 160
Judson, Sarah Hall Boardman, 160, 250
Kane, Carol, 73
Kerns, Jan, 336

Kersey, Ruth, 76
King, Carl, 330
Kuhn, Isobel, 232
Kyzar, Melinda, 143
Lafferty, Todd and Susan, 159
Land, Mitch and Vivian Lea, 44, 242
Larson, Dave, 344
Laubach, Frank, 252
Laws, Robert, 62, 67, 337
Lee, Betty, 154
Lee, Wanda, 231
Levrets, Fred and Mary Lou, 61
Liddell, Eric, 2, 45
Livingstone, David, 67, 85, 131, 139, 201, 236, 245, 314, 337, 348
Livingstone, Mary, 139, 314
Lozuk, Mark and Carolyn, 44, 194
Lyon, Mary, 65
Macomber, Eleanor, 113
Mallory, Kathleen, 175
Manley, Stevan, 202
Marhenke, Larry and Sonya, 334
Marler, Malcolm, 166
Marquette, Jacques, 348
Marshman, Joshua and Hannah, 167, 295
Martin, Mike and Dawne-Marie, 88
Martyn, Henry, 67, 120, 285
Maury, Matthew and Susan, 20
Mayhew, Thomas, 155
McBride, Grace, 76
McCall, Dennis and Margaret, 10
McCone, Harvey and Sharon, 321
McCormick, Cyrus H. and Nettie, 210
McCoy, Isaac and Christiana, 327
McDaniel, Jean, 345
McFarland, Amanda, 311
McGuire, Lucy, 323
McKee, Gil, 69
Meredith, Jane Carole, 24
Miller, Paul, 228
Miller, Richard, 325
Mills, Samuel, 185
Miu, Siu, 307
Moe, Malla, 62, 97
Montgomery, Helen Barrett, 23, 151

Moon, Lottie, 2, 76, 177, 187, 353, 365
Morrison, Robert, 37
Mott, John, 210, 299, 351
Mueller, George, 19, 30, 111, 198
Mullis, Michelle, 225
Nichols, Robert and Deborah, 134
Nielson, John, 34
Nielson, John and Katherine, 106
Nommensen, Ludwig, 62, 110, 122
Norton, Anne, 155
Norton, John and Nancy, 233
O'Brien, Dellanna, 4, 11
O'Brien, Ross and Lisa, 246
Oglesby, Joy, 35
Olsen, Betty, 36
Padgett, Carol, 207
Parker, Peter, 297
Paton, John Gibson, 324
Patrick, St., 2, 83
Payne, Angela, 7
Peabody, Lucy, 23, 151
Peck, John Mason, 79
Pepper, Larry, 188
Pettigrew, Jessie, 76
Pierce, Bob, 2, 157, 162
Pollard, Dan, 273
Pollard, Samuel, 122
Presley, Don, 350
Quarrier, William, 198
Ramabai, Pandita, 3, 133
Randall, Maurice and Shirley, 278
Rankin, M. Theron, 256
Rankin, Melinda, 193
Rask, Giertrud, 208
Rawley, Cliff, 197
Reagan, Lucille, 292
Rebman, Johannes, 18
Rehn, Heather, 128
Rheuby, Betty, 342
Rice, Luther, 91, 275
Richard, Timothy, 190
Richards, William, 129
Rivera, Rosario, 360
Rochester, Annie Katherine Taylor, 141
Roseveare, Helen, 63
Ryder, Tom and Liz, 296

Scudder, Ida, 71, 72, 301
Scudder, John, 72, 301
Schereschewsky, Samuel, 74, 280
Schweitzer, Albert, 351
Seale, Dana, 55
Shaffer, Roy and Ruth, 312
Sheppard, Lucy Gantt, 58
Shuck, J. Lewis and Henrietta Hall, 258, 272
Simmons, Camille, 341
Simons, Karen, 266
Simpson, A. B., 232, 247
Slessor, Mary, 3, 12, 67, 81, 131, 187, 224
Smith, Amanda, 2, 205
Smith, Bertha, 267
Smith, Carrie Ann, 184
Smith, David and Dee, 229
Smith, Gail, 257
Smith, Ginger, 158
Smith, Kurtis, 57
Smith, Robert and Hanna Whitall, 98
Soderdahl, Doug and Nancy, 59
Solomon, Bishop, 132
Sonnenberg, Bruce, 342
Staines, Gladys, Graham, Philip, Timothy, 315
Stam, John and Betty, 349
Stark, Frank and Betty, 92
Stearns, Richard, 263
Stewart, John, 102
Strong, Stephen and Carol, 13
Studd, C. T., 19
Sutton, Mark and Susan, 288
Swain, Clara, 33
Tawney, Andrea, 114
Taylor, J. Hudson, 2, 19, 27, 139, 147, 183, 187
Taylor, Maria, 139
Teresa, Mother, 2, 51, 351
Thoburn, Isabella, 115, 299
Thoburn, James Mills, 115, 299
Thomas, Sally, 287
Thurman, Tom and Gloria, 77
Thurston, Lucy, 62, 195
Tidenberg, Tim and Ann, 313
Townsend, William Cameron, 279

Trasher, Lillian, 16, 62
Trotter, Isabella Lilias, 98
Trotter, Mel, 25
Tucker, Charlotte Maria, 137
Turnbull, Bob, 318
Underwood, Lillias, 364
Vanderkemp, Johaness Theodorus, 304
Van Dyck, Cornelius Van Alan, 62
Vines, Carolyn, 332
Von Zinzendorf, Nicolaus Ludwig, 95
Wakefield, Mark and Fran, 186
Walker, Johnny, 259
Wallace, Bill, 48
Warne, Francis Wesley, 306
Webb, Mary, 74, 289
Wertz, Lowell and Claudia, 356
West, Paul, 112
Whitman, Marcus and Narcissa, 340
Whittemore, Emma, 8
Wightman, Maria Davies, 125
Wilder, Robert, 74
Wiley, Elizabeth Reaves Wiley, 180
Wilkins, Jerry, 338
Williams, Hester, 43
Williams, John, 104, 331
Williams, Larry, 196
Williams, Mary, 139
Williams, Pam, 123
Williams, Rebecca, 231
Williamson, John and Sharon, 282
Wolff, Sam, 49
Wood, David and Tami, 47, 305
Wood, Jim, 126
Xavier, Francis, 234
York, Ted and Frances, 150
Young, Ken and Grace, 22
Zaqueu, Luiz, 78
Zeisberger, David, 62
Zwemer, Samuel, 100, 109

C. Joanne Sloan has written hundreds of articles for a variety of Christian and secular publications. She specializes in researching and writing about historical figures. She is the coauthor of three books and has written chapters for six other books. The Texas native received her master's degree from the University of Arkansas. As coordinator of the annual Southern Christian Writers Conference, Joanne loves to encourage other writers. She lives in Northport, Alabama, with her professor husband, David. They have two children and four grandchildren.

Cheryl Sloan Wray is a full-time freelancer who has published more than 350 magazine and newspaper articles. The author of the book *Writing for Magazines: A Beginner's Guide,* she has coauthored four other books. She often writes about religious topics and Christian personalities. Cheryl has a master's degree in journalism from the University of Alabama and teaches magazine writing classes at the University of Alabama at Birmingham. She lives with her husband, Gary, in Hueytown, Alabama. They have two daughters, McKenna and Delaney.